When Rape Goes Viral

When Rape Goes Viral

Youth and Sexual Assault
in the Digital Age

Anna Gjika

UNIVERSITY OF CALIFORNIA PRESS

University of California Press
Oakland, California

© 2024 by Anna Gjika

Library of Congress Cataloging-in-Publication Data

Names: Gjika, Anna, 1980- author.
Title: When rape goes viral : youth and sexual assault in the
    digital age / Anna Gjika.
Description: Oakland, California : University of California
    Press, [2024] | Includes bibliographical references and
    index.
Identifiers: LCCN 2023023369 (print) | LCCN 2023023370
    (ebook) | ISBN 9780520391031 (cloth) |
    ISBN 9780520391048 (paperback) | ISBN 9780520391055
    (epub)
Subjects: LCSH: Rape—United States—21st century. | Social
    media and teenagers—United States—21st century.
Classification: LCC HV6561 .G555 2024 (print) | LCC HV6561
    (ebook) | DDC 362.883920973—dc23/eng/20230720
LC record available at https://lccn.loc.gov/2023023369
LC ebook record available at https://lccn.loc.gov/2023023370

32 31 30 29 28 27 26 25 24 23
10 9 8 7 6 5 4 3 2 1

Contents

Acknowledgments

This project began as a dissertation at the CUNY Graduate Center, and I am grateful for all the support and encouragement I received there from friends and mentors alike. In particular, my dissertation committee—Lynn Chancer, Jessie Daniels, Jayne Mooney, and Walter DeKeseredy—helped me realize my ideas into a thesis and provided invaluable feedback and advice toward the writing of this book. Thank you, Lynn, for patiently reading all the drafts, and the gentle nudges along the way. I am also deeply indebted to the late Jerry Watts and Jock Young for their brilliant work and generous mentorship. I lost them both at the beginning stages of my dissertation, but my intellectual journey would not have been possible without their guidance and support.

Many colleagues have engaged with this project at conferences, in workshops, over coffee, and in long Zoom sessions, and I am lucky to have been able to refine my ideas on this topic alongside them. My thinking and this book have benefited greatly from your comments and insights. I am especially grateful to Swati Birla, Walter Dekeseredy, Bridget Harris, and Alison Marganski for the ongoing conversations and encouragement. Thank you, as well, to the anonymous reviewers who understood what I was trying to say in this book and offered deeply engaged and cogent commentary. I owe a huge thanks to everyone at the University of California Press particularly the publishing team, and to my wonderful editor, Maura Roessner, who had faith in this project from early days, and whose enthusiasm, knowledge, and support have helped me to make it a reality.

This project would not have been possible without the young women and men who took the time to talk to me. Thank you for so generously and enthusiastically contributing your voices to this project. I am also indebted to the parents and teachers who helped me connect with teenagers in their schools and communities. I further want to acknowledge and thank the attorneys and journalists who kindly agreed to be interviewed for this research, often because they believed in its broader questions and goals.

I owe much gratitude to the friendships and community that made it possible for me to complete this monograph through general support and encouragement during the writing period, including Rebecca, Ricardo, Adam, Megan, Julie, Kat, Logan, Kalle, Bronwyn, Rakhee, and Charlotte. Thank you, Martha, for giving me a home away from home where I could write during the semester. Erin and Sara, your friendship and advice during this process have been indispensable. I am grateful to the family I have surrounded myself with, whose love of knowledge and education have fostered and enabled my own. Most importantly, I want to thank my partner, Brandon, for the laughter, the distractions, and the unwavering love and support that nurtured and sustained me across the finish line. I love you.

Introduction

On a late August evening in 2012, students from Steubenville High School in Ohio hosted a series of house parties to celebrate the end of summer. Attendees included Trent Mays and Ma'lik Richmond, two star football players from the high school, and a 16-year-old girl from a neighboring town, whom the two young men sexually assaulted multiple times during the evening. The first of these violations occurred in the back seat of a car, Mays taking advantage of the victim's inebriated status during the drive between parties, while Richmond and two other male friends watched. The subsequent assaults, by Mays and Richmond, occurred in the basement of another boy's house, while the girl lay unconscious on the floor, once again in front of witnesses. Every stage of Jane Doe's abuse during that night was captured in pictures and videos, posted on YouTube and Instagram for popular consumption. The events were also circulated and commented on by the perpetrators and bystanders via text messaging and social media platforms, such as Twitter.[1]

Earlier that year, on a cold, January night, 14-year-old Daisy Coleman and her friend decided to join a handful of boys from Daisy's high school for a small house party in Maryville, Missouri. A few hours and many drinks later, a heavily intoxicated Daisy was (allegedly) assaulted by 17-year-old Matthew Barnett, while his friend watched and recorded the incident on his phone.[2] And only one month after the

1

Steubenville rape, 15-year-old Audrie Pott of Saratoga, California, was also sexually assaulted at a house party by three young men she knew.[3] Waiting until she was passed out drunk, the three 16-year-old boys dragged Audrie to an upstairs bedroom, drew and wrote on her body, sexually assaulted her, and took photos, which they shared with others at her school through social media and text messaging. As rumors and images of her abuse circulated among her peers, Audrie also became the target of their bullying; eight days after the assault, she killed herself by hanging.[4]

These three cases describe highly publicized incidents that dominated news media and public discourse in 2013. When they made headlines, most of the concern surrounding youth, technology, and sexuality centered primarily on problematic but legal activity among teens (i.e., sexting). The Steubenville rape, and the Coleman and Pott incidents that followed in its wake, however, featured non-consensual, sexually abusive, and criminal behavior by young people, introducing a new set of questions and anxieties about the consequences of digital engagement for teens. The stories were met with shock and outrage over the callous behavior and attitudes young people exhibited. Particularly bewildering and alarming was teens' willingness to brazenly share such activity across social media, without concern for repercussions. The question gnawing at everyone, myself included, was: What were these kids thinking? Public fears over the dangers of the digital turn for younger generations became more acute once the Steubenville trial started. The crucial role of social media in gathering evidence in the case raised serious concerns over the implications of the digital trail for young men and their futures. At the same time, Audrie Pott's suicide and the online harassment directed at Jane Doe after her assault also sounded alarms about social media platforms and cyberbullying.

The use of digital platforms to document and share sexual assault and perpetuate sexual harm and abuse presents important questions about youth peer cultures and sexual practices, as well as concerns over how this group is engaging with new technologies. Why would young people publicize such behavior on social media? What are the long-term implications of this activity for young victims and perpetrators of sexual violence? Public discourse in the ensuing months and years treated the incidents as a referendum on technological risk, as cautionary tales about cyberbullying, underage drinking, and the harms of digital engagement for adolescents everywhere and for young women in particular.[5]

The sexual violence central to these cases and the motives driving young people's digital participation remain insufficiently analyzed.

Research has likewise been slow to theorize image-based sexual abuse among youth, often subsuming instances of digitally mediated sexual violence into broader discussions of rape culture or technology-facilitated violence, citing them as examples of both.[6] This scholarship frames digital harm as an extension of unequal gender relations into the digital realm, but though true, this framework fails to explain the motives of the perpetrators of such abuse. More recently, scholars have identified power and control as reasons for image-based sexual abuse, however these studies are overwhelmingly based on violence in the context of dating and intimate partner relationships.[7] Multi-perpetrator sexual assault is a *group* occurrence, with its own unique motivations and power dynamics, one that requires a separate investigation of young people's digital activities in such settings.[8] Such assaults are not only about the relationship between victim and offender but also about those between co-offenders and bystanders, as well as men's relationships to each other. As peer-oriented behavior, these incidents necessitate a different explanation of technological engagement, one that centers identify and performance rather than coercion and control as the frame of analysis.

Although news media and public attention have moved on to other pressing social problems in recent years, instances of young groups of men assaulting young women and capturing and circulating this abuse via digital platforms continue to happen across the country (and the world). In 2017 a 15-year-old girl's rape by multiple perpetrators in Chicago was streamed on Facebook Live, watched by dozens in real time, without anyone reporting the event to the police.[9] In 2019 three 18-year-old boys assaulted an intoxicated, passed out 17-year-old girl in a hotel room in Deerfield, Ohio; filmed it; and shared the rape on Snapchat.[10] Three similar incidents made headlines in 2020 alone. In Georgia three young men recorded the rape of another girl and posted it on Snapchat.[11] In South Carolina two boys recorded the sexual assault of a 13-year-old on Facebook Live, and the video was shared dozens of times.[12] And in Providence, Rhode Island, eight young men posted on Facebook a video of their rape of a passed out 16-year-old girl at a house party.[13]

This is by no means an exhaustive list; rather, I offer these occurrences as examples that such behaviors are an ongoing feature of the adolescent sexual assault landscape and require our attention. In this book, I engage explicitly with such cases to provide critical insights into what these episodes tell us about the meanings and contexts of young people's digital activity. Further, I document how social media and digital evidence feature in social and institutional responses to the incidents, to analyze the consequences of the digital trail for victim-survivors and perpetrators of sexual assault. More broadly, I attempt to provide critical insight into the appeal of social media platforms for mediated representation writ large and the implications of this digital turn for our culture and society.

SITUATING ADOLESCENTS' DIGITAL PRACTICES

Digital media are now a ubiquitous feature of everyday life, with a vast majority of teens having access to a smartphone or computer. According to the latest study by the Pew Research Center, as of 2022, 95 percent of American teens have a smartphone or access to one, with ownership being nearly universal among youth of different genders, races, ethnicities, and socioeconomic backgrounds. Nearly universal mobile phone ownership also means heavy usage of social media and online platforms by teens, with YouTube, TikTok, Instagram, and Snapchat as the primary platforms regardless of demographic characteristics.[14] The explosive uptake of new technologies has been met with an equally expanding body of research and public debate on the implications of this digital engagement for youth. One area of concern has been the interface of technology and sexuality, with anxieties about how young people manage privacy and the damaging impact of digital engagement converging around sexting. Studies find that the news media frame sexting in a negative and alarmist discourse that suggests technology drives adolescents' engagement in increasingly sexual behaviors and may include harmful behaviors.[15]

Contemporary discourses about teens and social media are only the latest iteration in a long history of social concern and moral panics around youth and technology.[16] They are informed by a determinist view that sees technology as an autonomous force, operating outside of the control of humans and with the capacity to act upon and change society.[17] They also reflect an adult perspective of risk and safety informed by social anxiety about perceived problem shifts in youth values and behaviors. Historically, teenagers have been constructed as both risky and at risk; they are either vulnerable and dependent, and thus in need of adult protection, or delinquent and dangerous, and thus in need of control and discipline.[18] Both configurations engender risk anxiety in adults, often resulting in segregation and increased surveillance and control over adolescents' lives.[19]

Youth sexuality, in particular, is a key site fraught with fears for adult generations and subject to heavy policing by them.[20] The continued concern among adults regarding youth sex and sexual practices reflects assumptions about young people's immaturity, "raging hormones," and their inability to make good sexual decisions. These understandings arise from the social construction of teenagers as emotionally and intellectually not adults and therefore in need of guidance and protection. But they also reveal our anxiety over the vulnerability of children and adolescents to being sexually exploited and the need to protect their sexual innocence, especially in an increasingly sexualized cultural and media landscape.[21] Digital technologies exacerbate these fears since they complicate and often undermine efforts to protect youth and their (sexual) innocence, both by facilitating access and communication between teenagers and by increasing the potential for harm through their ability to store, distribute, and replicate information.[22]

Rather than adding to current anxiety about teens, sexuality, and digital engagement, I suggest placing adolescents' social media practices into social and historical perspective and giving young people a chance to articulate their own ethics of engagement.[23] Today, the technological means to document behavior are far more dispersed throughout the general public than ever before, as is the over-sharing culture promoted and naturalized by social media platforms. As a generation that has grown up digital, young people's identities and ethics are being fundamentally shaped by these new norms and cultures, both positive and negative. At the same time, teens are trying to navigate the precarious and highly gendered social landscape of adolescence, and we must be sensitive to this fact, and to the ways digital practices are often embedded in these dynamics, if we are to understand the motives and values informing their digital praxis.[24] What does it mean for youth to grow up in a world where social media and mobile technologies are key sites and tools of self-presentation and identity work, including expressions of gender and sexuality? A world where disclosure is increasingly encouraged, routinized, and rewarded, not least of all by the logics and affordances of social media platforms themselves? Engaging with these questions is crucial if we want to understand why some teens digitally capture and distribute sexual abuse.

In this book, I examine how youth experience and make sense of these gendered worlds and the evolving social media landscape through an analysis of the gender dynamics, sexual ethics, and digital norms that inform young people's interactions and digital practices. I also investigate the ways teens' practices and ethics intersect with, and are informed by, the logics of digital technologies and broader economies of attention and humiliation. My analysis is based on qualitative interviews with 35 young men and women between 16- and 18 years old. I find that for many adolescents, dominant gender norms and heteronormative sex scripts inform their interpersonal relationships and peer cultures, including interactions with the opposite sex, and that such dynamics also extend to their digital praxis. My conversations with teens further reveal a world where digital production and sharing is primarily individualistic and heavily driven by likes and peer validation. The principal consideration behind much of their social media activity focuses on the potential consequences for oneself: Will I get in trouble if I share this image, for example, or will sharing it get me likes? And are the rewards of sharing worth the risks? This is not to say youth are thoughtless in their digital production and decision-making, just deeply self-focused.[25] Such a narrow focus has implications for who their imagined audiences are and what they perceive as the consequences of their actions, including what their actions mean for others, and informs their overall ethics of digital participation. My analysis suggests young people record and share their behavior on social media—including negative activity—with immediate contexts in mind, often with the goal of receiving peer validation. This approach to digital engagement extends to sexual activity, I argue, including sexual assault. Instead of focusing on the criminal aspects of teens' behavior in such instances, I propose centering the *social* nature of the assaults and the *rewards* of digital sharing. Doing so enables us to understand the digital documentation and sharing of this behavior not just as evidence of a sex crime but also as a means for young men to perform hetero-masculinity for their peers' gaze and approval.

Digital platforms and activity are instructive because they reflect, magnify, and make more visible the structural factors and inequalities that shape everyday life. When social relations and cultural systems are shaped by misogyny, racism, and other forms of prejudice, for example, this becomes visible online. Similarly, when young people record and share sexual violence or callously mock and bully victims of assault on social media, they are telling us something about the cultural values and beliefs that shape their views and experiences of gender, sexual norms, and sexual victimization. We have to use these incidents to determine how the social and cultural fault lines that structure American life impact young people. Understanding the abusive content created and disseminated by teens in these cases, the ethical dispositions displayed, and the lack of fear of consequences, I contend, requires us to address how their behaviors and ways of thinking are situated in and supported by patriarchy, heterosexism, and rape culture.

Also crucial to the discussion of why teens would share evidence of a sex crime on social media is the design of these platforms. It is easy, between discussions of young men's masculinity goals and the unequal dynamics that permeate our gender relations, to forget about how digital media influence individuals' behaviors. Much of the existing scholarship on gender and digital abuse treats social media as neutral phenomena whose application depends on the motives of their users.[26] Men turn to these platforms with the express purpose of asserting their power and control over women, whether in the context of an intimate relationship or in the public sphere. However, social media do not simply channel user interactions; they also structure the manner in which interactions take place by enabling and encouraging certain types of practices through their design and software architecture.[27] Digital platforms actively encourage the publication and circulation of private material and promote such practices without reflection, all in the name of profit. Hence, I argue here for theorizing sexual violence and its digital circulation at the intersection of localized gender practices with larger digital cultures and technological affordances. While these properties of technology certainly do not determine teen practices, I maintain that they can encourage diminished ethical responsibility, commodification, and an instrumental attitude among users that makes digital abuse possible. Established patterns of inequality and the attention economies and cultures of humiliation and exploitation in which media practices are embedded further destigmatize and sanction such harm.

HOW THE DIGITAL TRAIL MATTERS

The cases that serve as the focus of this book provide a rare opportunity to examine the implications of the digital trail for sex crime investigations and young people's entanglement with the criminal justice system. One of the more noteworthy—and concerning—revelations to emerge from the Steubenville trial was the astounding volume of evidence investigators were able to obtain through social media. Story after news story highlighted the thousands of text messages, photos, and social media postings that helped prosecutors build their case and successfully convict Mays and Richmond. Digital platforms in Steubenville, as well as in the Coleman and Pott incidents, were similarly instrumental for galvanizing public interest in the cases and pressuring local authorities to take the sexual assault allegations seriously. The ease with which new media gather, store, and distribute information, as well as their capacity to engage and mobilize publics, invites consideration of the possibilities of technology for institutional responses to sexual violence. How useful is the digital trail for sexual assault investigations? The scholarship on sexual violence shows rape myths, gender stereotypes, and victim-blaming attitudes continue to permeate the criminal justice system's treatment of survivors and perpetrators of sexual assault. Does digital evidence hold any potential for disrupting these patterns?

Reliance on smartphones and social media to capture evidence of criminal activity and of the digital trail in the criminal justice system is increasingly common and encouraged. Nevertheless, youth and legal scholars have been slow to examine the role of new technologies in investigating and prosecuting sexual violence, including juvenile sexual assault. Most of the research in this area focuses on cyberbullying and sexting to highlight the inappropriate charges and draconian penalties young offenders often face in such cases. Researchers warn about the risk of over-regulation and criminalization of young people's consensual, digital sexual interactions as states struggle to develop or revise laws to properly deal with these practices.[28] But what of the law's response to non-consensual and sexually abusive image sharing by this population? What are the consequences of the digital trail for young perpetrators of sexual assault and for the punishment meted out to them?

When the three cases that open this book made headlines, I also worried over the repercussions of the digital trail for victim-survivors. Sexual violence can be a severely traumatic event; having evidence of that violation and humiliation shared for the world to see can deeply amplify the harm to survivors, especially young and vulnerable victims. While social media played a crucial role in elevating the cases to the national sphere and generating public interest in the incidents, they were also used to circulate the artifacts of their abuse for broader consumption, as well as make fun of, shame, and bully the victims in each case, with tragic results for some of them. What promises and pitfalls do new technologies pose for young survivors of sexual violence and their justice goals, then? Are social media and digital evidence the solutions to victim-survivors—and the problem of sexual violence more broadly—being taken seriously?

My analysis reveals the contradictory potential of digital media for sexual assault survivors and offenders, as well as larger cultural and socio-legal responses to gendered violence and image-based abuse. New technologies provide valuable information in criminal cases, helping to corroborate victim allegations, critique attitudes and myths about rape, and generally aid in overcoming long-standing barriers in processing sexual assault. Their utility, however, is compromised by obstacles resulting from the inability of criminal justice actors and the law to keep up with the constantly evolving state of technologies, as well as ongoing issues surrounding the admissibility and reliability of digital evidence. For young survivors, social media's potential is context specific. Digital evidence helps victim credibility, can offer powerful visual evidence, and may contribute to allegations being taken more seriously by the criminal justice system. But technology also creates new forms of social consequences for survivors, often amplifying their suffering and future victimization, particularly due to the law's failure to account for the gendered nature of the harm perpetuated through these platforms. For both survivors and perpetrators of sexual assault, ongoing gender, race, and class biases across the criminal legal system continue to limit the efficacy of the digital trail in improving responses to gendered violence. Still, social media present some survivors and advocates with new opportunities to seek justice through extralegal avenues, to engage broader publics, and to engender cultural shifts in discourses and solutions to sexual violence and image-based sexual abuse.

HOW TO READ THIS BOOK

The chapters that follow are dedicated to exploring the interplay between gender, status, technology, and sexual violence among youth, as well as the consequences of these relations for responses to juvenile sexual assault, both through and outside of the criminal justice system. A dialectical approach to the relationship between technology and society informs my arguments and analysis throughout this book. Influenced by media theorist Raymond Williams, this social constructivist view conceptualizes digital media as both socially shaped and socially shaping.[29] According to this perspective, the consequences of technologies arise from a mix of the "affordances" or "logics" that limit the ways technologies can be used and the unexpected and emergent ways people make use of those affordances.[30] Writing specifically on gender, science and technology studies scholar Judy Wajcman describes this framework as technofeminism, referring to the mutually shaping relationship between gender and technology, with technology conceptualized as "both a source and consequence of gender relations."[31] Such a framework allows for a flexible approach to social media that accounts for both how people's engagement with technology changes over time and the ways technology (re)shapes other practices. In the context of multi-perpetrator sexual assault and technology-facilitated violence, this perspective helps identify the ways the objectifying tendencies of social media and their inducements toward visibility and social exposure intersect with existing inequalities within peer groups and social contexts to sanction or create new forms of sexual harm and abuse.

The first chapter engages directly with the question of what would motivate teens to record and share sexual assault on social media. I begin with an analysis of how the selected incidents, as well as the relationship between technology and youth, are presented and explained by the mainstream media. I then consider the group aspects of the assaults, and the rewards of documenting and sharing rape and sexual abuse within those peer relations, to identify the motives driving some teens to digitally capture and disseminate these crimes. I detail how gender norms, peer cultures, and masculinity, in particular, shape young people's sexual practices and ethics, including their digital activity, to explain why risky or criminal sexual behaviors may be recorded and shared by some of them.

Understanding the reasons some adolescents document and distribute sexual abuse on social media also requires us to make sense of the behavior and norms exposed by technologies in these cases. Drawing from interviews with teenage participants, chapter 2 situates young people's behavior in the broader context of gender inequality, rape culture, patriarchy, and digital humiliation. It further explores the ways technological design and logics impact teens' disclosure practices and create an ecosystem of commodification, humiliation, and exploitation that sanctions digital abuse. My analysis in these first two chapters provides a theoretical framework for examining technology-facilitated sexual violence that recognizes the dynamic ways social and technological factors inform and shape each other, impacting practice and norms.

The changing disclosure norms and ethics resulting from the digital turn have serious legal and social repercussions for perpetrators and victims of sexual violence. Chapters 3 and 4 examine the uses of the digital trail in the investigation and prosecution of the selected cases and in juvenile sex crimes more broadly, based on interviews with prosecuting and defense attorneys with experience in juvenile sex crimes, including those involved in the incidents described in this book. Chapter 3 details the utility of digital evidence for police and prosecutors, particularly for corroborating allegations, gathering proof of the assault, and helping challenge rape culture across the criminal justice process. The chapter further discusses the socio-legal challenges relating to digital evidence that restrict some of the potential of the digital trail for sexual assault investigations.

Chapter 4 considers the implications of shifting digital cultures and practices for young victim-survivors of sexual assault. In this chapter I investigate whether the potential of the digital trail highlighted by criminal justice officials and the news media is realized in juvenile sexual assault cases, as well as what digital technologies mean for survivors going forward. I argue that a fundamental paradox exists for survivors where digital evidence is concerned. New technologies can help make reporting easier for some survivors, providing evidence that contributes to their cases being taken seriously by investigators. At the same time, the ongoing threat of harm that social media present and the law's inability to account for this abuse risk further victimizing this vulnerable population.

Chapter 5 extends the conversation on the justice-seeking possibilities of the digital trail beyond the criminal legal system. I discuss the potential of social media platforms and digital participation, writ large, to mobilize pressure and support in instances of sexual assault, improve state and public responses to sexual violence, and provide survivors with alternatives for seeking justice through informal mechanisms. The chapter considers potential pathways to justice in the context of recent social media movements, such as #MeToo, and addresses the implications of digital evidence for news media reporting and public discourses on the issue.

In chapter 6 I consider the implications of my findings for addressing and preventing sexual violence and image-based sexual abuse. I propose a model for responses to sexual and technological harm in the digital era that includes prevention strategies across individual, institutional, and cultural levels. To this end, I outline several specific interventions in education, law, and the tech industry to help young people better navigate the gender, power, and technology nexus and to improve responses to gendered violence and digital abuse. I conclude the book with a summary of my main arguments and key takeaways, reflecting on what has changed since I started this project and what remains to be done by future scholarship in the field.

Throughout this book, I draw on mixed qualitative research that I conducted from 2014 to 2016 to provide an analysis of how crime, gender, and status intersect with technology for young people growing up digital. This includes in-depth analysis of high-profile juvenile sexual assault cases, group interviews with teens, interviews with criminal justice professionals and reporters covering the selected cases, and critical analysis of news media coverage of the incidents. A full discussion of my methodology is included in the appendix.

Two further points of clarification are needed. I have opted to reproduce the text and social media evidence from the Steubenville case, as well as the other incidents discussed in the book, while anonymizing the identities of their authors, except when the messages are authored by the perpetrators in each case. My goal in doing so is not to be sensationalist or further perpetuate harm against either the young victims or offenders in each instance, although I recognize this is a possibility. Rather, the messages and social media postings provide context for the perpetrators' actions and state of mind and are evidence of the rape culture, gender inequality, and gender policing that enable the sexual violence and digital abuse occurring in these cases. Not depicting these exchanges runs the risk of minimizing these issues and reproducing the very rape culture this book is criticizing.

The sexual assault incidents that inform my analysis all consist of heterosexual accounts of sexual violence and include primarily—though not exclusively—white victim-survivors and perpetrators. This does not mean that men, LGBTQI+ youth, and/or youth of color are not victims of sexual violence and image-based abuse, and my goal here is not to reproduce the hegemony of white, heterosexist research. I focus on female victims and male perpetrators because the extant scholarship on sexual violence and digital abuse shows these practices remain highly gendered, and also because these are the instances that generated public interest. The lack of more diverse cases underscores the lack of media and public attention to these forms of violence among such groups and the need for further research in the field. In many ways, this book is a critique of such inattention to technology-facilitated juvenile sexual assault, arguing that we need to examine this ongoing phenomenon especially because it has extended to vulnerable and marginalized populations. I hope the arguments I make here provide a starting point for new directions of inquiry and a robust theoretical framework for explaining peer sexual assault and image-based abuse upon which to build such future investigations.

Contemporary youth are growing up in a social and cultural moment where many aspects of their lives are mediated by digital media, and many of their experiences and opportunities will be shaped by their engagement with technology. Warning younger generation to abstain from social media participation does little to help them deal with the realities of the digital age, including managing its risks. In writing this book, I hope to help the public better understand what teenagers are doing when they engage with social media and why cases of mediated juvenile sexual assault have much to tell us about how technology intersects with teens' sexual ethics and practices and the gender norms governing their peer cultures. Moreover, the incidents matter because they reveal how the objectifying logics and routinized sharing that new technologies foster extend to include and sanction harmful behavior, displaying the broader implications of the digital turn for our interactions and practices. Considering that digital media are here to stay, it is likewise important to understand what the consequences of digital engagement and digital evidence are for younger generations. While we may still be wrestling with the meanings of digital media for our lives, we are nevertheless increasingly turning to their surveillance capabilities to improve responses to crime and to the publics on these platforms to advocate for equity and justice. Through the examples and analysis in this book, I also hope to detail the ramifications of social media platforms and digital participation for perpetrators and victim-survivors of sexual violence, as well as to identify ways the public and the state are being forced to change their understandings of and responses to gendered violence and image-based sexual abuse.

KEY TERMS

This book defines *social media* (and social media platforms) as the wide range of web-based (and increasingly, mobile) services that allow users to participate in online exchanges, connect, interact and build community, and contribute user-generated content.[32] Examples include social networking sites such as Facebook and Twitter, user-generated or media-sharing sites such as YouTube, and other web-based communication forums. *Digital media technologies*, on the other hand, is the umbrella term used throughout to refer to both social media and the broad array of technologies and devices enabling access to and the flow of information into and from these platforms (*digital media*, *technology*, and *digital technologies* are used interchangeably with *digital media technologies*).

I use *technology-facilitated sexual violence* as an umbrella term to capture "the diverse ways in which criminal, civil, or otherwise harmful sexually aggressive and harassing behaviours are being perpetrated with the aid or use of digital communication technologies."[33] *Image-based sexual abuse*, more specifically, refers to Clare McGlynn and Erika Rackley's definition of the concept as the "non-consensual creation and/or distribution of private sexual images."[34] Informed by Liz Kelly's pioneering conceptual work on the continuum of sexual violence, their concept of image-based sexual abuse similarly emphasizes the connection between the non-consensual use of private sexual images and other forms of sexual violence, including rape and sexual assault, and acknowledges the real, embodied harms of technology-facilitated sexual violence.[35] This definition of image-based sexual abuse is broad and flexible enough to account for new ways of perpetrating and experiencing these forms of abuse and of enabling better recognition and responses by legislatures and policy makers to the harms experienced predominantly by women.

The terms *rape* and *sexual assault* have different legal definitions. Rape usually refers to penetration, and sexual assault refers to any degree of unwanted sexual contact. Nevertheless, in this book I use both terms interchangeably, to reflect media depictions as well as the language used by criminal justice professionals in the cases. I tend to use the term rape more frequently in reference to the Steubenville case, as the incident meets the legal definition of rape in the state of Ohio.

Throughout this book I also refer to *victims, survivors*, and *victim-survivors* interchangeably. While I acknowledge the feminist critiques of binary categories such as "victim" and "survivor," I move between these terms to reflect their usage across different contexts and social actors.[36] The terms *victim* and *survivor* dominate media and public discourse in the sexual assault cases, while the use of *victim* is more pronounced across legal actors, including the ones interviewed for this book. The strength of those who have been sexually victimized should be recognized and respected. However, it is also true that some of the young women whose cases I discuss tragically did not survive this abuse, and the "victim" label is a more accurate representation of their experiences.[37] Similarly, while I have attempted to be non–gender specific at certain points, the majority of my analysis uses gendered terms because so much of sexual violence and digital abuse disproportionately impacts women and girls.

Understanding the Youth, Identity, and Technology Nexus

In many ways, the three cases at the center of this book can be characterized as typical examples of peer sexual assault among teens—alcohol and flirting were involved, and a heavily intoxicated girl was taken advantage of by young men she knew and trusted. Such incidents are sad examples of teen partying gone wrong, an all too familiar story that we find warnings about throughout popular culture and in our discourses with and about young people. This routine aspect of sexual assault is one of the main reasons the Steubenville rape did not make headlines until January 2013, although the incident had occurred in August of the previous year. National attention turned to Steubenville following an article by the *New York Times* discussing the digital trail in the case and leaked social media postings and a YouTube video about the assault by hackers. The social media posts included a photograph on Instagram of the victim being carried by the two young men who later abused her, shared by one of the partygoers. In it Trent Mays is holding her wrists, while Ma'lik Richmond grips her ankles; her head is drooped backward, her hair trailing on the floor, and she looks completely limp. Mays is grinning. The young man who posted the photo also tweeted:

Whore status. Hahahahhaaha.

Never seen anything this sloppy lol.[1]

Tweets from that night also feature exchanges between other partygoers disparaging the young victim, including comments like these:

> I have no sympathy for whores.

> Whores are hilarious.

> If they're getting 'raped' and don't resist then to me it's not rape. I feel bad for her, but still.

> Some people deserve to be peed on.

> Song of the night is definitely Rape Me by Nirvana.

> RIP to the person that died, you went out doin it big.[2]

A similar tone pervades the YouTube video, which depicts a number of young men drunkenly joking about the assault and laughing at the victim. The video is over 12 minutes long, and one young man in particular jokes about the victim's "dead" status at length, openly acknowledging that she has been raped. Here are some quotes from the video:

> You don't need any foreplay with a dead girl.

> They peed on her. That's how you know she's dead, because someone pissed on her.

> She's deader than O.J.'s wife. She's deader than Caylee Anthony.

> They raped her harder than that cop raped Marcellus Wallace in Pulp Fiction.

> They raped her quicker than Mike Tyson raped that one girl.

> They raped her more than the Duke lacrosse team.

> She is so raped right now.

> Her puss is about as dry as the sun right now.

> It isn't really rape because you don't know if she wanted to or not.

It is unclear how many boys were in the room at the time of the video recording, and we do hear at least two of them admonish the young man featured prominently in the video off-camera for making light of the rape. "What if that was your daughter?" one of them asks. "But it isn't," he replies, and the laughter and joking continue.[3]

REPRESENTING TECHNOLOGY-FACILITATED
JUVENILE SEXUAL ASSAULT

It is difficult to imagine most people not being shocked and disturbed by the appalling behavior and flippant attitudes depicted by the teens in these exchanges. In fact, the use of digital technologies to document, share, and callously discuss the rape helped transform Steubenville into a highly dramatic incident, with the case featured prominently across news outlets during 2013. Reporters, law enforcement officials, and parents across the country—and the world—were stunned and fascinated by the brazen online discussions of the assault; the crude text messages and social media exchanges between the teens; and the callous attitudes toward the incident, as well as the victim, that many of them exhibited. As Tina Susman of the *LA Times* explains:

> The Steubenville case got a lot of attention because of the social media aspect. . . . [W]ithout the social media element, a case like Steubenville could just come down to—sadly—another he said, she said situation, and vary rarely do those stories get a lot of attention because there are so many of them to begin with—which is unfortunate, but . . . there's only so much interest you can generate. . . . When you have the pictures . . . it's the fact that they're out there, the fact that they were obviously shared and seen by so many people, especially at that, you know, relatively young age. . . . [I]t just seems so unbelievably callous and vile, and . . . that is one reason it makes such a compelling narrative story.

Many of the journalists I spoke with who covered the assault similarly described the incident as "very eye opening" for the community and the adults impacted by the case as "mortified" by the digital activity and "pretty stunned by . . . the raunchy texting that was going back and forth between everybody." Digital technologies in Steubenville, and subsequently the Audrie Pott case, created a trail that helped lift the veil on youth subcultures, exposing aspects of adolescent behavior previously hidden from adults. The practices social media revealed in these instances—the underage drinking, the risky sexual behavior, and the casual objectification of women—ended up confirming many of the fears and anxieties parents have about what their kids are up to away from adult supervision. This made Steubenville and similar instances that occurred in its wake, including the Audrie Pott and Daisy Coleman assaults, more compelling and more worthy of attention for the public and the news media alike.

Nevertheless, despite the sexual abuse and "ugly" teen culture on display in these instances, most of the news coverage about Steubenville, as well as the Pott and Coleman incidents, focused on the dangers social media platforms pose to adolescents.[4] Stories following the Jane Doe and Audrie Pott assaults expressed alarm over the willingness of teens to incriminate themselves by recording and sharing the assaults. The question of the negative consequences of digital participation for teens became particularly salient following the Steubenville trial, when the public was informed of the thousands of text messages, photos, and social media postings law enforcement was able to examine in the case.[5] The Pott and Coleman incidents furthered these generational and technological anxieties. Both Audrie and Daisy were subjected to intense bullying from their peers on social media in the aftermath of their abuse, contributing to Pott's suicide by hanging a week after the assault and multiple suicide attempts by Coleman in the months after her case became public. As reporter Julia Sulek of the *San Jose Mercury News* explains regarding her decision to write about the Pott story:

> [The case had] so many lessons for young people and their parents. . . . Because we're living in this digital age that—the parents' generation, anyone over 40, are not native digital people, right? We were in our twenties or thirties. So with these kids growing up with it, parents don't realize how bad it can get. . . . I thought [the story] had tremendous reader appeal for those reasons. It was a story of our culture and our time that was a bit mysterious to the parental generation. . . . This thing is happening, how do we stop it, how do we teach our children to behave with the phone in every pocket?

The questions and themes informing reporting on the selected cases reflect narratives of fear about the role of social media in young people's lives that have featured prominently in the news over the last 15 years as digital technologies have increased in ubiquity. One heavily scrutinized area has been the intersection of technology with adolescents' sexual practices, with stories relating to digital shaming and cyberbullying, sexting, online harassment, and porn consumption among youth dominating headlines. Studies consistently find that the media frame young people's digital activity in a negative discourse that highlights social media's capacity to endanger youth as both "victims" and "perpetrators" of risky behavior, with particularly dangerous consequences for young girls. Such stories frequently highlight the inexperience of young people and their parents when it comes to social media, acting as cautionary tales for a generation often depicted as dependent on digital technologies and vulnerable to the access and connectedness they provide. In turn, the media promote surveillance-based solutions, such as increased parental monitoring, as the most effective tool for ensuring teens safely engage with digital platforms.[6]

Retelling the Cautionary Tale

This risk discourse is also evident in the media's reporting on the Doe, Pott, and Coleman assaults, framing the lens through which these incidents are interpreted for broader audiences. As I have argued elsewhere, the focus by the press on the novel role of social media in each crime results in these technologies becoming the story, eclipsing the overarching problem of sexual violence evident in the episodes.[7] By centering digital media in its coverage of the three cases, the press ends up reproducing many of the prevalent cautionary narratives on youth and technology in its portrayal of the incidents. For instance, initial reporting by the *New York Times* represents the Steubenville case as showcasing the "ugly" reality of teen culture and being indicative of the age of social media "when teenagers are capturing much of their lives on their camera phones . . . and then posting it on the Web, like a graphic, public diary," rather than an incident that exposes issues of gender inequality and sexual abuse among youth.[8] Throughout their coverage, journalists reserve adjectives such as "repugnant," "callous," and "revolting" to describe the lewd text messages, heavy drinking, and lack of ethics exhibited by the teens during and after each assault, rather than the sex crimes themselves.[9]

Articles during the final days of national coverage reinforce the message that what is significant about the incidents is how new technologies feature in them. Both the *New York Times* and the Associated Press quote the presiding judge in framing Steubenville as "a cautionary lesson" in how teens conduct themselves when drinking and "in how [they] record things on the social media so prevalent today."[10] The *Los Angeles Times* similarly summarizes Steubenville as an incident that "touched on a range of social issues, among them teen drinking, abuse of social media, parental responsibility and youthful ignorance of what constitutes rape."[11] Subsequent reporting on Audrie Pott and Daisy Coleman reiterates the "cautionary tale" theme. Coleman's case is portrayed as focusing a harsh light on "underage intoxication" and its consequences, while articles about Pott repeatedly stress cyberbullying, describing her assault as "underscoring the seeming callousness with which some young people use technology."[12] This emphasis by the news media on digital technologies and teen drinking in their reporting works to recast the cases as episodes of alcohol abuse and bullying amplified or possibly caused by technology, rather than as examples of a social problem.

Opinion pieces published in mainstream outlets during and after each assault further reproduce this interpretation of events. Many of these stories, penned by journalists as well as parents, educators, religious leaders, and academics, address the failure of parents and schools to properly educate and/or monitor children and binge drinking—particularly by young women—as the major takeaways from each incident.[13] A number of these authors mention rape culture and male privilege; however, their advice is typically limited to the need to instill respect for women in young men and ways adults can better educate children about technological engagement and bystander intervention.[14] Some mainstream sources did speak at length about patriarchy, masculinity norms, and rape culture, but in the context of explaining why we should feel compassion for the offenders and why other women did not help stop the sexual assaults, rather than as causes of the crime.[15]

The cumulative effect of these media portrayals is a reframing of what the three cases are really about—from sexual violence to "cautionary tales" and "teachable moments" for teens and their parents about underage drinking, dangerous technologies, and parental responsibility. The sex crime in each instance is stripped of its violence and severity, and the incidents are reconstructed as episodes of regrettable, drunken sex, or of unsophisticated teens using technologies that are beyond their control and mastery. The narrative focus on the role of technology in the assaults also reproduces existing media discourses about youth and technological risk, reinforcing deterministic explanations that frame technology as responsible for the assaults. Portraying the incidents as a consequence of naïve youth using digital platforms whose capabilities are beyond their comprehension suggests that digital media are partially responsible for the sex crime occurring. This framing reflects historical fears about adolescent sexuality and what Nora Draper describes as "the seductive ability of technologies to promote increasing sexual behaviors among youth," including aggressive and violent behaviors.[16] Such a framework fails to situate young people's digital activity in these cases in the context of male dominance and gender inequality, masking the ways we use technologies to fit our needs and goals. Discursively, this representation further works to exclude the perpetrators—and young men, more generally—from any responsibility in the assaults.

ADOLESCENTS, TECHNOLOGY, AND IDENTITY

The media commentary on the selected cases offers one more example of adults speaking for teenagers and cautioning them on the consequences of digital engagement, rather than explaining what social media practices look like among youth and their peer cultures. Framing the digital activity in these instances as a consequence of youthful immaturity and digital inexperience, alongside representations of technology as a risky, outside force on human behavior, works to restrict public understandings of the selected assaults and of image-based sexual abuse more broadly. The ethics and practices enabling some teens to digitally capture and disseminate sexual abuse are not separate from the gender norms and hierarchies that enable the crime to occur in the first place. Social media document these dynamics and help make them visible, but they did not cause the assaults. To understand what might motivate teens to share such activity requires us to identify what young people gain from sharing behavior online. What is the relationship between technology and identity for adolescents, specifically as it relates to their gender and sexuality performances?

In *The Presentation of Self in Everyday Life* (1959), sociologist Erving Goffman builds on the work of symbolic interactionists who conceptualize the self as social and collaborative, constructed in constant interaction with others, by framing identity as performance.[17] Using a dramaturgical metaphor, he posits individuals as actors who strategically tailor their interactions based on context and audience, aspiring to present an identity that is credible and fulfills the expectations of the audience and the definition of the interactional situation. Of course, self-presentation is not constructed in a vacuum; as a conscious and interactive act, it requires both an awareness of and participation from broader collectives, from audiences of individuals who work together to ensure a successful performance.[18] The collaborative aspect of this performance, maintains Goffman, becomes a process of "impression management," in which individuals habitually monitor how others respond to their self-presentations and continually adjust their performances based on these responses to foster the desired impression.

For young people growing up in the digital age, impression management and identity performances increasingly take place on social media platforms. Over the course of the twentieth century, media have played an increasingly significant role as the conduits through which a unique self is asserted, is displayed, and seeks social recognition and esteem. We see evidence of this in the onset of the "society of self-disclosure" and the rise of celebrity culture, which prize social skills that encourage performance and reward people with both economic gains and social esteem for displaying themselves in engaging and easily consumed public ways.[19] The digital turn has only made this imperative toward visibility stronger. According to criminologist Majid Yar, in the current configuration of mediatized society, "'to be' is 'to be seen'—one exists as a socially recognizable (and noteworthy) subject insofar as one is available and visible to others through mediated representation."[20] Increasingly, he goes on to argue, everyday individuals seek "to assert their selfhood and seek social recognition ('to be somebody') through mediated self-presentation." Digital media and networked technologies provide people with both the tools and the platforms through which to exercise their desire for representation and recognition, reconfiguring social interaction and identity performance. Audiences become more important for identity performance, and recording and broadcasting daily behavior becomes necessary and naturalized, since social recognition and status are increasingly garnered through mediated self-presentation.

Social Media as Lived Experience

Young people's engagement with social media reflects this cultural shift and the increasing importance of digital platforms for the presentation of self. A long-standing problem with mainstream narratives on youth, sexuality, and digital praxis is that they reflect adult concerns about adolescents, rather than seeking to understand their digital sexual cultures as situated in and informed by new economies of self-presentation. Research with teens shows this group uses social media and mobile technologies to support, experiment with, and reinforce key development processes, such as identity formation, enhancing their social lives, and connecting with their peers. It is by now well established that adolescents find digital platforms appealing because they facilitate impression management and enable immediate feedback, evaluation, and validation from their peer groups. In particular, the ability to "like," comment, and circulate content on mobile devices and social media platforms allows teens to maintain social ties and construct a visual form of recognition that is valuable for their efforts at popularity and status in their peer networks.[21]

This does not mean teens are always successful at navigating the social and technological environments of digital media. On social media, audiences are less visible than in face-to-face interactions, making it particularly challenging for individuals to understand who is observing their performances, and when. Teens are concerned with managing their privacy, but like most social media users, these concerns extend primarily to interpersonal relations rather than institutional or governmental surveillance. Control is also difficult in an ecosystem where content is constantly uploaded, tagged, and shared by other users, often without permission. Digital platforms can result in context collapse—a flattening of separate contexts and audiences due to the persistent, searchable, and replicable nature of social media—which makes it difficult for users to differentiate or adjust their self-presentation strategies and negotiate their multifaceted lives.[22] Nevertheless, the value placed on identity expression and peer connection and affirmation means we need to understand young people's social media practices as *purposeful* and teens sharing details about themselves as a result of having something to *gain* from being visible. Some of the social rewards users gain for engaging with digital platforms are impression management, recognition and social status, stronger social ties, and increased social and cultural capital.[23] When youth disclose online, they do so with the goal of having their media performances evaluated; they seek feedback from their social groups, which they use to adjust their digital practices and (re)presentations in an effort to attain peer approval and social validation.

The teens I spoke to while undertaking this research similarly described social media as integral to their daily lives and communication and a key medium for sharing experience and establishing a valued sense of self.[24] Their responses also reveal young people who are actively thinking about their audiences, managing the sorts of activities they share and the platforms they share them on for maximum desired effect, even if they do not always get it right. Contrary to popular discourses, this suggests adolescents are not victims of technology or unsophisticated users of it. Instead, echoing the scholarship on youth and technology, I discovered that teens exercise agency and skill in their digital engagement, but their expectations of privacy and disclosure are different from those of previous generations, defaulting toward public sharing.[25] The consensus among participants, regardless of gender, race, and class differences, was that capturing and sharing behavior was a regular part of young people's daily interactions, a "way to stay connected" and communicate to others "this is who I am" and "this is what's going on with me." Girls often constructed their digital activity in relational terms, as a way to connect with friends, stay current on each other's lives, and maintain relationships. For many, this activity was also primarily driven by peer feedback, judgment, and status over their identity performances. Young women were particularly explicit in linking their digital sharing to peer group status. When asked what they share online and what types of activities they post about, they offered the following answers:

> *Amanda*: I feel like you share when you go out, so people know that you go out.
>
> *Logan*: Like if I go somewhere interesting, I'll post a picture on Instagram.
>
> *Jen*: Yeah. I use social media just to, like, show that you're social. Like, that's a thing.
>
> *Kayla*: Honestly, I've been to parties before where literally it's like, you'll get to the party, everybody'll be drinking, doing their thing, and taking, like, all these, like, pictures with each other, like, looking they're having so much fun and stuff, and maybe after, like, 15 to 20 minutes of picture-taking, everyone's just kind of like sitting in different areas of the room, like, silently drinking, not looking at each other.

Communicating their presence and sociality was important for these participants; they engaged with social media to show they were not missing out on activities their peers were participating in, such as parties. One young woman best summarized these practices as posting so that "everybody knows what you're doing and everybody can, like, see."

Male participants initially framed their digital praxis as instrumental rather than linked to identity and performance. They used social media as tools to achieve specific outcomes, which frequently included amusement or "entertainment," turning to digital platforms to share "goofy" or "funny" behavior with their friends. Although they presented their participation as more neutral and less performative than the girls' social media activities, the boys are nevertheless using digital media as an impression management tool. The selective activities and images of themselves they are sharing with friends on social media seek to portray different and desirable masculinities, specific to their peer group. In fact, as the interviews progressed, the young men admitted to the importance of getting likes and positive feedback on their digital activity, showing that social media matter to their identity—for being accepted and being perceived as cool or interesting or funny by one's friends, thus reaffirming the primacy of peer validation and status as influencing digital sharing. As Sonia Livingstone and David Brake noted more than a decade ago when writing about teens and new media, "At the heart of the explosion in online communication is the desire to construct a valued representation of oneself which affirms and is affirmed by one's peers."[26]

Performing Gender and Sexuality Online

Digital media and mobile technologies have also proven particularly useful in facilitating the exploration and performance of gender and sexuality among young people. Researchers have noted the importance of social media platforms for providing teens with spaces where they can express sexual thoughts, explore questions about sexual practice and identity, and seek sexual gratification. Additionally, many teenagers use digital technologies to develop and maintain romantic or sexual relationships, including connecting with people they find attractive in their peer groups and flirting with current or potential romantic partners.[27] These interactions include the exchange of sexual messages and images between teens (i.e., sexting), which studies reveal is becoming a more common practice among youth and an increasingly normalized aspect of intimate relations in the last decade. A 2018 review of the research on youth and sexting found that approximately 15 percent of teens 12 to 18 years old had sent a sext, and about 27 percent had received one. The study also revealed that 12 percent of teens had forwarded a sexual image without consent from the original sender.[28] Recent scholarship with young adults similarly finds that sexting is a common practice among the 18- to 26-year-old population in the United States, with about half of this population having sent nude or seminude photos of themselves to others. Overall, this research maintains that young people's sexting practices are often consensual and experimental in nature and are increasingly equally prevalent across the sexes, as youth negotiate their sexual needs and boundaries.[29]

At the same time, there is the emergence of a blurring between the fun/experimental and coercive dimensions of sexual digital communication among youth. Studies across the United States, Australia, Europe, and the United Kingdom highlight that non-consensual sharing of intimate sexual images is seen as common and acceptable behavior among teens and young adults.[30] While both sexes share sexual images for fun, because the person depicted is attractive, or as a joke, young men are more likely than women to perceive dissemination as harmless, reflecting their privileged position at experiencing minimal negative consequences from sending sexts. Women and girls experience particularly harmful impacts when their intimate images are shared with others because the meanings and consequences of intimate image sharing—consensual or otherwise—are inextricably bound up with unequal power relations between the genders. These risks and vulnerabilities are further structured in predictable and long-standing ways by factors like race, sexuality, social status, class, and cultural background, among others. Unlike boys, girls do not elicit peer approval for producing and sending sexually explicit messages but are seen as behaving irresponsibly and putting themselves at risk through their behavior. They also face harsh criticism because of their actions, often being labeled "sluts" and "attention whores" by their peers for violating gender and sexuality norms.[31] Consequently, young women and girls are more likely to view sexting and non-consensual image sharing as harmful and causing serious negative consequences. For young men, on the other hand, collecting and sharing nude images of girls is motivated by a desire to display sexual prowess to other young men and to increase their social status and popularity among their peer group. This is what scholars describe as an abusive homosociality, whereby boys distinguish themselves among their peers through competitive displays of their "collections."[32]

In my group interviews with youth, participants also highlighted the significance of digital platforms for their everyday sexual communications and the exploration and performance of gender and sexual identities. Teens explained they use social media to connect with attractive peers, flirt, exchange sexual images, and maintain romantic relationships. While not necessarily universal, exchanging sexually explicit and/or nude images among their peer group was discussed as common practice by both young men and women, although the expectations, value, and consequences of such images were deeply gendered. Many of the young women, for instance, described being frequently solicited for sexually explicit or nude photos by male peers and significant others and noted the pressure to do so in intimate relationships was high. Both sexes were also familiar with a range of incidents in which boys and young men solicited girls for nude or intimate photos and then exploitatively and non-consensually circulated these images via text messages, social media, and email:

> *Rob*: So a few years ago, there was this . . . Instagram page of around
> a thousand girls from the high school, where everything was shared.

And people went to jail, or prison, whatever, people got in big, big trouble, got expelled.

Julie: I'd heard in another school in (nearby town), apparently that they were sending pictures around to get free pairs of shoes from each other. That whoever got the most—everyone pooled in money, and whoever got the most pictures of naked girls got the shoes that they had bought.

Becca: Like in our school, . . . it was, like, a while ago. Like, the boys would share nudes that they had from other girls. So they would, like, . . . send each other the ones they had. . . . And they would all do the same thing. So they would all have the girls. So they would all see it.

Neither the young women nor the young men thought such behaviors were healthy or acceptable, but they did recognize the value of women's bodies—and images of their bodies—as currency in young men's masculinity performances and peer groups. When explaining what may have prompted boys to request such images, show them to others, or share them with friends, young people rarely spoke of sexual desire. Rather, their answers emphasized that collecting and exchanging nudes were valuable forms of social and cultural capital for boys, enabling them to demonstrate hetero-masculinity and gain recognition and approval from their male peers:[33]

Hannah: Like, if a guy came up to me and showed me that kind of picture, I'd be like, "Are you kidding me? Like, what do you think you're doing? That's disgusting." But to a guy, a guy's like, "Yo, that's awesome."

Jasmine: Because, like, guys like to talk about their numbers. Like, how many girls—they like to make that public, because it makes them look—

Ashley: Like, other guys can be like, "That's on point!"

Justin: I think that they're thinking that, like, if I show this person [a photo], I'm going to look more like a big shot, kind of. Like, the man, so to speak.

Max: Like a reputation, yeah.

Young women seemed resigned to the fact that such new media practices put them at risk, that boys would probably betray their trust, and they did not necessarily frame such behavior as abusive.[34] In part, their attitudes reflect dominant conceptions of gender and heterosexuality that posit boys as natural sexual aggressors (e.g., boys will be boys) and women as responsible for protecting themselves from aggressive male desire. However, their position also reveals their understanding of the cultural value of the female body, especially in the new digital landscape they are navigating. They recognize that demand for images of women's naked bodies renders girls and women more vulnerable to having their images shared by men, regardless of consent.[35] Overall, they abstained from any harsh judgment or moral assessment of the young men who put them in such a position, framing the behavior as a consequence of boys "not thinking" or not understanding the ramifications of sharing nudes for women. As Sophia put it:

> They're thinking, like, the picture they see of the girl who's really conscious about that, they see it as they would see a picture of themselves. And they don't mind sending a picture of themselves around, but the girl minds. They're only thinking in their point of view, and not—they're not thinking about how sending that around affects the girl.

Rather than emphasizing the responsibility of the boys to act ethically in these situations, girls focused on strategies to protect themselves, including refusing to send nudes, avoiding the boys who made the requests, or sending images but not including their faces in the photos. Male participants, on the other hand, did not endorse the non-consensual sharing of intimate or nude photos and framed such behavior as something done by *other* boys. When asked if they looked at photos their friends shared with them, however, they admitted to looking and did not see this behavior as problematic or supportive of male dominance and women's exploitation.[36] In their responses and attitudes toward the manufacture and exchange of nude images, both sexes communicate the neoliberal logics informing contemporary gender relations. The self-interested, market-based approach and the language of value and currency used to explain boys' non-consensual image sharing individualize blame and responsibility, helping minimize the role of masculinity in the perpetration of digital abuse. The asymmetrical power relations between the genders and the derogation of women are normalized, creating the context in which abuse becomes more likely and can extend to include the sharing of sexually violent behavior.

Capturing the Moment: (Hetero)Masculinity on Display

It matters that young people recognize the collection and circulation of nude images of girls as a method by which boys can show off for each other, as a means of attaining status and respect. Implicit in their answers is an understanding of masculinity as a homosocial and het-erosexual performance, enacted for the approval of one's peers.[37] While the norms and definitions of masculinities are multiple, fluid, and dynamic, hegemonic notions of gender and sexuality inform much of young people's identity work.[38] Not all teens take up hegemonic gen-der identities or take them up to the same degree as others; race, class, and cultural location all impact how masculinities are constructed, and men shift in out and out of different gender performances depending on context and operating power relations.[39] Nevertheless, studies of school and peer cultures and sexuality show that heterosexuality is an impor-tant requirement for a successful gender performance among youth across race and class lines, and that heterosexual performance remains an essential criterion for "doing masculinity" and status achievement among young men.[40] Of course other men have to witness this activity, as it is their validation that marks a successful masculinity performance.

If young men's gender performances are directed toward attaining a heterosexual masculine ideal and peer approval, including through the digital exchange of intimate images of girls, there is no reason why the recording and distribution of sexual assault cannot be understood as motivated by the same goals. Teens already share risky and illegal behaviors on social media, such as alcohol and drug use, as well as gang affiliations. They are driven to do so by the same ambitions as previous generations of teens who drank or did drugs in group gatherings and later bragged to their friends about it: a desire to be cool, to project a valued identity, and to attain status and acceptance among their peers.[41] We have a hard time seeing technology-facilitated sexual violence as a gendered performance because we keep focusing on the sex crime, on the abuse and the unequal gender dynamics and misogyny that allow it to happen. But young people's sexual practices and digital ethics are localized and self-oriented, informed by the gender norms and commu-nities of practice within their peer group. When sexist attitudes, sexual boasting, women's objectification, and image-based abuse are normal-ized and accepted practices of masculinity in young men's peer networks and part of how power and social capital circulate among them, the sharing of sexual assault becomes an extension of these peer norms.[42]

In fact, asked to explain the reasons the Steubenville assault was digitally circulated, teen respondents were quick to identify the per-petrators' primary goals as trying to "look cool" and "show off," to say "look what I got, look what I did" to other guys. This explanation indicates an awareness, a purpose in the actions of the male offenders similar to the motive surrounding nudes: the performance of hetero-masculinity. When the young men in Steubenville or Saratoga recorded and shared their actions on social media, they did so in the immediacy of the moment; what they were saying was "here is me, doing this, now." The photos provide unambiguous proof of their sexual conquest, and heterosexuality, to their group. This extends to male bystanders, whose own hetero-masculinity performances are bolstered by being a party to the act, by recording and commenting on it, as well as through their association with the sexual actor(s). Like many of their peers' social media activity, the primary consideration among these boys is the self and the consequences of sharing for one's identity.

Teens turn to social media to share these performances because, as discussed earlier in the chapter, they consider social media a component of their lived experience—their lives are lived in and through these platforms. Given the rapid exchange of information and the instant reaction social media enable, *sharing an experience has become an integral part of that experience.* During the focus groups, participants were not surprised by the fact that the first reaction of the offenders and bystanders in Steubenville was to record and share the assaults via their phones. They explained this sharing as being "of the moment," ephemeral, like their own impulsivity and lack of thought when capturing or posting risky, embarrassing, and/or illegal behavior on social media, rather than seeing the photos as a form of archival production. Their answers as to whether the young perpetrators thought about the consequences of their actions were quite similar:

GIRLS

Jen: And [the recording] is like a moment, thing.

Yeah. [general agreement]

BOYS

Damien: I don't think there's much of a thought process when they do it.

Justin: I don't think they were standing there like, "Should I post it?" It was just like, "Oh, it's happened—post it!"

Mike: It's just an instinct. People just have an instinct—

Luke: It's just a thing that happened.

Digital platforms and media technologies feel personal. The fact that we can tailor and highly individualize them, wear them on our bodies (e.g., smartphones), and constantly interact with them means we increasingly think of them as "extensions of the self."[43] The features and settings of these platforms make us think we exercise choice and control in our digital activity. We feel as if we are engaging in private communications— what we share feels intimate, and within our control. As a result of these imagined technological affordances, we become blind to the potential of social media for exposure and surveillance. Instead, we disclose more thoughtlessly, without deliberating on the contents of the message, thinking settings and features will minimize leakage. And often we share with local contexts in mind, failing to connect our everyday digital activity to potential negative long-term consequences and institutional surveillance, although this is complicated by race.[44] This is also how the teens in Steubenville, and in similar incidents across the country, are engaging with digital media. The choice by the young offenders to record and distribute evidence of what happened with each of the young women discussed here was made with immediate contexts in mind, motivated by the desire to display that performance to their peers for recognition and legitimacy.

The masculinity performance and homosocial rewards that boys gain from sharing images of sexual activity—consensual or otherwise—are significant because they trouble current assumptions that image-based sexual abuse is always about asserting dominance and shaming and humiliating young women.[45] This is not to say that the circulation of such images does not harm the women and girls pictured in them, or that humiliation is not part of the exercise. The exchanges and language used to refer to the victims in these instances demonstrate the young men enjoy debasing women and their bodies. Rather, I want to make the point that in cases of juvenile sexual assault and image-based sexual abuse, the motivation is peer status and approval—it is self-oriented; the digital trophies and the denigration of women that accompany the incidents are the means to achieving those rewards. The group aspect of such cases attests to this. Reflecting on incidents like Steubenville, philosopher Kelly Oliver writes that "rape has become a spectator sport worthy of candid photographs to be disseminated during and after the event."[46] But multiple-perpetrator rape has always been a spectator sport. Studies by Bernard Lefkowitz and Peggy Sanday show that young men assault women in group settings so as to be seen by other men who are present when these assaults take place. The social dimension of these rapes demonstrates the importance of peer attendance and the male gaze for the performance of masculinity.[47]

Voyeurism and trophy taking are central to these performances— boys want a visual record of such experiences, to offer as proof to their friends. Historically, men have taken photos to show each other or circulate at school; they have created non-consensual recordings and videos to play for their friends at a later date. Social media and mobile technologies offer the latest evolution of this practice.[48] Majid Yar's point, that individuals share their behavior on social media because, increasingly, status and recognition are obtained through self-mediation, is particularly salient here. New media contain significant potential for men's efforts at performing a desirable identity. Smartphones, readily available and capable of taking and displaying pictures anywhere, help document and share visual proof of boys' sexual encounters. Social media further facilitate the circulation of evidence of one's hetero-masculinity, extending the performance and its representation across highly visible platforms and for broader audiences, enabling approval and esteem at a much faster pace.

The group dimension of such assaults also facilitates an intense form of bonding between the boys, whether through the sex act or the shared risk and transgression, cementing cultural bonds among peer groups.[49] In addition to increasing group cohesion, sexual violence, along with misogynous talk, bragging, and sexist humor, also become practices through which young men display and reassert heterosexuality and male dominance and further attain validation from other men. Women and women's bodies, in these encounters, are simply currency, objects men share among each other or use to enact their masculinity performance.[50] According to masculinities and gender violence scholar Michael Flood, males use "ritualized sexual humiliation of a woman for men's collective amusement."[51] This helps explain why the perpetrators in the Audrie Pott case described the assault as a prank, and why the boys who sexually victimized Savannah Dietrich though it would be "funny" to take photos of her abuse. It is why some of the young men in Steubenville created a 12-minute video in which they laughed at the victim. It also provides an additional reason why male bystanders in each case failed to intervene to stop the assaults. The mutual bonding through women's objectification and denigration and the ways this shores up young men's masculinity performances are the point here. As writer Elizabeth Schambelan further explains, for these young men "sex is something you do to a woman, with your friends. . . . The woman's responsiveness or lack thereof is irrelevant, because it is the responsiveness of the rapists' male friends that matters—whether the friends are standing right there during the act or are brought up to speed afterward."[52] We see this abusive peer bonding play out in Steubenville, in the text messages between Trent Mays and his friends following the assault:

Trent Mays (picture image of a naked Jane Doe sent to two of his friends; has caption): Bitches is bitches. Fuck 'em.

Friend 1 (to Trent Mays): I wanna see the vid of u hitting her with your weiner.

Friend 2: What did u guys do lol
       Did u fuck her?

Trent Mays: Yes.

Friend 2: Yeah boy!

Friend 3: She looks dead lmao

Unknown Party: Lmao

Trent Mays: She is

Friend 2: Shoulda moved her around and got a better angle

Friend 4: Do anything with Jane Doe?

Trent Mays: She was a deady, and I needed sexual attention just like u lol. I shoulda f*cked her.

Friend 4: Why no head?

Trent Mays: She woulda thrown up

Trent Mays: Yeah dude it was bad, but she was naked so It was all good.

Trent Mays: I fingered her before you asked though

Friend 4: She's loose as fuck tho

Friend 4: You got any naked pics?[53]

The notion that the woman, and her willingness, are irrelevant to the boys is also evident in the responses offered by the teens I interviewed, who repeatedly highlight *sex*—regardless of consent—and *peer approval* as central to the young men's actions and the digital documentation of the assault:

Anna Gjika (AG): What do you think some of the reasons are that people took photos and videos [of the assault]?

GIRLS

Megan: To show off. To be like, "Look what I got, look what I did."

AG: To their friends?

Megan: To the other guys.

BOYS

Chris: To be like, "watch this!"

Jake: Attention.

Damien: I would say—yeah, exactly. You want attention, you want people to say, "Look at how cool I am, I get to have sex with people and go to these really cool parties where this kind of crazy stuff happens."

Sexual violence, consent, and deviance are minimized, if not altogether missing, in these accounts. This suggests that the boys are *conforming*, rather than transgressing—what they are documenting, and sharing, is evidence of sexual activity, not criminality per se. The young men are "doing masculinity" in a culturally specific, hypermasculine way that makes sense and is rewarded within their peer groups. Walter DeKeseredy and Martin Schwartz have written at length about the significance of male peer groups for encouraging and legitimating sexual violence. They explain that if one's peers value and support the objectification, exploitation, and abuse of women, then non-consensual sex becomes acceptable and justified among the group.[54] The celebratory and enthusiastic responses by Trent Mays's friends over text messaging and their lack of regard for the victim attest to the abusive and sexist norms of their network. Approaching the offenders' behavior through this lens could help us understand why young men are not always preoccupied with self-incrimination when creating a digital trail of sexual violence. What matters to these boys is the sexual conquest, and for all intents that masculine performance is all the perpetrators were documenting on their phones—as evidence, for others to see.

The social setting and the primacy given to performing heteromasculinity can also help explain why such incidents are occurring across race and class lines. Although adolescents are similar in their usage of social media and mobile technologies, studies find youth of color and poor/working-class youth are generally more aware of the surveillance potential of these platforms and more cautious in their digital engagement. Young black men, especially, are aware of how myths about black male sexuality and aggression, as well as the specter of false rape accusations, inform their gender performances and sexual interactions.[55] However, in cases of sexual assaults occurring in group settings, this awareness might be compromised, subordinated to young men's gender and/or sexuality concerns in relation to their peers. If boys are digitally sharing their participation in sexual activity as a way of demonstrating their heterosexuality for other boys, for social rewards, there is no reason for us to expect that racialized and classed fears of surveillance will trump their gender goals in that moment, or that these concerns will be given proper attention among peer and cultural norms that require immediate digital engagement and disclosure to validate one's identity and experience.

If we listen to how young people explain their social media practices, we need to move beyond narratives that posit teens as victims of technology, incapable of understanding the consequences of their actions, and focus instead on examining the aims and motives of their digital praxis, particularly as it relates to their identity performances. Specifically, their responses indicate that we need to account for the role of gender and masculinity in explanations of image-based sexual abuse. The text messages and social media posts by perpetrators and bystanders during the selected assaults, as well as my interviews with teens, suggest there are specific hegemonic gender and sexuality goals informing these young men's digital sharing: they are performing and displaying a desirable gender identity (i.e., hetero-masculinity) with immediate contexts and audiences in mind—for approval and status from their (male) peers.

While identity goals and peer norms matter for understanding young people's digital practices, including technology-facilitated sexual violence, they are also informative for what they reveal about the cultural values and broader social patterns that shape adolescents' views of gender, sex, consent, and digital engagement. In the next chapter I detail how teens' local practices intersect with gendered sex scripts and rape culture to help normalize sexual violence against women and sanction image-based sexual abuse. I also examine the ways new media logics, evolving disclosure norms and ethics, and a growing culture of digital humiliation work in tandem to foster male entitlement and women's objectification, further destigmatizing abuse and digital harm.

Missing Cultures of Consent

Gender Inequality, Digital Commodification, and Youth Ethics

The *Los Angeles Times* summarizes Steubenville as an incident that "touched on a range of social issues, among them teen drinking, abuse of social media, parental responsibility and youthful ignorance of what constitutes rape."[1] I like this quote because it succinctly captures the dominant sentiment repeatedly echoed in public narratives about Steubenville and the subsequent cases involving Audrie Pott and Daisy Coleman. It also does a lot of discursive work, minimizing adolescents' culpability for the sexual assaults through alcohol and sexual ignorance as justification for their behavior. Simultaneously, the sexual violence is decontextualized, the role of toxic masculinity, entitlement, gender inequality, and rape culture missing from explanations of the assaults and how these factors may contribute to young people's recording and distributing the abuse on social media.

The media's representation of youth as ill-informed on definitions of rape is largely based on the testimony offered by the witnesses in the Steubenville case. One of the young men who witnessed Jane Doe's first violation in the back seat of a car testified that he recorded the incident because he was "being stupid, not making the right choices" and as the result of being "under the influence." He explained that he did not try to stop the assault because "at the time, no one really saw it as being forceful."[2] Many news stories during the trial repeatedly and uncritically reproduced this testimony, although I am not sure what other socially and legally acceptable explanation one could provide in the situation. Compared to this testimony, the teens I spoke with were quick to label the Steubenville case study as a rape, or at least as "messed up," noting the victim's drunken state and inability to consent to sexual activity. It is possible their understanding may be indicative of the health and sex education standards adopted by the state of New York.[3] It is also possible they interpreted the scenario in a way they thought would best meet my expectations, presenting a performance of appropriate teen ethics and sexual practices for an adult figure. However, I would also argue it shows young people are more aware of sexual norms than they are given credit for and can typically identify a problematic sexual encounter when they witness one, even if this knowledge does not necessarily translate into their sexual practices.[4]

This holds true for the bystanders in the Steubenville and Coleman cases as well, if we interrogate their actions further. In his testimony for the Steubenville trial, the young man who recorded Jane's assault in the car due to intoxication indicated he was too drunk to act appropriately in the situation, but not so incapacitated that he was unable to assess whether the incident met his definition of rape. Moreover, his inebriated status did not stop him from recognizing that *something* worthwhile was going on in the car, which is why he took out his phone to document it. Another of Trent Mays's friends testified he was "stunned at what I saw" in the basement, where Doe was assaulted for a second time, and left the house abruptly because he "just wanted to get out of there." Yet after he left, he went back to the second party and made the video that was posted on YouTube; you can hear him laughing in the background, encouraging the principal participant in that video with the question "How do you feel on a dead girl?"

Another football player, and Mays's best friend, also witnessed Doe's rape in the basement and testified that he "tried to tell Trent to stop it. You know, I told him, 'Just wait—wait until she wakes up if you're going to do any of this stuff. Don't do anything you're going to regret.'" His statement indicates he was aware the girl was unconscious (and therefore could not consent) and that Mays's actions were possibly wrong. When Mays told him not to worry, he proceeded to take photographs of her and of the two young men abusing her, then left the house, going back to the original party and showing the photos to a few of his friends. He deleted the images, but at no time did he actually try to stop Mays or report the incident to the police or any other adults. Instead, he texted the young victim in the following days to say, "I seriously felt so fucking bad for you and I couldn't do shit about it. I'm so sorry."[5] Similarly, the young man who recorded Daisy Coleman's assault admitted in his police interview to deleting the video shortly thereafter because he "didn't want that on my phone." Like the bystanders in Steubenville, his statement suggests he recognized he was witnessing problematic sexual behavior, which is why he did not want video evidence of it on his phone.[6]

These exchanges attest to the fact that throughout the night each of these young men was neither too naïve nor too incapacitated by alcohol to recognize they were witnessing bad behavior. While I think there is a very real possibility these teens have muddled definitions of rape—and the comment about the lack of force certainly implies this—I still maintain they were aware that what they were witnessing was not okay. Why else did they document this behavior through photos and videos? Why else were they so quick to leave the house and their friends behind? Why delete the recordings from their phones? Their actions suggest that when they witnessed how their friends were treating Jane Doe and Daisy Coleman, they knew enough about what healthy and consensual sexual activity is supposed to look like to distance themselves physically and mentally from the events, even if they did not intervene to stop the abuse.[7]

It is quite possible that bystander responses in incidents like the Steubenville, Maryville, and Saratoga assaults are impacted by the collective action (i.e., multiple offenders) and the social setting surrounding the abuse (i.e., party). Social psychologists have identified several group processes that may contribute to violence, including diffusion of responsibility and deindividuation.[8] Some young men witnessing the assault may have failed to intervene because they thought someone else would, while others got "caught up" in the events, their own self-awareness temporarily overcome by the spirit of the group. However, the peer group norms demonstrated by the boys in these cases, especially in the exchanges and actions following the assaults, also suggest they did not perceive these events as particularly troubling or unethical. Rather, as others have suggested, the joking and derogatory messages and references to the victim as "dead" indicate the young men approve and support the actions of the perpetrators.[9]

Notably, when discussing the Steubenville incident during the group interviews, many of the teen participants likewise failed to attach any lasting stigma to the young perpetrators, either for sexually assaulting the girl or for taking and distributing images of that abuse, despite initially identifying the events as rape. Why might young people's knowledge about risky and non-consensual sexual behavior not translate into their sexual practices? How do incidents like Steubenville initially get recognized as rape, or as wrong, only to then have the sexual violence disappear from teens' explanations of the recording and dissemination of the assault? Gender ideology and heteronormative sex scripts are important here to help us understand how hegemonic discourses inform adolescents' descriptions and interpretations of sexual violence and account for young people's ethical ambivalence and the sanctioning of image-based sexual abuse among this population.[10]

GENDER INEQUALITY AND ADOLESCENT RELATIONS

Sex Scripts and Sexual Consent

In her analysis of compulsory heterosexuality, Adrienne Rich explains that heterosexuality is not simply about attraction to and engaging in sexual behaviors with the opposite sex. Rather, it is a pervasive institution comprised of unwritten but clearly codified conventions that organize male and female relationships, and is understood as natural and unproblematic.[11] Further, it is a political institution, functioning to serve the needs and desires of men within patriarchy through gender norms and beliefs that produce and require male dominance and female subordination.[12] Heteronormative discourses, for example, help link female sexuality with passivity, submissiveness, and vulnerability, while male sexuality is linked with dominance, aggression, and desire.[13] One enduring theme is the idea that men are always eager and ready for sex, positing that all healthy, normal men have a strong, almost overwhelming need to have sex, and they will go to great lengths to do so. Within this matrix, women's role is to receive or reject men's sexual advances; their own sexual desires are of no consequence.

Dominant discourses of heterosex also help provide what Nicola Gavey calls the "normative scripts for the practice of sex"—parameters for who does what to whom, and how. Sexual consent is negotiated and interpreted with this understanding of men as sexual initiators and women as sexual gatekeepers, such that men's sexual needs are privileged over women's sexual desires.[14] This privileging of male sexual desire and agency can lead men to feel entitled to sex and women to feel they do not have the right to deny men access to their bodies. By limiting women's responses in sexual encounters to "just saying no" or not, gendered sex scripts may lead men to read women's lack of resistance (verbal or otherwise) as consent.[15] Further, the gendered binary of male dominance and female submission that normative scripts enable can also work to legitimize unjust or non-consensual sex taking place and provide a smokescreen for interpreting rape as "just sex." Boys' and men's overwhelming sexual urges toward intercourse are presented as normal, as simply "boys being boys," naturalizing and encouraging male power and aggression while also helping minimize their culpability for abusive sexual behaviors. Women's exploitation, on the other hand, is justified and normalized through this explanatory framework, and women are expected to endure men's aggression as part of normative heterosexual relations.[16]

Young people are socialized into this patriarchal culture and accompanying heteronormative scripts that presume boys will be sexually demanding and act as predators, while girls are expected to act as sexual gatekeepers of male desire.[17] Adolescence is a time when youth start to develop a sense of their sexual identity and engage in sexual activity for the first time. It is also a period of development when gender socialization—what it means to be considered masculine or feminine—is prominent. However, because many teens in the United States lack access to comprehensive and formal instruction on gender inequality, sex education, and the negotiation of sexual consent, they rely on dominant notions of gender and heterosexuality found in the wider culture to inform their identity work and sexual norms.[18]

This also held true for the youth in my study, many of whom expressed essentialist understandings of gender, conceptualizing heterosexual relations as consisting primarily of male entitlement and female objectification. Often it seemed as if sexual aggression and harassment were integral to the construction of a heterosexual male identity. When discussing the actions of the boys in Steubenville, for example, most female participants spoke of young men as natural sexual aggressors, predatory, untrustworthy, and exploitative of women. They repeatedly noted that in sexual situations, boys "don't care what you say"; they are typically "just trying to get some." Male respondents offered similar notions of hetero-masculinity, citing the boys' "lust" and "sexual needs" as causes for the assault. Additionally, they highlighted the victim's drunkenness as providing "an opportunity" for the young men to "take advantage" of the situation. Elliot's comment is exemplary of these views:

> I mean, it could be, too, where like, you know, teenagers do have their hormones, and they won't—sometimes they won't think before they do. They just let their penis do their thinking for them. So this could have been that case, you know, where like, the guy was just probably—he was probably

feeling on it, he was like, "Oh . . ." taking advantage of the moment. He probably wasn't thinking with his head.

We see here a deeply gendered explanation, one that prioritizes men's sexual needs exclusive of women or their consent and simultaneously frames male desire as a biological drive, justifying their efforts at satisfying these urges. Such sex scripts could also inform the actions of young men in cases of sexual assault, enabling them to focus on what matters most to them in that moment: the sexual act. Heteronormative discourses further help minimize issues of male dominance and aggression. If boys are being driven by their hormones, their actions are outside of their control, and they cannot possibly be held responsible for their behavior. Rape is reconstructed as boys "taking advantage" of the situation. Interpreting their actions through this lens may have gone some way in helping the young perpetrators to see their behavior as normal or excusable and the risk of digitally documenting it as minimal. It also helps explain why some of the boys who witnessed the sexual assaults failed to intervene, and why many of the teens in my study did not hold the young men fully responsible for the abuse.

Rape Myths and Victim Blaming

According to Gavey, rape culture consists of two central interlocking elements. The first of these comprises the gendered heteronormative scripts detailed earlier that make a man's rape of a woman possible. The other key element entails the collection of rape myths and trivializing depictions of sexual violence that render certain categories of women rapeable and certain categories of men above suspicion. Rape myths are the widely held beliefs about rape, rape victims, and rapists that serve to downplay, justify, or condone sexual assault and abuse.[19] They often take the form of blaming the victim, such as "she asked for it," and minimizing perpetrator culpability through this attribution of responsibility to those targeted. These narratives reinforce hegemonic gender norms by helping normalize and legitimate men's violation of sexual and ethical boundaries. When such violations become visible, these myths further work to obscure them, trivializing the seriousness of the sexual violence or helping to excuse and deny the abuse.[20]

Young people's responses to sexual assault are therefore also influenced by their acceptance of these cultural rape myths and victim-blaming ideologies. During our interviews, teens drew heavily from established discourses to minimize the seriousness of the Steubenville assault and sanction its documentation and dissemination. For instance, even though participants initially identified the case study as rape, as the discussion progressed, resistance to this definition emerged in focus groups with both sexes. Among the girls, the hesitation often came from popular girls, like Kayla, whose concerns related to the ambiguities of consent:

> *Anna Gjika (AG)*: So, you think it was rape?
>
> *Kayla*: I mean, the thing is, it doesn't say that, like. . . . I don't think it says that she said no.
>
> *Megan*: Doesn't say that she said yes.
>
> *Kayla*: But it doesn't say that she said no.
>
> *Megan*: She was so out of it that she didn't know, like, what was happening, and she couldn't say yes or no.
>
> *Jen*: Right—It said that she was unconscious . . .
>
> *Kayla*: It says she was semi-conscious.
>
> *Megan*: In the beginning. But then she lay unconscious on the floor.
>
> *Kayla*: Right. But when she's in the back seat of the car, when he took off her shirt and bra, and all that, she was semi-conscious, so she had to have known what was going on, somewhat.

The exchange between the girls reveals resistance to victim-blaming while also highlighting the mixed messages adolescents often receive from adults, schools, and the broader culture about healthy and positive sexual activity and norms. Moreover, the discussion illustrates the persistence of the myth that a clear "no" is required for an incident to count as rape, that a woman would do her best to stop the interaction if she really did not want it. Some adolescents, like Kayla, have internalized the gendered belief that women are the ones responsible for setting the limits on sex and controlling male desire. In sexual situations where women do not verbally say no (or physically resist) or *cannot* do so because they are incapacitated by drugs or alcohol, this passivity may be interpreted as consent. They become, following Gavey, "technically unrapeable."[21] Where the young men are concerned, on the other hand, the lack of a clear "no" creates ambiguity in the interaction and can help render them less blameworthy.

Male participants were more likely to explicitly blame the victim in Steubenville and to cite her intoxication as a reason to hold her accountable for the sexual assault. As in the case of female participants, the popular boys in the focus groups were more likely to voice these objections:

> *Noah*: It was also the girl's fault for getting just drunk out of her mind.
>
> *Elliot*: Like, come one, you put yourself in this situation, you know? You became a stupid drunk bitch and went to the party and put yourself there. Nobody told you to go to that party.
> You already put yourself at risk . . .
>
> *Chris*: Honestly, I would probably be one of those people who felt really bad for her, but at the same time, be like, well, you know, it's your fault. Maybe you shouldn't have been there. It's a messed up thing to say, but it's like, who else can you blame besides yourself for being there? Like, yeah, you wanted to go to the party and have fun. All right. Be responsible. Don't make yourself so vulnerable.
>
> *Andrew*: They didn't roofie her or anything. She got drunk herself.

These teens are not alone in their views. Recent studies with young people indicate victim-blaming and rape myths are common in adolescents' understandings of, and responses to, sexual violence. In a national study about prevalence rates of male and female sexual violence perpetration among youth, Michele Ybarra and colleagues found that 50 percent of teen perpetrators of sexual violence blame the victim for the assault.[22] Research consistently finds that alcohol consumption blurs definitions of consent and resistance for bystanders and can shift perceived culpability and rape myth acceptance. Women who drink are often seen as acting irresponsibly, engaging in behavior that increases their risk of rape, and are thereby "asking for it."[23] Similarly, Jane Doe's drunkenness compromises her status as a victim in the eyes of youth, and she is perceived as somewhat responsible for her abuse. This extends to the other young victims discussed throughout this book, all of whom were heavily intoxicated when they were assaulted. The derogatory and sexist characterization of Jane as a "stupid drunk bitch" also suggests she was punished for violating appropriate femininity norms by going out, partying, and drinking, and works to excuse the boys for treating her badly.

The focus on the actions of the victim by both male and female participants demonstrates teens tended to at least partially blame Jane Doe for the rape. The repeated stress on Jane putting herself at risk reveals young people deploying a neoliberal risk discourse informing current cultural discussions about young women's sexuality and alcohol consumption. This is a gendered discourse that frames behavior as a matter of "choice" with no attention to power or structural issues, and in the context of sexual assault it works to implicate women and girls in their victimization.[24] Noticeably, this narrative does not extend to the young men in these cases. Their actions are not identified as unusual, harmful, or blameworthy, but rather expected. Once again, the notion of men as sexual aggressors is naturalized and reproduced; it is women who need to protect themselves in situations where men are present, because boys will be boys and they will take advantage.

Moreover, drinking by the boys is not seen as inappropriate or irresponsible behavior, and instead of increasing blame, it reduces the perpetrators' culpability.[25] Male respondents were particularly vocal in referencing alcohol use as a primary consideration for excusing the offenders' behavior in Steubenville:

Max: The two boys are drunk, too.

Ryan: I mean, even though we all do that [drink] . . . it's just not going to hold up in court, because like, you shouldn't have been there in the first place, you know, you probably led him on, you know?

The suggestion here is that because the guys are inebriated, they did not realize what they were doing. Their drunkenness compromises the intent of their actions—they did not mean to rape Jane, and so the incident cannot be considered rape. The comment about the victim probably leading the boys on reinforces this interpretation: because everyone was drinking, the boys likely got mixed sexual signals and cannot be held accountable for their behavior. These answers were particularly interesting because while the case study mentioned the boys were drinking, the only actor described as drunk or intoxicated that night was the victim. By reframing the events to increase the severity of the offenders' inebriation, the young men in these focus groups were able to diminish the boys' responsibility in the assault.

One additional victim-blaming narrative that emerged in the focus groups with male participants was the myth that previous consent by a woman signals her ongoing and future desire for sex. A number of the respondents referenced the prior sexual relationship between Jane Doe and Trent Mays as a reason that the boys may have deemed the sexual activity consensual. The weeks of flirting between the two was reinterpreted as Jane Doe "leading him on" in their conversation. Ma'lik Richmond, one of the two perpetrators in Steubenville, employed an almost identical rationalization in his interview with the *New Yorker*. Asked to explain why he failed to realize what (he) and Trent Mays did constituted rape, Richmond replied: "I wasn't really thinking about, Oh, this is rape. I was just thinking, He talked to her, so I don't really care what they do. . . . They were *texting*."[26]

The presence of alcohol came up again when teens moved beyond the assault to discussing the young perpetrators and bystanders recording and disseminating the abuse. This time, both male and female participants cited intoxication as an excuse for the boys turning to their phones and to social media to document the events:

AG: Do you think these boys thought about, should I record this? Will I get in trouble if I record this?

GROUP I (GIRLS)

No. [general agreement]

Sophia: Because I think if they're drunk, too, they're just trying to have fun.

Jake: The thing is. . . . In my head, I'm trying to find the scenario that gives them the benefit of the doubt. Like, okay, they're drunk, they have phones. . . . Typically when they have phones, and they're drunk—I don't know, it kind of makes people record things for some reason when they're drunk. They'll record anything.

It matters that teen girls were more likely to reference alcohol consumption when explaining the image-based abuse rather than the sexual assault. It suggests they do not find intoxication a good enough excuse for rape but can understand how it can foster bad social media engagement, perhaps including in their own practices. Their answers also align with earlier observations on the non-consensual sharing of intimate sexual images—young women are aware that boys are thoughtless and selfish in their digital sharing but appear resigned to the unequal gender dynamics informing digital participation as a new "normal."

Not every teen that participated in this study expressed these views, and I do not mean to imply here that their responses are representative of all youth. But I found it significant that gendered sexual scripts and rape myth acceptance were more frequent among the popular and sociable teens, considering that in the cases analyzed in this book, it is also typically the popular, high status boys who commit the assaults. The presence of such discourses among my respondents, and their deployment in interpreting the Steubenville rape, suggests similar narratives may exist among their peer groups and could help explain why such cases are trivialized, not perceived as sexual assault (or criminal behavior), and why there is willingness to digitally record and share them. Youth internalize the rape myths and dominant discourses of heterosex available in the wider culture, and these scripts aid teens in reconstructing sexual assault as sex, reducing both the violence and the criminality of incidents like Steubenville. This helps explain the disconnect between adolescents' theoretical knowledge of rape and consent and their behavior in real-life contexts, including how they respond to others' experiences of sexual violence.[27]

NEW MEDIA LOGICS

A discussion of the reasons young people may record and disseminate sexual violence is not complete without considering how social media's architecture and evolving digital norms impact teens' disclosure practices and facilitate image-based sexual abuse. Technology is not making teenagers behave badly, as the dominant narrative surrounding the selected cases may suggest, but it is actively influencing how and what they share about themselves, how they interact with others, and their relationship with ethics and consent.

Social media have altered the structural conditions of privacy, making disclosure the default in digital participation.[28] Generating and publishing content, so as to commodify that information in a variety of ways for profit, is coded into the design of social media platforms. New media are constantly inviting users to share massive amounts of personal and intimate details about their lives, opinions, and experiences. This information includes images and video, as cameras, broadband, and mobile wireless technology become more integrated and accessible. The "constantly on" nature of smartphones and the countless apps available on them promote increased—if not continuous—contact and availability and increasing disclosure among users.[29] Further, in making cameras so easily available and omnipresent, smartphones also routinize the impulse to document and share every aspect of our daily lives. For many, and not just teens, it has become a reflex to pick up the phone when something happens, no matter how trivial. There is societal evidence of this in the rise of selfies and the snapshot culture that has emerged among users. This is a culture of instant photo-taking, from the food we eat, to what our kids are doing, to the places we visit, and so on—everything must be mediated, captured, and shared.[30]

This reflex is even more naturalized among young people, who are consummate mobile phone users. Their response when noteworthy incidents occur is to document first, rather than processing events and assessing how to react. As Brian observed:

But that's, like, another negative about social media. Now, with all this, like, phones and all this happening, all this social media outlets, people don't react like they used to back in the day, where like, if you see kids fighting, you'll stop the fight, rather than pulling out your phone, and recording the fight, and then posting it on World Star Hip-hop, or Snapchat.

Social media also alter our relationship with consent, dulling the impulse to ask others for their permission when disclosing information about them, given that sharing is a normal and expected practice. In the larger discussion about digital sharing norms, the teens I spoke with did not mention consent or ethics as points of consideration. When I inquired if they asked for permission from others before they tagged them in photos or shared embarrassing content about them, all focus group participants answered with a resounding "No." "I don't think anybody cares about that," exclaimed one young woman, followed by general agreement from the rest of the group. The assumption among youth is that anything that happens in their presence is subject to capture and distribution on social media.

Like other social media users, teens share things they find interesting and that will grab the attention of others. They have learned about the enormous social and material value of attention through the celebrity cultures, reality TV programming, and attention economies surrounding them, which have increasingly seeped into everyday life.[31] Social media are also situated within this attention economy, with technologies built to capture and sustain the interest of users. Revenue for tech companies is driven by user-generated content, traffic, and user information, which is commodified for profit in various ways and used for targeted advertising. To reward users for the information they provide and the data they share, social media companies have quantified popularity and attention. The visibility of metrics such as "likes," "shares," and "followers" provides an immediate feedback mechanism for users that communicates their ranking in the digital marketplace and ensures their ongoing engagement with social media.[32] By commodifying attention, technology incentivizes users to share more, garner more followers, and raise their profiles, but it also creates a competitive space where people jockey for visibility and status because they matter for both social and financial rewards.

A Digital Culture of Humiliation

The turn toward self-mediation and status seeking through digital platforms is not without consequence for other values. Claims for status and attention can occur in the context of normative or "good" behavior, as well as in the transgression of social norms and values, as both are rewarded. The line between what constitutes good attention versus bad attention gets blurry. On commodified platforms like social media, shocking or humiliating content gains attention and drives traffic in a manner that other types of content do not. This creates an environment where users are incentivized to create or circulate harmful or abusive material to enhance their status online. Consequently, the digital age has also been accompanied by a cultural trend toward objectification and the celebration of cruelty and degradation, together creating a digital culture of humiliation.[33] Examples of this cultural turn abound in viral images and videos: Abu Ghraib, the recording of "happy slapping" incidents in which strangers are hit in public for the camera, the explosion of "fail" and "prank" footage compilations on YouTube, the posting and commentary on everyday fights on World Star Hip Hop, and the innumerable gross and humiliating "challenges" shared and promoted across social media, just to name a few.[34] We also see evidence in the rapidly increasing rates of gendered, racialized, and homophobic violence online, including online abuse and harassment, cyberbullying, the leaking of private photos and sex tapes, "revenge pornography" and image-based abuse, and the growth of rape and humiliation porn, among other practices.[35]

Young people learn to use technologies and navigate sharing practices and claims for attention within this ecosystem of commodification, humiliation, and exploitation. Their ethics, in turn, are informed by, and reflective of, these larger cultural patterns of engagement with new media technologies. Although teens can and do share helpful or entertaining content online, they also disseminate embarrassing, humiliating, sexual, and shocking material because they know this will be interesting to their peers. Many of my participants, for example, noted that recording and sharing risky/illegal behavior across social media was common among their peer groups. This included images and videos of drinking, hook ups, fights, marijuana use, and intimate sexual images, as well as other embarrassing but more low-stakes occurrences, such as physical mishaps and pranks. As in the discussion of nudes, sharing practices among the teens were similarly gendered. Generally, boys were more likely to create or capture and initially share embarrassing content, often for "entertainment"; this was true even if the content featured them or one of their friends, highlighting the privileges of masculinity in digital interactions. Female respondents, on the other hand, were more cautious about the types of behavior they shared, especially if the content pertained to sexuality and/or featured one of their friends, expressing an awareness of the stigmatization and reputational risks that new media pose for young women. Across all groups, however, when elaborating on why youth may publicize risky, provocative, or abusive content, most teens spoke of sociality, as well as peer responses and approval, as key motivators:

> *Chris*: You want to share it with your friends. You want to either get a laugh out of it or say how crazy something is.
>
> *Luke*: I mean, I guess basically you want people to know. You want people to see how cool I am, this is what I do on a daily basis, this is how you should see me.
>
> *Sophia*: Because it's, like, the norm, I guess. Like, everybody's doing it, and just like. . . . People do things to be cool.

These answers emphasize how objectification and humiliation have become a regular and accepted occurrence in youth peer contexts and the role of social media's commodifying logics in promoting and normalizing abuse as a strategy for improving one's status. Teens are prioritizing what will get the most "likes" or make them "look cool" and "interesting" to their peers when sharing on digital platforms, signifying that self-validation and the pursuit of likes take precedence over concern for others.

The denigration of others on social media is further facilitated by the various layers of software and hardware that dehumanize human-to-human interactions and create distance between users. In instances of sexual assault, but also in cases of technology-facilitated abuse and mediated violence more broadly, these layers of software and hardware work to distance the victim and the offender. This is both a physical and an emotional/moral distancing—the perpetrators and bystanders are removed from the live, in-person experience of the assault through the barrier of the smartphone. Rather than perpetrators or witnesses, these individuals become producers, as well as *spectators/consumers* of the events. Something like rape goes from being a violation one commits or witnesses to an experience one watches on a screen. The technology deepens the objectification of the victim and removes offenders and bystanders from the act, at the same time minimizing their responsibility and their capacity to care for her.[36] What matters is sharing and receiving approval for the activity they share, rather than the ethical implications of what they are actually doing or the human consequences (i.e., victims) of their digital sharing. Social media are flooded with stories of smartphones short-circuiting human decency, with people opting to record a car accident or a violent beating rather than helping the victim.[37] People fixate on capturing and mediating the "spectacle" because they want the thrill and the reward of that instant reaction to their postings on social media.

On technological platforms that normalize, commodify, and reward the mediation of everyday activity, struggles for attention increasingly blur the boundary between ethical/unethical, consensual/nonconsensual, and legal/illegal behavior for young people. Social media further complicate these efforts by increasingly celebrating and rewarding a culture of online humiliation, creating an environment that promotes objectification and abuse and sanctions the public sharing of all types of transgressive and harmful activity, including sexual assault. Consequently, rather than framing the actions of the young men who recorded and disseminated the sexual assaults as counterintuitive or self-incriminating, we can approach the digital record the offenders created of their sex crimes as routine activity on the extreme ends of the continuum of disclosure and digital humiliation.

RAPE CULTURE

Feminist scholars called Steubenville "rape culture's Abu Ghraib moment," the images in the case, and in incidents like it, revealing the norms and values shared by those behind the camera as well as those who circulate and comment on the photos. This thoughtlessness, argues Alexa Dodge, suggests the young men did not appear to recognize their actions as "morally corrupt" and saw the images as "something other than evidence of sexual assault."[38] However, it is difficult to imagine the young perpetrators and bystanders taking and distributing images of the abuse and joking about it online if there were not also a social tolerance of rape in our culture. Regardless of the nature of their behavior (egregious and criminal), the boys involved in these incidents felt it was acceptable to boast about sexual violence because our culture has signaled to them they will not be punished for it or for perpetrating image-based sexual abuse; in fact, they may even be rewarded for it (at least by their peers).

This is not so far from the truth if we look at the rape-supportive attitudes expressed by parents, communities, and the media in the aftermath of the assaults. In a text message to his friends, Trent Mays noted that the head coach of the football team, Coach Reno Saccoccia, told Mays he would "take care" of the problem, and that he "was joking about it so I'm not that worried."[39] The same coach allowed players who witnessed the rape to continue playing on the team until the eighth game of a 10-game season because he could see no reason for benching them. Another volunteer coach at the school, Nate Hubbard, responded to the rape allegation by saying, "The rape was just an excuse, I think. What else are you going to tell your parents when you come home drunk like that and after a night like that? She had to make up something."[40]

These rape myths were repeated on social media even after the volume of digital evidence attesting to the boys' abusive behavior came to light during the Steubenville trial. Following their conviction, social media users continued to sympathize with the offenders, lamenting their "destroyed lives" and the loss of their "promising futures":

> I honestly feel sorry for the boys in that Steubenville trial. That whore was asking for it.

> Disgusting outcome on #Steubenville trial. Remember kids, if you're drunk/slutty at a party, and embarrassed later, just say you got raped!

> Cause come on, they're not even 18 and their lives are seriously screwed up now because of that. It's uncalled for.

> Ya way to go now these 2 guys lives are ruined . . . her vag would have been fine #Steubenville.

> There is no justice in Steubenville today. The girl asked for it and wanted it, in my opinion. They gave it to her. No crime. Appeal!

> Steubenville: Guilty. I feel bad for the two young guys, Mays and Richmond, they did what most people in their situation would have done.

> The Steubenville story is all too familiar. Be responsible for your actions ladies before your drunken decisions ruin innocent lives.

> Young girls acting like whores there's no punishment. Young men acting like boys is a sentence.[41]

They also frequently and harshly blamed Jane Doe for her rape. Like some of the teen participants in my interviews, these public tweets highlighted Jane's intoxicated state as the reason for the assault taking place, attesting to the prevalence and ease with which these narratives are mobilized against "unworthy" victims:

> Maybe if you don't want to get raped, don't get blackout drunk. Just a thought.

Yeah, it's sad about what happened in Steubenville, but the boys aren't completely at fault. don't get sloppy drunk homegirl.

So you got drunk at a party and two people take advantage of you, that's not rape you're just a loose drunk slut.

If only the victim would be charged for underage drinking herself . . . her actions led to everything else.[42]

Explanations that help minimize the sexual abuse, excuse offender behavior, and blame the victim were also voiced by key adults in the Pott and Coleman incidents. Speaking to *Rolling Stone*, one of the parents of one of the boys accused of assaulting Audrie characterized the young men's actions as "a prank by a few kids, . . . blown out of proportion" and dismissed their role in her suicide by noting that "Audrie had a lot of other problems in her life."[43] In Maryville, it is Robert Rice, the county prosecutor in the Daisy Coleman case, who diminishes the boys' culpability in the 14-year-old's abuse and helps sanction sexual violence. Discussing why he declined to file charges against the perpetrators, he explained: "They were doing what they wanted to do, and there weren't any consequences. And it's reprehensible. But is it criminal? No."[44] Young men stripping an unconscious girl naked, drawing on her body, inserting foreign objects into her, and taking pictures of it can only be interpreted as a "prank" if their desire (to play a joke, bond, humiliate) is more important than the young woman's desires or personhood. Boys plying a 14-year-old girl with alcohol, assaulting her, capturing the act on video, and then dumping the girl outside in the freezing cold is only "reprehensible" but "not criminal" behavior if the subordination and exploitation of women and women's bodies is seen as natural and accepted practice. It is not a coincidence that the adult actors protecting, supporting, and justifying the abusive behavior of the boys in each case are other men.

Mainstream media reporting on the incidents employed many of the same rape-supportive attitudes as social media and community reactions in each case. An *ABC News* episode about Steubenville focused on the families of the two young men and framed the case as "every parent's worst nightmare."[45] Following the Steubenville verdict, outlets such as CNN and NBC News similarly centered on the devastating consequences of the verdict for the two young men's "promising futures" as football players, rather than on the well-being of the survivor.[46] The attention and concern surrounding the offending boys in Steubenville suggests they matter more than the victim, and that their behavior was not particularly egregious or out of the ordinary. Additionally, as I detailed in the last chapter, news stories repeatedly highlighted the party environment in which the assaults occurred, as well as the intoxicated state of the victims, framing the incidents as cautionary tales about underage drinking and technological risk. While less explicit than the social media commentary, such depictions similarly suggest the young women may have invited the assaults by consuming alcohol, helping minimize the culpability of the young perpetrators.[47] Finally, traditional media end up perpetuating rape myths and victim-blaming attitudes by uncritically reproducing the previously cited quotes from parents and community members in their reporting of the stories, without a broader discussion of rape culture and the long-standing factors that contribute to sexual violence.

The public responses to the selected assaults are not unique occurrences. Our culture is replete with examples of men abusing women and getting away with it; of judges, politicians, athletes, and celebrities repeatedly excusing male aggression; and of media, advertising, and pornography that celebrate women's sexual objectification.[48] Politicians argue over "legitimate rape." Fraternities publicly chant "No Means Yes and Yes Means Anal" and circulate emails about luring "rapebait" without consequence.[49] Facebook groups such as "Abducting, Raping and Violently Murdering Your Friend, as a Joke" amass thousands of followers and likes, while topics like "Reasons to beat your girlfriend" trend on Twitter, and violent misogynists become TikTok superstars.[50] Women accusing athletes and celebrities of sexual violence are publicly shamed and criticized for trying to "tear men down."[51] Judges dismiss rape cases because the accused "came from a good family, attended an excellent school, had terrific grades," and the girl should have understood that "pressing charges would destroy the boy's life."[52] Online abuse and harassment and rape and death threats against women on social media have become everyday occurrences, without police or platform intervention, but certainly with more followers for the perpetrators in the manosphere. Teens get that people who troll and bully online are rewarded socially and financially. They understand that the men who created and own these platforms are celebrated billionaires. And they see how men accused of sexual violence, men who publicly admit to assaulting women, who espouse racist, sexist, and transphobic views and condone the expression of those views through violence, are elected Supreme Court judges and president of the United States of America. Why would our youth be immune to these messages, these very public displays of (white) patriarchal impunity? Why would they think their behavior wrong or immoral, when everything around them indicates they will be protected?

The insights offered by the young men and women in this study reveal that we have to understand teens digitally capturing and distributing sexual assault as both an extension of everyday practice and social dynamics onto the digital realm and indicative of the shifting disclosure norms and ethics fostered by new media technologies, and to theorize digital harm at the intersection of the two. Young men recording and sharing sexual assault is not deviant or transgressive, but rather hyper-conformist; it is the performance of heterosexuality for the consumption and approval of male peers, often with their support. The digital documentation of such episodes is facilitated by mobile technologies and evolving digital norms that prioritize self-validation, routinize sharing as central for identity performance and status, and foster objectification among users. Finally, gender scripts and a rape culture that trivialize and normalize sexual violence against women further help sanction the distribution of the assaults and work in tandem with a growing digital culture of humiliation to foster male entitlement and women's objectification, further destigmatizing abuse and digital harm.

Even if teens do not perceive the documentation and sharing of sexual assault as problematic or unethical and rarely think of the consequences of this activity for the victims, or for themselves in the long term, these shifting disclosure norms have serious legal and social repercussions for both offenders and victims, as well as public and institutional responses to technology-facilitated violence. In the next chapter I consider these implications in detail, focusing on the consequences of the digital trail for young perpetrators of sexual assault and digital abuse and the implications of digital evidence for sexual assault investigations.

A Gold Mine of Information?

The Digital Trail in Sex Crimes

When the Steubenville rape initially made headlines, much of the media reporting on the case centered on the astonishing volume of digital evidence the police were able to collect and the emerging power of new technologies as an evidentiary tool in criminal justice proceedings, including juvenile sexual assault cases. Article after article credited digital media with providing much of the evidence in the investigation and prosecution of the incident. The *Los Angeles Times*, for instance, maintained that "without social media, the case might have never come to court."[1] Dan Wetzel, in his coverage of the case for *Yahoo! Sports*, observed that the group of teens filming and documenting the assault "essentially took real-time crime-scene photos for the cops," and that "Mays, in particular, essentially confessed to the crime via hundreds of text messages over the next few days."[2] Similarly, during the trial proceedings the *New York Times* reported that "scores of text messages and cellphone picture provided much of the evidence" for the prosecution.[3] Most stories about Steubenville, in fact, highlight digital technologies as the primary source of ascertaining proof and bolstering attorney arguments and witness accounts in the case. Such articles describe Steubenville as "hinging on" the social media evidence and this digital "gold mine" as being "at the heart of criminal charges" against the two football players.[4]

Digital information is, in fact, increasingly being used as valuable evidence in criminal investigations, including sexual violence.[5] This is not surprising; the more we engage with technology, and the more we extend our lives into the digital realm, the greater the importance of digital evidence in both criminal and civil litigation. As users of social media and mobile technologies, we are constantly creating massive amounts of data, resulting in a wealth of potential evidence: text messages, social media postings, friend lists, photos and videos from our smartphones, GPS locations, chat logs, "likes," and more—information that is accessible and searchable by the police.[6] Emerging research on the role of digital evidence in sex crimes reveals that digital archives now play an extensive role in the investigation of sexual assaults, as victims and offenders may communicate with each other or with friends, before, during, or after an offense.[7] For many investigators, and prosecutors, the search for digital evidence has become a first step for information gathering in such cases, and technology is perceived as a useful tool for overcoming some of the long-standing barriers in the processing of rape and sexual assault cases.

BARRIERS TO SEXUAL VIOLENCE REPORTING AND INVESTIGATIONS

Decades of scholarship on criminal justice system responses to sexual violence have documented the system's historical failure in encouraging survivors to report their abuse, as well as the difficult and often victimizing investigative process and the low rates of prosecutions in cases of rape and sexual assault.[8] Cultural and legal definitions of rape have consistently demanded proof of forcible sex or evidence of aggravating factors for an allegation to be taken seriously. Although the Department of Justice finally updated the legal definition of rape in 2013 to reflect the spectrum of sexual violence experiences more accurately, in practice, the old requirements continue to influence many public and legal perceptions of, and responses to, rape.[9] As a consequence, survivors face much stricter scrutiny at all stages of the legal process, and evidentiary thresholds are much higher in sexual assault cases. In their investigations, police and prosecutors focus heavily on determining whether there is adequate evidence to pursue a case and will only file charges if they believe a conviction is possible. This sufficiency standard requires corroborating evidence beyond the victim's testimony, such as bodily injury to the victim, witnesses who can substantiate the victim's allegations, physical or medical evidence consistent with the victim's account of the incident, or DNA evidence establishing the identity of the offender.[10] Sexual assault incidents that do not meet these parameters, what law enforcement call "he said/she said" scenarios, often involving acquaintance rape or the presence of drugs and/or alcohol, are not investigated, as they are seen as too messy and difficult to pursue.

Factors such as whether a weapon was present during the sexual assault, the timing of reporting, the availability of witnesses, and the victim's credibility and behavior are not legally relevant for ascertaining if someone committed the crime. Their influence over sexual assault investigations reflects the stereotypes and rape myths that circulate in our cultural and political discourse about sexual violence; these same myths also inform the American legal process and the decisions of legal actors. One such prevalent myth is that "real" rape is typically perpetrated by strangers, men who use or threaten to use deadly weapons, and is often accompanied by extreme physical violence.[11] In these cases, it is easier for courts and jurors to accept that the victim did not consent, although exceptions arise in instances where the woman's behavior, lifestyle, or demographics impact perceptions of her character or credibility and can contribute to victim blaming.[12] The false belief that only rapes that fit this narrow and stereotypical model are "real" reinforces the notion that sexual assaults that fall outside of this definition—for instance, cases where the victim knows the attacker, where drugs and/or alcohol are involved, or where there are no visible injuries—are not "real" rapes.

A related myth is the belief that most rape allegations are false. This myth is informed by long-held cultural attitudes of women as deceitful, and the false belief that victims are lying or have ulterior motives. Established and accepted explanations for why a woman would falsely accuse someone of rape include to cover her infidelity, protect her reputation, seek revenge, and/or as an attempt to punish the alleged male rapist(s).[13] If women delay reporting sexual assault or are inconsistent in their recollections, this behavior is seen as evidence the rape did not occur and that they are lying; a true victim, someone who has really been raped, would want to report it immediately and would have a clear and detailed memory of the incident. People also hold false beliefs about perpetrators, such as that "good' men do not rape, or that the man did not mean to hurt or violate the victim, most of which work to excuse the offender's behavior.[14]

Rape myths are called myths not because the beliefs they express may not be true in specific instances of sexual assault, but because the data generally do not support these common stereotypes. Most rapes, for instance, are what is known as "simple" or "acquaintance" rape, involving someone the victim knows and who does not use a weapon or significant force against her. Research also shows that survivors often delay reporting for a number of reasons, and that traumatic events such as a sexual assault impair rather than enhance memory performance.[15] Finally, while false allegations of sexual assault do occur, studies indicate the prevalence of this is relatively low, between 2 and 10 percent of all reported cases.[16]

Nevertheless, cultural myths and stereotypes about rape are prevalent and embraced at all levels of the justice system, impacting decisions about the merits and processing of a rape case.[17] Studies show many police officers and prosecutors believe these stereotypes themselves, and even if they do not, are aware of the influence that assumptions regarding "real rapes" and "genuine victims" can have on judges and potential jurors in sexual assault trials.[18] For this reason, they point to the need for incontrovertible evidence in the form of physical evidence or corroborating witnesses in order for them to pursue a case, and they see digital technologies as useful toward this end. Social media have created new sites of communication and interaction, as well as the means to capture and store this information. This capacity, noted the prosecutors I interviewed, is valuable for helping police and prosecutors overcome some of the murkiness of sexual assault investigations.

Challenging Evidentiary Insufficiency and Rape Myths

For law enforcement, new media are seen as providing a way to get at "the truth" of an incident, helping them reduce some of the challenges they face in meeting the sufficiency standard in sexual violence cases. Social media and mobile technologies, by gathering evidence of the crime, can help establish timelines and whereabouts and substantiate allegations. Most significantly, and most frequently cited by the attorneys I spoke to, new technologies are appealing to investigators because, as one prosecutor succinctly put it, "the digital evidence speaks for itself, and witness credibility is no longer an issue." Victims can be unreliable and imperfect witnesses, and in sexual assault trials, perceptions and assessments of their truthfulness are further influenced by the intersection of extralegal factors and cultural myths, such as the victim's attire, attractiveness, lifestyle choices, and behavior before or after the assault, as well as their race and class.[19] On the other hand, it can be more difficult for juries or the courts to dismiss rape allegations as "bad sex" or not "real" rape when confronted with photos or videos of unconscious victims being sexually violated by their peers. Digital evidence offers an immutable subject, one that is permanently injured and helpless, providing prosecutors and jurors with an ideal, gendered victim.[20]

Let us consider Steubenville as a case study in the power of digital evidence and the capacity of new technologies to help prosecute sex crimes. Jane Doe, the young victim in Steubenville, was too inebriated to recall the details of the night she was raped. Physical evidence was also lacking, since it took the girl and her family a couple of days to find out about the assault and report it to the police.[21] The time lapse between an assault and the victim's decision to report the crime is one of the biggest challenges police and prosecutors face in rape cases, as physical and biological evidence degrades or disappears during this period. In contrast, digital evidence does not disappear in the same way, unless permanently deleted. Even then, if the crime is shared on social media, the digital trail is beyond the control of the perpetrator or his accomplices, making it easier for investigators to obtain this evidence. In Steubenville, despite the lack of physical evidence, social media were crucial for documenting the sequence of events on that night, including the movements of the young men who assaulted Jane, the individuals present during her rape, and aspects of her abuse at the hands of Trent Mays and Ma'lik Richmond. Following Doe's complaint, prosecutors seized and analyzed 13 smartphones as evidence and reviewed 96,270 text messages, 3,188 phone calls, 308,586 photos, and 940 videos, uncovering several implicating photos, videos, and texts about the assault.[22] According to Adam Nemann, defense attorney for Mays, "without the digital evidence, there would've been no Steubenville rape case." He elaborates:

> Yes, because without it, it would have been basically rumors that caused a girl concern or her parents concern, who would then go to the police, and unless individuals that are questioned came forward and admitted to doing anything improper or sexual, there was no evidence that anything improper occurred, outside of the digital evidence. And so, this case was born with digital media. It became a national sensation due to the YouTube video by Nodianos. So, the whole ball got rolling from there. . . . [P]eople would ask, "Trent, what happened?" through a text message on his phone, and he would respond, "Oh, nothing." I believe his response to the messages was, "I just fingered her, that's all." Well, that's an admission to rape. [laughs] In Ohio, if there's no consent, and you know there's no consent, any penetration, ever so slightly, even digital, is rape. And so, something that, in his mind, is harmless as a statement is what convicted him, along with other things.

Nemann noted that Trent Mays's cell phone, in particular, was a trove of information that, once legally seized and searched, irrefutably implicated him in the rape:

I can tell you that when they seized my client's, Trent Mays, [phone] from a search warrant, the phone itself had photographs on it and text messages and tweets, some of which were verified through other people's phones as having received them or having had conversations with them. So, he didn't delete anything. He kept everything on his phone, even two or three days later. So, the evidence was all on his cell phone. There's nothing to dispute.

Metadata from the pictures found on his smartphone show the images were taken and sent by Mays. This technology was then also able to serve as a witness during the trial, testifying on Jane Doe's behalf. There were two photographs used by the prosecution—one of the girl being carried by her hands and feet by the two perpetrators, her head fallen back, clearly unconscious; the other of her naked, passed out face down on the floor, hands awkwardly tucked beneath her, with semen on her body.[23] The prosecution used the first of these images to demonstrate Jane's intoxicated state and inability to consent, and the second as proof that sexual activity (abuse) had occurred while she remained unconscious. The defense attorney for Richmond argued context was missing from both photographs, that it was quite possible the first photo was staged, the victim faking being passed out when the boys were carrying her. He further maintained Jane could have consented to sexual activity before the second photo of her awkwardly lying on the floor naked was taken. But as various attorneys repeatedly explain, visual evidence—photos, video, and even text messages/ social media posts—can be difficult to disprove, and more notably, hard for juries and/or judges to overcome:

> Well, as a criminal defense attorney that's been doing this for forty years, I can tell you it's pretty hard to cross-examine a video or a picture. And you couple that with the testimony of a young victim who says, "I was passed out and I may have been drugged or I drunk too much," it's awful hard to overcome that evidence (criminal defense attorney).

> But where you have it in print, or on pictures, or a video of it, I think it has two effects. One, it removes any doubt. Sometimes the digital evidence speaks for itself, and witness credibility is no longer an issue. And second, to see some of the things that people do to each other, in my experience, is far more moving and difficult than to hear about it. . . . (and a bit later). . . But I think being forced to see it, and have the crime have a little more context in that sense, can be very valuable, persuasive, and sometimes very damning evidence at sentencing, at trial, and anywhere (judge, former prosecutor).

> Yeah, well, I mean, I can tell you, you know, pictures of crimes being committed are extremely powerful, there's really no way to refute them. And they [defense attorneys] will go to any effort they can to make sure these images are not presented before a jury . . . because once they are, they realize they're

extremely powerful, that there is no defending something that can be seen by a jury with their own eyes (civil victim attorney).

What these lawyers are highlighting is the role of imagery in influencing the production of truth and legal objectivity in the courtroom. The authority of visual evidence, its potential to communicate "the truth," as well as to inflame, is presented as useful for victims in sexual assault cases, helping to undermine some of the more entrenched rape myths and biases impacting the prosecution of sex crimes. For attorneys, the digital trail and visual evidence provide a means of truth-knowing in a way that verbal testimony cannot offer. Static and incontrovertible in their nature, digital data are perceived as capable of offering a rendering of the events—of the sexual violence—uncontaminated by the passage of time and memory. As one prosecutor put it, when "you have a contemporaneous recording or contemporaneous picture of the situation, that's gonna typically be more helpful than, you know, someone's just memory alone. I think that we can all admit . . . that sometimes memories fade or they adjust over time but usually that picture or that video remains, you know, what happened at that situation." More to the point, Dawn Moore and Rashmee Singh explain that when the living victim speaks, "her narrative cannot escape the artificial tinge it acquires as a second story delivered far after the initial incident occurred."[24] She is distant from her abuse and has had too much time to reformulate it, reconsider the implications, and give an accurate account of it. Human memory, here, is constructed as fallible or false in a way that images of human bodies and of-the-moment exclamations made through social media posts, text messaging, and so on are not. David Mejia, defense attorney for Ma'lik Richmond, explains:

> The availability of e-mails and public photography and text messages and tweets and instantaneous kind of commentary on what they see is good because it's revealing of the truth. We have what's called spontaneous declaration. Excited utterance, you know, these things are reliable, these things are dependable. What somebody says without an opportunity to rehearse or to prepare is more reliable and credible than what they say a year and a half later in a courtroom.

Conventional wisdom tells us that memory and words can be manipulated and confused, particularly when coming from a woman—a subject that has been historically constructed as inherently unreliable; the visual image, on the other hand, is perceived as bypassing all these risks.

I want to pause here for a moment and note that the use of digital evidence, and the privileging of visual evidence in the courtroom, is not uncomplicated. By privileging the "truth" new media technologies provide over the narratives and testimony of victims, police and prosecutors are also indirectly reproducing rape myths and misconceptions about the veracity and untrustworthiness of survivors of sexual violence.[25] If the message from these actors is that images do not lie, the implication is that women do. The fact that a survivor's allegations require additional corroboration through digital communication further reifies the notion that her words are insufficient and unreliable. The capacity of digital evidence to offer the "truth" is also limited. Broader assumptions that "seeing is believing," such as the ones voiced by the attorneys here, often contribute to the construction of digital and visual evidence as an objective and neutral witness in trials. Images, however, do not speak for themselves; the idea that seeing is believing does not hold up against research that examines the use of images in law historically and finds a legacy of contestation and the reality that courts do not always take visual evidence at face value.[26] Socio-legal scholarship on visual evidence, in particular, demonstrates that images occupy an ambivalent position in the courtroom, as the visual is a contested field, with factors like race, class, sexuality, ability, and other social categories impacting what juries and audiences see and what they perceive as truth.[27] Relatedly, and as discussed further in the next chapter, the emotion that images of harm and abuse are assumed to evoke in judges and juries is not always guaranteed—whether or not we extend sympathy to a sexual assault victim depends both on our subject position and on theirs.[28] Nevertheless, dismissing the potential of new technologies and digital evidence for investigating sex crimes risks trivializing the multiple victimizations and harms that survivors experience in the digital age and perpetuating the ongoing institutional apathy toward the problem of sexual violence.

Contesting Perpetrator Stereotypes

Digital evidence further bolsters victim credibility through the repository of self-incriminating social media communication, photos, and text messages it offers law enforcement. The direct quotes and images digital media preserve, and avail, are "irrefutable" for the defense. "Those are his words. That's his communication, and it's recorded, and it's documented forever. That's very difficult. There's nothing I can do," explains one attorney. Digital exchanges are particularly useful for revealing the motives and intent of defendants. In Steubenville, for example, prosecutors recovered text messages from Trent Mays admitting to his friends he "just fingered her [Jane Doe]," a statement directly attesting to his guilt. In some of these exchanges, Doe is described as "a dead girl," which Mays affirms by texting back "LOL, she couldn't even move," a response that communicates his awareness of her heavily intoxicated state, as well as his callousness over her inability to consent.

Not only do such statements undermine his character and further solidify his culpability in Doe's rape, but they also demonstrate that the assault was a crime of opportunity. Such evidence can help chip away at long-held rape myths that assailants are often motivated by lust, are pathological in their sexual needs, or did not intend to harm the victim. More generally, digital evidence can be useful for overcoming the *mens rea* element—the intention or knowledge of wrongdoing that constitutes part of a crime, of which many rape cases fail to convince a jury.[29] There can be little question of an accused "not knowing" he was acting without the victim's consent if a message shows the perpetrator is aware of—and sometimes even boasting about—a victim's unconscious state, or if there is a photograph depicting him violating a clearly unconscious person. This also helps challenge young men's claims of "misunderstanding" around consent, or not realizing that they were participating in illegal behavior. Bob Allard, attorney for the Audrie Pott family, describes how this played out in Audrie's case:

> There was—through the Facebook—through the texting, messaging, that we did uncover from the police that it appears there were great lengths made to destroy the evidence. Just outright messaging between two of them [the perpetrators] saying, delete all photographs, make sure so and so has deleted them, make sure so and so has deleted them too, there was a conscious effort to cover their tracks.

This intent and efforts to cover up on behalf of the three young men went a long way in proving their guilt, according to Allard. Similar tactics are evident in the Steubenville case, where multiple text messages from Trent Mays to his friends show he was trying to orchestrate a cover-up by urging them to conceal what transpired the night of the assault:

> Her dad knows, and if our names get brought up, if asked, she was just really drunk.

> They knew she stayed at Mark's. You just gotta say she was asleep by the time you got there.

Nodi's running his mouth saying how dead she was. If anyone asks, we just took her to Mark's, and she fell asleep.

Just say she passed out at your house if anyone asks.[30]

Prosecutors and civil attorneys can further use digital evidence to undermine claims of a defendant's remorse and to counter arguments that a crime was a one-time behavioral aberration. For instance, when arrests were finally made in the Audrie Pott case, seven months after her assault, new pictures of other nude teenage girls were found on the phones of two of the offenders. Prosecutors used the photos to demonstrate the young men refused to accept responsibility or show regret for Audrie's assault, or her suicide, and continued to disrespect and abuse women.[31] In addition to the criminal conviction, Audrie's family also brought a wrongful death civil suit against the three young offenders and their families. Allard, the Potts' family attorney, relied on the digital trail of these young men soliciting and distributing nude photos of girls, even after Audrie's death, to successfully argue the defendants' behavior was part of a larger pattern of digital abuse and to settle the lawsuit with all three families.[32]

These case studies and attorney insights reveal that digital media have the potential to be productive for state responses to sexual violence. Digital evidence is very useful for police and prosecutors because it helps make their cases stronger, whether by improving victim credibility, by providing better evidence of the crime, or through the powerful visual proof it offers juries and judges. New technologies enable prosecutors to disrupt some of the cultural stereotypes judges and juries draw on when faced with uncertain or limited information, offering concrete evidence to fill in gaps where otherwise rape myths might prevail. Moreover, visual depictions of unconscious women being assaulted by their peers may provide a powerful counternarrative to the "real" rape myth and victim-blaming discourses informing so many popular understandings of sexual assault. Photos of the unconscious Jane Doe and Audrie Pott being sexually assaulted, for instance, show that force is not necessary for a rape to occur, and that victimization often happens at the hands of someone familiar to the victim. These images also offer incontrovertible evidence of missing consent, and that these young women were not "asking for it" as they were incapable of participating in consensual sexual activity. There is nothing ambiguous about a passed-out teenager, and by capturing this, often alongside the boastful confessions of offenders, technology helps refute any suggestions that a rape allegation is not real or is merely a misunderstanding. As such, legal actors place high evidentiary value on the digital trail because it can be useful at every phase of the criminal justice process, facilitating the investigation of sexual assault allegations and challenging commonly held assumptions and stereotypes about rape victims and what constitutes a "real" rape, as well as persuading courts and juries that a rape occurred and the accused is guilty of a crime.

NEW MEDIA, NEW OBSTACLES

Despite the opportunities digital technologies provide for investigating and prosecuting rape and sexual assault, the use of digital data in this area is not without multiple new challenges. Legal scholarship consistently shows that most of the legal challenges on the sorts of digital evidence that can be accepted into court proceedings arise in the form of *discoverability*, *admissibility*, and especially *authentication* and *reliability* issues.[33] A combination of a lack of resources, training, and cultural lag relating to the rapidly changing technological landscape contributes to these hurdles for both law enforcement and legal professionals. One major complication resulting from the digital turn is that new technologies require police to dramatically recalibrate the skills they require during investigations. Although the process of collecting evidence during an investigation has not changed, the knowledge and skills required of law enforcement to effectively handle digital evidence are new and evolving. Police in sex crime units are now required to have the know-how to access a variety of social media sites, applications, and mobile technologies to find and correctly document evidence of the crime.[34] Dedicated units or personnel trained in digital forensics—the systematic and scientific methods for collecting and preserving data—therefore are needed across police departments to ensure the authenticity and integrity of digital data. But available funding for such units varies across jurisdictions, leaving many departments without digital forensics specialists or the training required for officers to accurately access and document digital evidence.[35]

Data Collection and Discovery

The lack of adequate resources and expertly trained staff in digital forensics is well documented in the broader policing literature. While social media are increasingly used by police as an intelligence gathering tool for investigations, a 2021 report sponsored by the National Institute of Justice finds significant challenges to successfully using digital evidence in prosecutions, including officer inexperience in preserving and collecting this evidence, as well as a lack of familiarity with digital evidence on the part of court officials.[36] The authors also reveal that digital forensics examiners are overwhelmed by the volume of work during such investigations. Research from the United Kingdom, Australia, and Canada similarly shows police officers citing under-sourcing and the lack of training on digital technologies as major barriers to effectively responding to technology-related offenses in sex crime investigations.[37]

Such findings suggest many law enforcement personnel are primarily self-taught in their usage of social media, including the use of digital platforms for investigations. The average person, meanwhile, has five connected devices, each containing potential for information. Most investigations involve several devices consisting of different infrastructures, operating systems, firmware, and software; data can be stored locally or on a cloud service, and in different formats, and may be encrypted or password protected.[38] For these reasons, many cases require multiple investigators with specialized knowledge working in tandem. The training and time needed to remain current with the rapidly changing technological landscape are daunting, particularly for law enforcement and legal personnel faced with limited resources.

Lack of digital literacy among officers increases the risk of *spoliation* of evidence during the discovery phase. Phones and other digital devices may get lost or damaged, data—text messages, photos, video, email—can be erased, or accounts deleted, because the officers responding to an incident may not know how to secure or use digital evidence to preserve chain of custody and ensure that evidence is later admissible in court. According to one prosecutor, when it comes to digital evidence:

> I think the biggest challenges are, do we get that information in time? I mean, people are destroying phones. You know, I think people now realize, you know, take your SIM card out, destroy it, um, throw the phone away. That doesn't always stop everything but it delays, often, law enforcement agencies from being able to get vital pieces of information whether it includes text messages—a lot of cell phone providers don't maintain text messages for a long period of time, and so if you have something that's a late report, you don't realize what happened and you're only getting the information three months later and when you service a search warrant on someone, a lot of that data may have been deleted already.

During the Audrie Pott investigation, for instance, the police took over a week to collect cell phones from the perpetrators, giving the young men plenty of opportunity to delete evidence of the crime (or in this instance, to damage one phone and lose another). The Pott family claims the loss of these devices delayed the investigation for up to seven months, while the police tried to recover enough evidence to charge two of the offenders.

The increasingly ephemeral nature of social media applications, as well as growing user sophistication, can also frustrate the collection and discovery of digital evidence. Several of the prosecutors I spoke with described spending hours online researching how young people are communicating with each other, creating social media accounts to look for evidence, and the ongoing effort they have to make to stay current on emerging technologies. Moreover, while young people, and social media users in general, continue to capture and share all types of activity through new technologies, they are, as one attorney observed, "starting to get smarter about how they use that information, deleting that information, finding an application that won't maintain their data for very long, etcetera." He goes on:

> I'll say, as a prosecutor, what we're always facing is there's always going to be new applications, digital applications, like the WhatsApps, the GroupMes, SnapChats, where the app is, you know, not developed for criminals to hide or make it more difficult to prosecute cases but where that digital imprint is not left as much, or not as much information is there, and that makes our job more difficult because you could send 50 SnapChats of pictures to your friends and there may not be a record of exactly what the picture is if we don't get to that in a certain amount of time, because that's not kept and they, you know, erase those pictures relatively quickly.

These comments hint at the police and prosecutors always being one step behind those using technology to offend, especially social media–savvy youth, and having to catch up to the technical expertise of perpetrators. Consequently, investigative responses to the digital trail and gathering evidence on social media often reflect an ad hoc approach, rather than a consistent, systemized response.

Even if investigators can successfully obtain access to digital devices in a timely manner, the sheer volume of data they must process, validate, and analyze is overwhelming, time-consuming, and resource-intensive for already overburdened sex crime units. The large volume of digital information in these cases, combined with shortages in personnel and digital literacy training across police departments, results in backlogs that considerably lengthen many investigations, delaying trials and potential resolutions for both victims and offenders.[39] Moreover, the increase in wait time may contribute to victims of sexual assault remembering fewer details at trial, which could compromise the successful prosecution of their case, or in survivors becoming frustrated with the criminal justice system and opting to no longer pursue the case.

Investigations may be further slowed down or impeded as law enforcement personnel wait for access to information involving technology companies, outside sources, or different jurisdictions. There is a lengthy wait time to obtain warrants for all digital devices and (known) social media platforms or to subpoena tech companies and third-party providers to preserve and/or turn over users' data, increasing the likelihood of spoliation. Sometimes, companies that run or host social networking sites are located overseas (e.g., Kik) and may be slow or altogether unwilling to cooperate with law enforcement efforts. Other telecommunications companies or social media platforms, like Snapchat, may not keep records of the required information. Historically, companies such as Facebook have been generally willing to cooperate with law enforcement in their investigations, as long as they are showed legal cause for access to the information being requested.[40] However, as users in recent years have become more aware of privacy and surveillance concerns, tech companies have also turned toward "privacy" and "data protection" in their newer product offerings, to meet user demands. Companies like Apple and Signal, for instance, provide users with end-to-end encryption services that limit access to user data, including from the companies themselves (e.g., when a file is deleted from an iPhone, the data is scrambled, and the file cannot be recovered). I am not arguing for a closer relationship between technology companies and the police state, here, or an expansion of the surveillance dragnet. The privacy concerns expressed by users are certainly warranted; as the storage capacity of digital devices continues to increase, digital investigations are gathering larger amounts of information, often well beyond the specific evidence needed in a case. Nevertheless, it is worth noting that these new technological developments frustrate the investigative and evidentiary potential of digital media for sex crimes, and for victim-survivors more broadly.

Admissibility of Digital Evidence

Assuming the challenges just discussed are overcome, and digital evidence is discovered and collected in time, lawyers next come across admissibility issues. Judges make decisions about admissibility in terms of reliability, veracity, and accuracy.[41] Data needs to be authenticated before it is admitted into evidence, and legal scholarship finds that courts doubt the authenticity of digital evidence because they distrust and/or do not understand new technologies. Although most judges use digital platforms and the Internet, they are not necessarily more knowledgeable about the underlying technologies of the hardware, software, and applications than the general population of social media and computer users.[42] In their interviews, attorneys also cited authentication issues as the most common challenge to digital evidence. One juvenile sex crimes prosecutor best articulates the multiple issues with reliability, veracity, and accuracy that attorneys encounter when working with new technologies:

> Additionally, let's say you screenshotted everything. You know, you've got some classmate who's been posting nasty things about you on Facebook or Instagram, and you screenshotted every time they do it. So I can show, you know, okay, good. That's the date it posted on; it was posted on this account. How do I prove that the person whose account in whose name it is, is the one who did it? . . . Because if I leave my phone unattended, you know, everybody's been, you know, Facebook hacked, where someone leaves a gross status response—status update—because you were careless enough to leave your phone unattended without a password lock. So, that is often a defense, is that, "I'm not the one who put it up there." And the burden is not on a defendant or a suspect to prove they didn't do it; the burden is on me to prove that they did. . . . Even if I can tie the account to that person, how do I prove that, you know, that the keystrokes that actually put that on were done by the client? I can't, unless they admit to it, or someone else can testify that they were with them when they did that, you know, status update or posted that photo or whatever.

Attorneys often rely on a forensic examination of the data to prove authenticity and reliability of social networking evidence. Web content, social media postings, and multimedia messages may be embedded with metadata—data about data that describes when and by whom data was created, accessed, modified, formatted, and stored—that help establish the data is what it purports to be. However, origin issues remain, as metadata cannot always identify the individual who created the data. In the Steubenville case, for instance, the media focused heavily on the volume of digital information available to law enforcement officials, framing this digital trail as a "gold mine" for prosecutors.[43] The probable cause hearing transcript, however, tells a somewhat different story. The forensic expert in the case repeatedly testified the EXIF information—that is, metadata identifying the make and mode of the phone camera taking a photo, the data/time the image was taken, saved, and so forth—was stripped from the photos. This meant the forensic expert was often unable to tell who took a photograph, only being able to identify if the image was sent or received through text messages. Further corroboration from bystanders and text messages from Trent Mays's phone were needed to ascertain the origin of the two images included in the criminal prosecution.

Sometimes authentication challenges arise because judges and juries lack an understanding of how new technologies work, or because these actors are aware of the existence of fake and shared online accounts and the risk of inaccurate or incomplete information.[44] A California prosecutor elaborated on this point:

> I mean, I think there's always the—the general defense strategy and this applies to, you know, DNA, all evidence, which is, how do I know—how can you prove that this is what it says, okay? Or what it purports to be, you know? How do I know that this is a forensically sound way to, you know, retrieve this information? . . . So, you know, we have to convince juries and judges sometimes of the evidence and that it is what it says, what it purports to be. And I think just understanding how the evidence works, understanding when a picture goes in the cloud, understanding why I know something was sent. For example, I know a text message was sent to these people and it was a picture, but I can't recover the picture, and being able to explain that. So I think you have all of those issues that we deal with, you know, as technology advances in general.

Accuracy and veracity issues can also be the result of missing context or lack of information. For example, the prosecutor who described the challenges of proving the source of a message further noted that she often also has to prove "what it [the message] actually means," given young people's use of slang and/or coded language. This is in line with earlier critiques that suggest we need to be careful to interpret digital evidence in the context of digital forms of expression. It is common, for example, for social media users to attempt to portray a happier and more likeable version of themselves in digital exchanges, regardless of how they are feeling. Likewise, youth, and young men especially, have a tendency to engage in outrageous talk over text messages and social media postings that is not necessarily honest. Legal scholars similarly observe that digital evidence can be difficult to interpret because of the decontextualized space of social media, where social cues, figurative speech, and offline dynamics make meaning difficult to parse.[45]

The lack of context surrounding digital evidence was often brought up by defense attorneys as a strategy to exclude or rebut such evidence. Walter Madison, Ma'lik Richmond's attorney in Steubenville, for instance, repeatedly argued over context on the two pictures of Jane Doe. He maintained that it was difficult to ascertain whether the pictures were staged (as a joke), or if the victim consented to sex sometime before the photo was taken, challenging their presentation as depictions of her heavily intoxicated status or proof of rape. Although cited frequently during the interviews, one former prosecutor astutely observed that context in the case of digital evidence is no different than any other type of evidence:

> In an investigation by the prosecution or the defense, and in the courtroom, the thought is, you never are relying on any single piece of evidence without any context. You're always aware, just like when a witness testifies live, that they may not be giving the whole picture. And so, we believe in cross-examination, we believe in corroboration. You look for other materials to either support or contradict what they're saying. That's the very same thing in digital media evidence. If you're getting emails, you want to get all of—you want to get a large portion of them, not simply the one email. Because of course it might be that it's a joke, it might be it's taken out of context. A Snapchat is particularly challenging, since in theory they disappear right away. You might not be able to get that context. Same with text messages, where somebody texts one person on this phone, but then they may be texting—since many people have 16 phones and devices—you may be getting one part of the conversation, when it turns out that the rest of it is occurring somewhere else. But again, I think that that's something, certainly as a prosecutor, I would not rely on any individual statement to make an entire case, without looking to corroborate it, or contradict it with other evidence.

These interviews highlight that although digital evidence may require more due diligence than other types of evidence, the unique investigative and courtroom challenges pertaining to it are primarily the result of human limitations, whether that is because criminal justice personnel lack the resources or the technical know-how to effectively use such data. The industry as a whole—law enforcement officers, prosecutors, defense attorneys, and judges—needs to do more to stay abreast of technological changes. Rather than increasing personnel or budgets, however, these efforts should focus on reallocating existing resources toward training criminal justice actors to update and improve their knowledge of the role of technologies in sexual violence perpetration.

INSTITUTIONAL RESISTANCE

Of course we cannot assume the criminal justice system and its actors are interested in taking a more proactive approach toward digital evidence in their responses to sexual violence.[46] Ad hoc approaches in many sexual assault investigations reveal persisting generational gaps in attitudes toward technology among police units, with some older officers and supervisors not fully understanding the length and complexity of investigations in the current digital landscape.[47] Other officers display an unwillingness to take digital abuse seriously, perhaps in part because of a lack of training on digital technologies or as a result of the same generational gap previously cited.[48] During our interview, Carry Goldberg, a NYC-based victim attorney specializing in sexual privacy violations, described her encounters with the police in cases of digital abuse as often met with a dismissive, "Oh, you know, with these cybercrimes, it's just so hard to investigate." The underlying assumption informing these practices, as well as the approach of institutional actors who do engage with digital technologies and evidence when responding to sex crimes, is that sexual violence and its subsequent digital circulation are discrete rather than interrelated events. Just as the incidents discussed in this book provide the public with examples of the technological risk youth must contend with, so too for many officers and prosecutors the digital trail is simply more proof of a sex crime. They fail to account for the harm new technologies and digital evidence may cause vulnerable victims and for the ways that harm is gendered. And because many criminal justice professionals do not conceptualize the non-consensual sharing of intimate images—including images of sexual assault—as a type of digital sexual abuse, as potentially also a crime, they approach digital evidence simply as one more *optional* tool they can engage with, effectively or not, in their responses to sexual violence.

For law enforcement personnel who do recognize the value of the digital trail for investigating rape and sexual assault, the opportunity to use it may be limited, as the volume of digital evidence in sex crime cases has not been met with an equal shift in staffing and resources for digital forensics training and units. This delay is particularly striking considering police departments' enthusiastic embrace of digital surveillance across other crime categories. Scholarship in the last decade has provided numerous examples of the growth in "big data" policing and the increasing reliance of police on social media to identify and corroborate criminal behavior and networks, as well as the use of algorithms to map and predict crime.[49] Recent events, such as the unchecked expansion of gang databases, the investigation of the January 6 attack on the Capitol, and the uses of people's digital activity to criminalize abortion, offer instructive case studies in law enforcement's comfort with and access to the digital trail and the increasing frequency with which digital evidence and communications feature in the courtroom. These realities suggest the slow response to incorporating new technologies in sex crime investigations is not simply about more resources and knowledge development. There is also a cultural and institutional problem across the criminal legal system, a resistance to acknowledging the ways sexual violence and technology are increasingly enmeshed in the digital age, that signals an institutional unwillingness to address sexual violence and the subsequent digital harm resulting from its circulation. The state has a long history of failing survivors, and its lack of interest in engaging with technology to respond to sexual violence and digital abuse signals one more instance of institutional abandonment.

REPRODUCING INEQUALITIES IN PRACTICE?

Institutional attitudes and varying approaches to digital evidence and technology-facilitated abuse also matter for how young offenders are treated by the criminal justice system, potentially exposing them to differential treatment depending on jurisdiction. A major concern for both parents and legal scholars is that increased reliance on digital evidence in juvenile sex crime cases may contribute to harsher punishments and the overcriminalization of youth. The law has been slow to recognize digital harms and inconsistent in its responses to issues such as non-consensual pornography. Many states use already existing laws on sexting, stalking, voyeurism, and harassment to address image-based sexual abuse, and as of 2022 all but two states had passed "revenge porn" laws, although these do not specifically engage with adolescents.[50] Instead, youth who non-consensually distribute an intimate or sexual image may face child pornography charges—especially in cases where the images being distributed feature a sex crime.[51]

Legal scholars have thoughtfully argued that child pornography laws were designed to address pedophilic behavior and protect children from sexual exploitation involving a power imbalance between adult and child. Using them in instances of image-based abuse may contribute to severe responses by law enforcement, including decade-long sentences and the placement of minors on their state's sex offender registry. There is also the possibility that such criminal charges will likely disproportionately penalize racialized, queer, and low-income youth, given our long history of using criminal law as a tool through which we emphasize racial, class, and sexual inequalities and punish the most marginalized among us.[52] Research from surveillance studies on youth gangs, drugs, and big data and policing already finds that new technologies exacerbate current inequalities in criminal justice responses.[53] More recently, scholars have suggested that digital evidence may add a further layer of inequality to the criminal justice system, as public defender offices struggle to access digital evidence and forensic technologies.[54] In the United States, the people most dependent on legal assistance are the poor, who disproportionately consist of people of color, immigrants, and LGBTQI+ populations.[55] Currently, public defenders struggle to gather digital evidence because social media companies only cooperate with law enforcement requests. Even when they do obtain the evidence, they lack the staff and resources to process this data. As a result, most public defender offices outsource requests for digital evidence assistance to third parties, a costly and time-consuming process that cannot be used in every case. The inability of public defenders to mount a strong defense for their clients means further increasing the vulnerability of indigent defendants in a system that is already biased against marginalized groups.[56]

When it comes to sexual violence, however, where disbelief that a crime has occurred and an institutional unwillingness to investigate persist, the issue is murkier. Emerging research from socio-legal studies on youth sexting and non-consensual intimate image sharing reveals that prosecutions for child pornography offenses in these instances are rare, and that discretion is widely used over how to charge youth violating pornography laws. Discretionary practices are evident at both the law enforcement and prosecutorial levels. For example, a recent study by Alexa Dodge and Dale Spencer on police responses to image-based sexual abuse found that while Canada continues to utilize child pornography charges in cases involving youth, investigators see these statutes as harsh and stigmatizing, and they often use discretion to avoid the criminalization of young men by utilizing extra-judicial means to respond to the offense.[57] The prosecutors I interviewed for this study similarly acknowledged the "catchall" nature of child pornography statutes. They expressed concern over the severity and implication of child pornography charges for young people and their futures and over the law's failure to account for varying degrees of culpability with different image-based sexual abuse scenarios. As a result, most of them exercise wide prosecutorial discretion when dealing with such potential charges in juvenile sex crimes. Most attorneys noted that in cases of image-based sexual abuse among youth, rather than criminal punishment, they often opt for diversionary programs and more corrective approaches, such as counseling, especially since most of these teens are first-time offenders.

Although the Jane Doe and Audrie Pott cases cannot provide a generalizable conclusion, it is worth noting that in Steubenville, Trent Mays was charged with "illegal use of a minor in nudity-oriented material" and sentenced to an extra year in a juvenile facility for transmission of nude photos, serving a total sentence of two years for the rape.[58] Both he and Richmond were initially required to register as sex offenders, but by 2018 they both had successfully appealed to be removed from the registry altogether, as Ohio law allows those convicted as juveniles to request removal. The three young men who assaulted Audrie Pott were also charged with—and pled guilty to—felony possession of child pornography, in addition to the sexual battery and abuse charges pertaining to the assault; no additional or harsher punishment resulted from this charge, nor were they required to register as sex offenders.[59]

More data is needed on how child pornography laws are applied in incidents involving sexual assault *and* image-based sexual abuse among adolescents. The preceding case studies and interviews do suggest some legal actors recognize the complexity of cases that exist at the intersection of youth sexualities, violence, and technology and are aware that punitive responses may not be the best approach. At the same time, it is unclear how race and class factors may complicate prosecutorial decisions in such cases. Previous research on sexual violence has shown how biases based on race and class—of both perpetrators and victims—impact the investigation and prosecution of sex crimes.[60] More recent scholarship with public defenders suggests digital evidence also contributes to the admission of selective and prejudicial evidence in the courtroom, which often plays into negative, racial stereotypes for defendants.[61] It is not hard to imagine how these biases and practices may extend to digital abuse, considering that law enforcement and legislators are still trying to develop a consensus about how to engage with digital media and manage technology-facilitated sexual violence.

Considering the criminal justice system's ongoing struggles with effectively responding to sexual violence, it is understandable why legal actors are hopeful about the potential of digital technologies in helping to investigate and prosecute sex crimes. The digital evidence in the Steubenville and Audrie Pott assaults clearly demonstrates the efficacy of the digital trail for providing proof of crime, corroborating witness testimony, and supplying offender motive and intent—key issues at the center of rape and sexual assault cases. The ongoing privilege awarded to visual evidence in the courtroom may further work in survivors' favor, as images and videos of their victimization can help bolster their credibility and garner sympathy from judges and juries, particularly in cases where the victim meets the "ideal" criteria of white, middle-class femininity.

As the cases and interviews discussed in this chapter indicate, however, such evidence is not without limitations. The rapidly evolving nature of technologies means law enforcement cannot always keep up with the skills or the resources needed to successfully mine these platforms for evidence. Even when digital evidence is collected in time, attorneys still have to contend with due diligence and admissibility issues, including verifying the authenticity and veracity of the data as well as overcoming knowledge limitations and cultural resistance in the industry. The role of visual evidence in the courtroom also remains ambivalent, its utility still limited by the same biases that challenge the veracity of other types of evidence in sexual violence cases. Research has repeatedly demonstrated the ways that race, class, gender, and sexuality, among other factors, impact reactions to visual evidence as well as victims and perpetrators in trial history and in sexual assault adjudication specifically.

It is unclear, in fact, what young survivors' experiences with digital evidence are in sexual assault investigations, and whether the potential of the digital trail is realized for teen victims who seek redress through the criminal justice system. These questions inform the discussion in the following chapter, where I explore how digital technologies impact disclosure and justice-seeking practices among survivors. Specifically, I investigate how intersecting categories, such as age, race, and class, as well as the capacity of new media to store, search, and circulate vast amounts of information, inform the experiences of this vulnerable population. The chapter also considers the implications of the law's inattention to digital harm for responses to sexual violence, and whether digital evidence is an effective solution for overcoming traditional barriers to addressing sexual violence through the criminal legal system.

4

Navigating Justice

Young Survivors and the Harms
of Image-Based Sexual Abuse

One of the earliest themes to appear in articles about the Steubenville rape is that of technology as a digital witness to the crime, with the incident described as "unfolding on the Internet, on Twitter and via text messages."[1] News stories present the social media activity from that night as testimony and regularly credit technology for uncovering the incident. The *New York Times*, for example, refers to Steubenville as the "rape that social media brought to light," seeming to suggest that without the digital witnessing, no one would have known about the assault.[2] This implication is particularly true in the case of survivors for whom, in bearing witness, new media enable the discovery of their abuse. The *Los Angeles Times* describes Jane Doe as learning about her rape "only after seeing text messages and viewing pictures and videos posted online from that night."[3] A similar "uncovering through social media" is depicted in the Pott case. Audrie woke up after the party to find her undergarments askew and writings on her body, but it was not until she went online that she discovered the full scope of her violation.[4]

The news articles do not explicitly discuss the challenges survivors of rape and sexual assault face when interacting with the criminal justice system, but implicit in their framing is the knowledge that sexual violence remains one of the most underreported crimes. Official statistics indicate that only 23 percent of victims report their crimes to the police.[5] For survivors under 18 years old, research suggests this number may be lower than the adult population. Adolescents make up 15 percent of all sexual assault victims, with more recent studies placing this figure at 20 percent for girls.[6] Reporting estimates among this group range from 8 to 19 percent of victims going to law enforcement about their crime.[7] Studies consistently show factors impacting women's reporting practices include fear of not being believed, self-blame, and fear that the police will not (or cannot) do anything to help, among others. These concerns are particularly acute in cases of acquaintance rape and instances where alcohol and/or drugs are involved, factors that increase the likelihood of victim-blaming.[8] As noted in the last chapter, while sexual assault by someone known to the victim and including the use of substances make up the majority of rape cases, research indicates law enforcement and prosecutors are less likely to investigate such incidents as they are seen as difficult to prove in the courts.

The presence of alcohol and the risk of victim-blaming are especially important aspects influencing young people's disclosure, given their age and dependent status.[9] Many young victims also must consider parental, school, and peer relationships when deciding to report, and studies show that sexual abuse disclosure is often delayed until adulthood for this population. The fear of getting in trouble with their parents, a lack of social networks and support, and the fear of being bullied about the incident by their peers at school may prevent survivors from disclosing an assault.[10] In their study on substance use and juvenile sexual assault, Amy Young and colleagues found that 12 to 20 percent of adolescents reported alcohol was involved at the time of the assault; for young women, this figure jumped to 29 percent when the victimization happened at parties or someone else's home. Victims who were incapacitated when they were assaulted may be more likely to partially blame themselves for being raped and less likely to report the crime.[11] The presence of alcohol and heavy intoxication also mean victims may experience difficulty in remembering the assault or its details, further reducing the chances of disclosing to the police. These factors are compounded for young survivors of multiple perpetrator assaults, whose victimization often occurs in social settings, such as house parties, and frequently involves alcohol, further decreasing the likelihood of reporting. In their study with adolescent gang-rape survivors, Laurel Edinburgh and colleagues discovered that most victims did not come forward in the aftermath of the incident; of the 32 young women they interviewed, only 4 reported their assault.[12]

REDUCING REPORTING BARRIERS

In the last chapter I detailed the utility of digital evidence for survivors of sexual violence during the investigative and adjudication processes, capturing evidence of the crime, and proffering corroborating evidence of a rape or sexual assault. In some instances, new technologies also provide insight into the offender(s)' state of mind or admissions of criminal behavior, further helping support a victim's allegations and testimony of events. For some survivors, however, the benefits of the digital trail may be felt earlier on in the process, in their decision to report and police willingness to investigate allegations.

Discovering and Reporting Abuse

Cases of multi-perpetrator rape such as the ones discussed here occur in social settings and frequently involve illicit substances, meaning often victims are not even aware of being assaulted while under the influence. They may wake up the next day with a sense of *something* having occurred the previous night, but lacking specifics, decide to ignore the feeling. Or, as in Jane Doe's case in Steubenville, they may not be aware anything bad has happened at all. One of the more useful unintended consequences of perpetrators and bystanders using digital technologies to capture an assault is that social media can bear witness (to the crime) in instances where the victim cannot do so, enabling survivors to discover their abuse. Digital media aided both Jane Doe and Audrie Pott in finding out about their assaults, as well as the details and extent of their abuse. By documenting the context in which these incidents occur, social media may also facilitate better parental and community responses in such cases. As I observed earlier, it can be difficult to dismiss rape allegations if there are videos and images of an unconscious victim or text messages and social media postings of the perpetrators admitting to the crime. While this may not be true for many in our society, as we saw in some of the social media responses to Steubenville, it may lead to less victim-blaming and more supportive responses by some parents and peers in adolescents' lives.

Furthermore, the evidence gathered by digital platforms in the Doe and Pott cases contributed to the parents of both victims reporting the crime to law enforcement, suggesting that such evidence may also increase the likelihood that other survivors of sexual assault who are interested in pursuing legal recourse will do the same. If there is a trail of photos, text messages, or social media postings documenting or attesting to their sexual victimization, survivors and their families recognize this evidence could increase the likelihood they will be believed by law enforcement. In Steubenville, for instance, when Jane Doe and her parents went to the police to report her rape, they brought with them a flash drive with Twitter posts, photos, and the YouTube video on it. Despite the time elapsed and the lack of physical evidence of the assault, the digital trail was sufficient to motivate Jane and her parents to report her abuse. Importantly, this evidence was also sufficient to convince police officers a crime had occurred and needed to be investigated, even if the physical evidence was lacking.

Law Enforcement Responses

Once an alleged sex crime is reported to the police, digital evidence can be useful for ensuring the crime is taken seriously by investigators. One of the many institutional hurdles survivors of sexual assault face when reporting their abuse is being believed by police officers. Law enforcement has wide discretion in their day-to-day activities at work and can decide whether a crime has occurred, how much time and effort to commit to the investigation, if an arrest should be made, and the charges to file.[13] In sexual assault case processing, officers are essentially the gatekeepers whose decisions largely determine the trajectory of the case, including whether a complaint results in formal charges against a suspect and whether victims have the opportunity for court resolution.

Research on police decision-making in sexual violence cases indicates officers are often skeptical of sexual assault allegations and concerned over proving consent and victim credibility. These attitudes reflect the gender bias and rape myths that continue to influence the way some police officers understand and respond to sexual violence allegations, as well as the legal requirements that need to be met to secure convictions in these cases.[14] Consequently, as the first point of contact, police remain one of the key contributors to the secondary victimization of sexual violence survivors. Victims who report to the police encounter barriers such as victim blaming, aggressive questioning, and refusal to continue with an investigation due to disbelief on the part of the officer.[15]

Digital platforms can help ease some of the challenges survivors face in their initial encounters with the police, in much the same way they help prosecutors meet the sufficiency standard in sexual violence cases.

The evidence these technologies make available can corroborate allegations of rape or sexual assault, which in turn may influence how police interact with a victim. Digital data from an assault can clear up issues of consent and culpability, possibly reducing the likelihood of victim-blaming and improving police attitudes toward a survivor and her credibility (i.e., less aggressive questioning, less skepticism about the claim, more inclination to investigate). This could hold interesting potential for victim-survivors whose behavior and lifestyle characteristics render them less than ideal, such as young victims or those assaulted while using illegal substances, and who are easily discredited by the police (and our culture, writ large).[16] Video of an assault, or text messages between an offender and his victim or between perpetrators and their friends, can confirm that a survivor did not consent prior to losing consciousness, for instance, making it harder for police to ignore a claim. Social media also gather information that may make it easier for police to investigate a case, providing officers with timelines, locations, and even potential witnesses to the crime, further increasing the likelihood of an allegation being taken seriously. Overall, the evidence captured by technology can work to reduce rape myth acceptance among officers and change police perceptions about the likelihood of success in investigating and prosecuting a sex crime, potentially improving their treatment of victims and their willingness to pursue a case.[17]

CIRCUMVENTING COURTROOM TRAUMA?
Testimony and Secondary Victimization

Feminist critiques of criminal justice system responses to sexual violence also highlight the deeply traumatizing courtroom experiences of victims, which often revictimize survivors with unrealistic expectations for clear, detailed, and consistent recollections of the events. Frequently, during courtroom interrogations survivors are required to recount details of the sexual violence that result in feelings of shame and guilt and force them to relive painful events, further compounding their trauma.[18] Testifying in court also opens survivors up to aggressive cross-examination by defense attorneys regarding their veracity and behavior, tactics aimed at discrediting complainants or implicating them in their victimization. Such practices disproportionately impact vulnerable and marginalized women, who are less readily identified as "ideal victims" and more easily stigmatized as "undeserving" victims. In fact, studies show that racialized and marginalized women are subjected to more questions and a more intense amount of questioning by defense counsel regarding their drinking, drug use, lying, and the levels of casual sexual relations in their communities.[19] Such hostile approaches make the trial process even more distressing and traumatizing for complainants, creating a cycle whereby their distress in the courtroom undermines their ability to "hold up" under legal interrogation in a way that is seen to be credible.

An important observation that came up in my interviews with prosecutors is that digital evidence often can save survivors from testifying altogether, as this sort of evidence can elicit a confession and reduce the stress on witness testimony. This was also a point made in the media coverage of the Steubenville and Pott cases, with stories positioning technology as giving voice to the young victims, testifying on their behalf. The *New York Times*, for instance, notes that "scores of text messages and cellphone pictures provided much of the evidence" in the Steubenville trial, offering testimony on behalf of the victim, who "did not remember what had happened" the night of her rape.[20] Digital media also helped Audrie Pott archive testimony of her pain and humiliation following her assault and subsequent peer bullying. According to Audrie's mother, by searching through Audrie's phone and social media, her family was able to "find statements made by Audrie herself in the last week of her life that draws a direct connection between her death and what the three young men did to her."[21] Here, new technologies did more than witness Pott's assault—in the aftermath of her suicide, they also enabled her to accuse her attackers from beyond the grave. By speaking on behalf of victims, new technologies have the potential to shield survivors from the burden of having to retell their stories, being scrutinized on the stand, and risking secondary victimization. In the long run, this may contribute to higher disclosure rates, particularly among youth and/or vulnerable populations who may be more hesitant to engage with the criminal justice system.

Additionally, digital data may protect survivors from testifying because it contributes to more cases being resolved through plea agreements. Although there is scant empirical evidence on this aspect of visual and digital evidence, the prosecutors I spoke with noted that often the digital evidence in juvenile sexual assault cases is sufficient to convince perpetrators to agree to a plea bargain. Defendants and their counsel realize, they explained, that if a judge sees the evidence against them, it will inflame them and possibly result in harsher punishment, so they opt for plea deals, instead. This is exactly what occurred in the Steubenville case, initially. According to Nemann, Mays's attorney:

I made a plea offer that they felt was reasonable to the attorney general's office, and it was being considered, and it would not have included jail time. And while it was under consideration, somehow, the [YouTube] video leaked, and Anonymous got involved, and as soon as this became an international sensation, they no longer were going to be offering any plea bargains. They wanted a conviction of rape, and we were moving forward with the trial.

This was substantiated by Walter Madison, Richmond's attorney, during our interview, who similarly highlighted the media's involvement in the case as the reason for a plea agreement no longer being an option for his client. The details provided by defense counsel in Steubenville are noteworthy because they raise questions about how politics and social responses may intersect with decisions about a case and the effects of social media in this process, regardless of what is best for the victim.

The case is also a stark reminder of just how little input teen victim-survivors have in how their assaults are handled by the criminal justice system. In their efforts to protect survivors from the possibility of further victimization at trial, prosecutors are making decisions regarding plea agreements without their consent, a strategy that risks further compromising victims' sense of control and may contribute to their revictimization. Moreover, there is an assumption made by the state that plea deals are the most desirable outcome for survivors, but as some victim attorneys noted, some of their clients want to proceed with a trial because they find this empowering and want their abusers to be criminally punished. Carrie Goldberg explains, "The victim's dedicated so much of herself into the case," but then, in juvenile cases, "it might plead down to some misdemeanor or something, . . . it's like, nothing. And so, it can be demoralizing" for the survivor. I offer this quote not to argue for more punitive responses by the criminal justice system, but rather to underscore the different justice goals that victim-survivors have and the need to consider their goals alongside organizational and political concerns in the adjudication of juvenile sex crimes.

Moreover, a discussion about plea bargain agreements would be incomplete without considering possible inequalities in practice. In addition to prosecutorial willingness, successful plea bargaining also requires an interest from the defense side to come to the table. In instances of juvenile sexual assault, it is worth bearing in mind that not all the young men accused of assault (or their parents) will be interested in a plea deal. Individuals with higher status (e.g., athletes) and support in the community, as well as those with more financial resources and better legal representation, may be more willing to contest the charges in court, opening the possibility of racial and class inequalities in plea agreements among this group of offenders. There is evidence of such inequity in both the sexual violence and criminological literature. Socio-legal studies on plea bargaining, as well as the war on drugs, are rife with examples of plea agreements disproportionately impacting poor and marginalized populations and communities of color, resulting in both higher incarceration rates and longer prison sentences among these groups.[22] Scholarship on bias in sexual violence trials has primarily focused on how victim characteristics impact blame attribution among judges and juries. However, studies on African American men accused of raping white women indicate that Black men are more likely to be wrongfully convicted than white men and more likely to be executed for the crime.[23] Research with white jurors (and mock jurors) also finds this group is often harsher in their judgment of out-group defendants and in their sentencing recommendations for Black defendants.[24]

It is perhaps unsurprising that both criminal justice actors and media outlets highlight the positive potentials of digital evidence for sexual assault investigations, considering the ongoing institutional challenges in effectively addressing sexual violence. While not explicitly stated, the implication in these discourses is that digital evidence may be *the* solution to our sexual violence problem. The data these platforms capture and retain is perceived as helping improve disclosure and reporting rapes among survivors, while also contributing to law enforcement's taking rape allegations more seriously by providing evidence of the crime and improving victim credibility, all factors that should result in better and more successful prosecutions of sexual assault.

Importantly, framing poor systemic responses to sexual violence as a matter of insufficient evidence or low reporting rates by victims once again shifts accountability from the criminal legal system onto the survivors. It reproduces the myth that unsuccessful sexual assault adjudication is about a lack of evidence rather than ongoing institutional sexism and racism, gender inequality, and the devaluing of girls' and women's bodies and lives. Turning to digital evidence as the solution further works to let the criminal justice system off the hook from effecting real institutional change, such as improving intake procedures, providing better training for police officers, or reforming the adversarial courtroom process.

Optimistic presentations of the potentiality of digital evidence are also rather selective in their understanding of the issues compromising sexual assault investigations. There is a clear assumption from criminal justice actors that victim-survivors want to report their abuse to the police, wish to involve the criminal legal system in attaining justice, and believe that such a system is the best way to obtain redress.[25] Additionally, there is the assumption that survivors have all of the support systems in place necessary to fight the legal and emotional battle of a criminal investigation and possible trial, and that this will be a fair and impartial process for victims regardless of the positions they occupy. Positionality, however, matters for who is deemed more or less credible, more or less vulnerable, and more or less blameworthy at every stage of the criminal justice system. Technology can help bolster a victim's allegations, but it may also expose them to invasive investigations and additional scrutiny. The same digital technologies that are used to gather information on defendants can also be used to gather evidence about survivors, exposing their sexual histories and reproducing all too familiar narratives of credibility and blame. The utility of digital evidence is further limited for young survivors due to the role of these platforms in perpetuating harm and abuse, as well as the law's continuing inability to account for the gendered nature of this harm.

THE THIRD ASSAULT

Considering technology-facilitated violence is a relatively new phenomenon, many scholars, legislators, criminal justice actors, and those in the general public are grappling with how to label and respond to such behaviors. The lack of physical contact between the target and the perpetrator(s) in many cases makes it difficult to conceptualize the harm of these interactions or to recognize them as existing on a continuum of violence that disproportionately impacts women and girls.[26] In practice, however, the use of new technologies to intimidate, threaten, access, or reveal information about victims means the harm directed at them can be significantly more acute, invasive, and distressing than traditional kinds of abuse, resulting in far-reaching psychological, social, and economic consequences for women.[27] While the extent of the harm will vary depending on a victim's life experience, social identity, age, and support networks, survivors share a common experience of the abuse as an extreme and pervasive violation. The creation and distribution of non-consensual sexual images, including images of rape and sexual assault, or the mere threat of such distribution, cause many women feelings of shame and humiliation, fear of reputational harm, anxiety, depression, paranoia, and suicidal ideation.[28] Such effects are particularly acute among young survivors of image-based sexual abuse, who are vulnerable because of their age and long-held cultural beliefs that closely link women's social status and reputation to chastity and feminine propriety.[29]

Moreover, the features of digital technologies, including accessibility, visibility, reach, and perpetuity, intensify and extend the potential for harassment and humiliation, amplifying the risks and consequences for victims of sexual violence. New media enable harm not only through the original violation and recording of the incident but also through the continuing and compounding trauma of the subsequent circulation, viewing, and downloading of images and videos they make possible.[30] The scale and unbounded nature of networked platforms often expose survivors to additional digital abuse and victimization through public shaming, intimidation, and harassment, further multiplying the harmful effects for many.

"It Makes One Really Bad Moment Last Forever"

For young survivors of sexual violence, this means that despite the potentials of digital evidence identified by the media and prosecutors, the negative consequences of the digital trail are ever present, particularly in the context of the sharing practices that social media foster. The increased vulnerability and ongoing risk of harm these technologies pose for many survivors was quite salient in my interviews with the civil attorneys representing this population. The digital artifacts of the abuse, whether images or video, extend the assault for victim-survivors, often compounding their trauma. One lawyer described the unique way in which images and videos of the assault amplified the violation experienced by her young client:

> [I]t made it feel like—Oh my god, I'm never going to be able to escape this having happened. And now it wasn't just a violation of my body, but it was also like, now my whole—like, my whole world is destroyed. Because everyone in my school has seen this. My whole family knows about this. The police were watching this, and you know, people are claiming that I was or wasn't, like, doing it consensually, and everyone has theories. And it just—And I don't understand how the Internet works, and now it's going to be everywhere, every—you know, forever, for perpetuity. And it's like, if—that's what really, like, took her to another level. . . . It makes one really bad moment last forever.

There are multiple concerns facing young women present in this quote. A traumatic moment lasts forever on digital media, and victims have to live with the permanency, longevity, and circulation of this record of their sexual victimization.[31] Social media's capacity to easily share and circulate photos and videos to wide audiences and across platforms also means more people discovering one's victimization. Survivors, as well as those responsible for their safety (such as the police), are unable to control the dissemination of this data once electronic distribution has begun. Victims are left exposed and vulnerable, their bodies and their violation readily available for others' consumption "out there" in the digital ether. Moreover, the threat of revictimization for young women is always present—even if the original images/video are deleted or social media platforms take them down, the ease with which mobile technologies enable the capture and recirculation of digital artifacts ensures their permanence and the possibility of that sexual violation coming up over and over again.

The underlying issue here for victims is control, or a lack thereof. When they are sexually assaulted, victims already experience a loss of privacy, of bodily integrity. The digital trail deepens this alienation for girls who are intoxicated or unconscious when assaulted. As Kelly Oliver observes, learning about their rape through social media means seeing their rape through the eyes of their abusers. Viewing their bodies being dragged and violated, as observers of the events, may intensify the damage to the survivor's "sense of their own identity and the coherence of their experience."[32] New technologies compound this objectification and privacy violation, as survivors have no control over how the record of their abuse is disseminated, who sees it and in what context, or how these digital artifacts are interpreted. Young women must cope with both shame and fear over how people will judge them, over how the incident—and their role in it—will be perceived. Studies show that women who are victims of sexual violence, including girls who are victims of privacy violations and image-based sexual abuse, often face negative reactions such as bullying, victim-blaming, and slut-shaming, further increasing their risk of revictimization.[33] There is also ongoing uncertainty, because they do not know where the digital afterlife of their assault lives or when these artifacts might be (re)discovered, a perpetual lifelong risk. The burden on girls to live with the knowledge that their violation is exposed, shared, and existing in a way such that they have no hope of ensuring those images will ever be erased can be devastating and difficult to bear.

There is evidence from academic scholarship on the experiences of adult survivors with image-based sexual abuse that for many these experiences are deeply traumatizing and perhaps the worst victimization. The narratives of the participants eerily echo those of teenage victims. Survivors interviewed by Nicola Henry and colleagues, for example, characterized their experiences of digital abuse as "life-ruining," "a nightmare . . . which destroyed everything," overwhelming and disrupting their lives and their sense of self.[34] Women in these studies also emphasize the relentless, constant nature of the harms they experience, as they worry about how the images are disseminated, what information is available about them on the internet, and the content of the digital communications they receive. Others spoke of being "haunted" by the images of them circulated online and being in a state of constant vigilance, obsessively checking their phones, social media, and the internet, waiting for the images or videos to reemerge; like the girls discussed in this book, some even admitted to attempting suicide.[35]

Particularly salient for young women is anxiety over the reputational impacts of the digital afterlife of their assault, which remain deeply gendered. According to Michael Salter, regardless of intent or context, images of female nudity retain "an inherently sexual and pornographic quality with deleterious effects on the social standing of the girl or woman depicted," often resulting in the woman being labeled a slut."[36] Girls are acutely conscious of these ramifications. Victim attorneys noted the primary concern for their adolescent clients is often to have pictures or videos of the assault deleted from devices and/or removed from online sites, so as to prevent or contain their circulation. This concern was often far more urgent than reporting the crime or their peers to the police, a theme appearing in other studies on youth and digital abuse.[37] We see this fear in Audrie Pott's frantic Facebook messages to her friends the day following her assault. She messages some of the boys who attended the party asking if any of them "still have any photos," terrified that images of her from that night are "gonna get out" to her peers. The humiliation and reputational damage this digital aftermath poses for Audrie are palpable; the "whole school knows," she writes to a friend on Facebook later that day. "Do you know how people view me now? I fucked up and I can't do anything to fix it. . . . One of my best friends hates me. And I now have a reputation I can never get rid of." Writing to another boy, she said, "My life is over."[38] Sadly, her statement proved prophetic; unable to live with the shame and ongoing trauma from the circulation of the record of her sexual victimization, Audrie took her own life only a week later.

Whether or not photos of Audrie's abuse were circulated among her peers is irrelevant. If a victim believes images of her naked body being abused are being (or at any time can be) shared and circulated, then the threat that her victimization will continue in perpetuity is real and can create lasting psychological damage, sometimes with devastating consequences. For Audrie, it was enough to know that a digital trail existed, and that it could be shared on social media, for her to imagine that everyone could see or eventually discover what had happened to her and blame her for it. Bob Allard, the Potts' lawyer, explains the damage of these digital artifacts for his young client:

> I strongly believe in—I'll rely on the words of Audrie and as published in her Facebook messaging, that it was the slut shaming that—that did her in. She felt overwhelmed that the whole school knew about it, everyone was talking about it. . . . So if that whole incident behind that closed door between the four of them had been kept private and no one else knew about it, I'm convinced she would've somehow found a way to persevere and live and try to fight it out. But once they started leaking it out with photographs, with rumors—vicious rumors about her, it spread like wildfire in her mind and she couldn't take it anymore. She decided that it was best just to end her life rather than, you know, be forced to endure the humiliation of being labeled the new hoe on campus.

Both Audrie and her family's attorney zero in on what is uniquely dangerous about digital platforms: their inability to forget. The permanency digital technologies enable has significant consequences for survivors of sexual violence. For an individual to move past an act or event that has caused them harm, a degree of not remembering is required. This does not mean being in denial or excusing the harms, but rather making the decision to work through the trauma and potentially letting go of feelings of resentment, so that the incident does not become central to one's identity.[39] The persistence of digital data, however, poses significant challenges to this goal, since there is no way of ensuring images and video are forever deleted, making it difficult for survivors to move on, to imagine a *post*–sexual violence reality.[40] Instead, digital memory risks reducing survivors to one identity, permanently defining them by their sexual victimization, with all the stigma and humiliation that carries for women and girls.

The harms new technologies make possible highlight that digital evidence is often a double-edged sword for survivors.[41] While these platforms can offer evidence of the sex crime and strengthen a victim's allegations, the digital trail can also be used to threaten victim-survivors, to insult and harass them, privately and publicly, as well as lead to additional abuse. Young women have to consider how to navigate these risks, especially in light of the varying degrees of support and resources available to them. For some vulnerable victims, this may mean less willingness to disclose sexual assault or bring charges against their assailants, in the hopes that the digital harassment, bullying, and reputational threat will be minimized.[42] For others, the primary concern is removing all evidence of their victimization from their peers' devices and from the internet. However, the police are not always helpful for accomplishing this goal because they prioritize the sex crime, failing to adequately recognize and respond to the harm that the digital trail poses for victims. They may also be limited in their responses by a lack of know-how or resources and slow responses from social media and internet companies, leaving survivors to try to take down images of their abuse on their own or through civil lawyers.[43] Consequently, this population of survivors may be less likely to turn to the criminal legal system to pursue their justice goals.

Moreover, victim-survivors of sexual violence who turn to the criminal justice system for help struggle with controlling who views photos and video evidence of their assaults, as well as with how this data is shared among criminal justice actors. While prosecutors may frame digital evidence as particularly useful in the courtroom and a means of shielding survivors from further revictimization, being confronted with visual evidence of one's abuse can be (re)triggering. Many of the young women discussed here had no clear recollection of being sexually assaulted. Filling in those memory gaps with graphic and invasive images or video can have a profound effect on survivors and risk further harming them. The use of digital evidence in courtroom proceedings, while valuable and effective, also means survivors have to witness their own victimization over and over again, which can result in significant distress, contribute to post-traumatic stress disorder, and risk further alienating survivors from their own experiences and bodies.[44]

Additionally, as Kaitlyn Regehr and colleagues remind us, the sharing and viewing of images and video of the assault during various phases of the criminal justice process, depicting survivors in sexually degrading and traumatic scenarios, "raises uncomfortable comparisons with the illegal non-consensual sharing of intimate images."[45] This is a rather significant observation, because while much attention has been given to the harm image-based sexual abuse can cause survivors in the public realm, there is an assumption that within the criminal justice system, digital evidence is rather safe and neutral. However, part of the violence victims experience is their loss of control over who will see evidence of their abuse, how many times the event is seen, and how that material will be interpreted. This is a concern that also extends to criminal justice personnel. The viewing and use of sexual abuse materials pertaining to children and juveniles may be controlled, but harm arises from the fact these artifacts are nevertheless circulated among criminal justice actors and depicted in courtrooms in ways that remain exploitative and gendered. As this digital evidence becomes part of the permanent record of the case, survivors are also left to contend with the risk of future leakage or exposure.[46] Scholars working on image-based sexual abuse are quick to explain the unique and pervasive ways the digital trail contributes to the disruption of victims' lives. Here, I want to raise the possibility that law enforcement, attorneys, and judges may also be contributing to this trauma by using digital artifacts during criminal justice proceedings, intensifying the harm victims experience and enacting an additional layer of state violence against survivors.

Digging for Digital Dirt: Victims on Trial

Even if a survivor decides to use textual evidence and/or images and video of her sexual assault to report the incident to the police, that digital trail can work against her. This happens because everything on social media is discoverable, and defense attorneys are increasingly turning to these platforms to "dig for digital dirt" against complainants, to perpetuate blame or suggest responsibility for their victimization.[47] Importantly, prosecutors can only use digital evidence in limited ways, as they are bound by restrictions on the type of evidence they can collect and present in court, so as to minimize the possibility of a wrongful conviction. Defense lawyers, on the other hand, have wide discretion to mine a victim's social media activity and pick apart her posts in an effort to weave a specific type of narrative that undermines the accuser's credibility or may present them as "untrustworthy." One juvenile sex crimes prosecutor explains:

> Complainants need to realize that the defendant and his lawyer will likely search through social media for pre- or post-event contact between the complainant and the defendant or with her friends and family. They're looking for anything that supports, however tenuously, inconsistent stories, collusion, fabrication, failure to express distress or to complain, or motive for reporting.[48]

For instance, if a victim discloses her abuse online, a defense attorney can take those comments and compare them to the disclosure she provided to the police in the official police report, to look for inconsistencies and undermine her credibility.[49] Attorneys are also checking digital platforms to raise questions about consent, as well as the victim's character and sex life. Images or video of a sexual assault often lack context—we do not always know what transpired right before or after their creation, a fact that defense counsel in sexual assault cases use to argue proof of consent rather than its absence. This is especially true in cases involving intoxication, where the victim has no recollection of the assault, enabling the defense to posit consent may have been given before or after the digital artifact was created. Further, complainants' call history and text messages are increasingly being used to undermine their claims in court and blame survivors for their victimization, even though research on sexual violence highlights the complexity of post-assault text exchanges and the varied meanings that might exist behind seemingly positive messages between the victim and defendant.[50] In a study from Canada on the use of digital evidence in sexual assault trials that feature underage victims and a mistake of age defense, Fanny Ramirez and colleagues found that online flirting, lying about one's age on social media, and posting sexualized photos facilitated victim blaming and strengthened the mistake of age defense. Of the 14 cases the researchers analyzed, 9 ended with judges rendering a "not guilty" decision.[51]

Using sexual content or sexualized photos of women from social media against them is already common practice in divorce and child custody cases and is now also being extended to sexual assault cases.[52] People may assume that rape complainants will be protected from questions about their sexual history during trial, a misconception most likely resulting from public understandings of rape shield laws. Scholarship in this area, however, consistently demonstrates these laws are not without crucial gaps, and defense counsel cross-examine complainants about their sexual history without much objection.[53] Because of its wide admissibility and the fact that we share so much of ourselves on social media, digital evidence actually increases the amount of information that is available on survivors. Defense attorneys are actively using this evidence to skirt rape shield laws and suggest promiscuity or prior consent in their efforts to discredit victims in court.[54]

This was, in fact, a strategy employed by Ma'lik Richmond's attorney in Steubenville. The malleability of digital evidence means the defense was able to find "provocative comments and photographs" Jane Doe had posted "on her Twitter page over time" and use them during the trial to demonstrate "she was sexually active and was clearly engaged in at-risk behavior."[55] Although this argument proved unsuccessful in Steubenville, it yielded more fruitful results in a similar rape case at Yale in 2015. In that case, defense attorneys parsed the victim's text messages with the accused to suggest she had been flirting with him in the days preceding the assault. They also mined her social media activity to find images of her in a "provocative" Halloween costume, to suggest her sexual promiscuity and implicate her in her assault.[56] The defendant was found not guilty.[57] Both instances draw on old rape tropes that depict sexually promiscuous women as unreliable and un-rapeable and conflate previous consent with future (and perpetual) consent, thereby minimizing the culpability of the male offenders in the assaults. But they also reveal a concerning trend whereby the digital trail is being used to subject sexual assault survivors to even greater scrutiny and may even potentially contribute to raising the bar on the evidentiary burden that survivors carry.[58]

In some instances, even when the digital trail offers evidence of a sexual assault, its reading is still subject to interpretation and bias. In 2012 Rehtaeh Parsons was sexually assaulted by several boys at a house party in Nova Scotia, Canada. A picture showing one of the boys appearing to violate Parsons from behind was widely circulated, yet local law enforcement did not move forward with formal charges, citing insufficient evidence. The investigating officers considered the scene depicted in the photograph unclear and open to alternative readings.[59] Their decision not to proceed with sexual assault charges was also based on a series of text messages between Parsons and her friends the night of the assault, in which she expresses that she "did a stupid thing . . . that she made a mistake and regretted it."[60] According to law enforcement, these exchanges indicated self-blame, thereby contradicting her earlier statements to the police. Because Parsons's comments after her assault did not conform to socially accepted and expected behavior by rape victims, criminal justice professionals used the messages to diminish her credibility and her abuse.[61]

Similar prejudices and hierarchies of victimhood influence courtroom proceedings. In their analysis of the use of text message evidence in sexual assault trials, Heather Hlavka and Sameena Mulla found that how such communications are interpreted in court depends on how the messages are animated and by whom, their meaning always embedded in long-standing gendered and racialized narratives of sexual violence, credibility, and victimhood.[62] More recently, in Spain, an 18-year-old woman was gang raped by five men; the assault was captured on video and showed the woman was "immobile and with her eyes shut" during the attack. In 2018 the trial judge in the case interpreted her closed eyes and lack of resistance as a sign of consent, resulting in a lesser charge for the perpetrators.[63] Such responses are not limited to the criminal justice system. In a particularly devastating case that occurred in Brooklyn in 2015, a 13-year-old girl was anally and orally raped by one of her classmates, who filmed the incident and shared it throughout the school and the borough. Even after the young, Black victim reported the rape and the video to the school principal, both the school and the police asked the girl why she had not fought the boy off, interpreting the video as consensual sex. Perhaps not surprisingly, no consideration was given to the *non-consensual* recording and distribution of the incident, even if the encounter had been consensual. Subsequently, the school sent the victim home on indefinite leave, for fear her presence would be "making things worse" on campus, while the boy faced no repercussions.[64]

This interpretative flexibility shows that notions of digital evidence as neutral and of the visual as a means of attaining the truth in sexual assault investigations are false. The critiques raised in the last chapter on the limits of the power of visual evidence to provide the truth bear repeating here. The authority of digital evidence, and of what constitutes truth, is compromised by the ways factors like gender, race, age, and class impact practices of observing, of being observed, and of extending sympathy to a sexual assault victim.[65] According to Nicola Gavey, sexual assault adjudication has long relied on the cultural scaffolding of gender and sexuality, including heteronormative, patriarchal, and racialized discourses.[66] Research on sexual violence against women has been particularly clear in identifying the ways in which victims belonging to marginalized groups (nonwhite, poor and/or working class, LGBTQ+, etc.) are disbelieved by police and jurors alike and more likely to be blamed for their victimization.[67]

There is every reason to believe these biases and stereotypes would also inform the adjudication of juvenile sexual assault. Digital evidence is presented, interpreted, and interrogated by courtroom actors. In the process, defense attorneys can leverage themes about teenagers as particularly rebellious, untrustworthy, and deceitful to undermine the narratives of young survivors. Additionally, they can draw on cultural stereotypes about Black and brown youth as hypersexual and out-of-control to sexualize young victims, implicate them in their victimization, and minimize the amount of sympathy extended to them in the court-room.[68] We cannot approach digital evidence as the solution to the criminal justice system's response to sexual violence because its efficacy has to be considered alongside questions of positionality and context; technology can often help corroborate a victim's statement, but it may also be used against the survivor to undermine their credibility, amplify harm, and perpetuate blame.

The criminal legal system, supported by the power of the law and promising punishment for the offender and validation for survivors' experiences, may seem an appealing avenue through which victims of sexual violence can secure justice. Where criminal justice actors are concerned, digital evidence holds great potential for further ensuring this goal is met. Social media and mobile technologies can certainly aid some victim-survivors to seek justice by proffering proof of a sex crime and, in doing so, potentially improving police responses to allegations of assault. There is also promise in the possibility that the digital trail may reduce the burden of testimony and courtroom trauma for certain victims. The fact remains, however, that survivors of all types of sexual violence are not well served by the justice system, and the instances discussed here further support this scholarship.[69] Their experiences with digital evidence reveal that, contrary to institutional expectations, the utility of digital platforms is context-specific, dependent on the positions victim-survivors occupy and their specific justice goals. Efforts at justice are further compromised by the risk technologies pose for survivors to scrutinize, blame, reproduce and amplify harm, without much protection from the law. Fear of harm and an unwillingness to engage with the criminal legal system may be particularly acute for young survivors who may not want their parents to find out about the abuse, may not have the resources and support networks needed to fight a legal battle, or are worried about the ongoing threats technologies present. As multiple attorneys observed, the law has not caught up with what young people are experiencing and fails to account for "how widespread the damage" of the digital trail can be for teen victims. There is also no guarantee that digital evidence will be able to successfully overcome the deeply embedded gender, racial, class, and sexual prejudices that continue to permeate and inform responses to sexual violence, but may instead reproduce the ongoing victimization and marginalization of survivors within the criminal justice system.

Yet survivor efforts to achieve justice and redress do not have to be limited to the confines of the law and its treatment of technology. Digital campaigns like #MeToo and Everyday Sexism suggest social media can also offer alternative tools and pathways for conceptualizing and seeking justice through online activism and feminist counter-publics. What opportunities, then, do these platforms offer victim-survivors for digital participation, mobilization, and improving state responses to sexual violence through informal mechanisms? And what might the implications of these extralegal efforts be for public understandings and discourses on sexual violence and image-based abuse?

Beyond the Law

Sexual Violence and Justice Practices
in Digital Spaces

The anti-rape and domestic violence movements of the 1970s and 1980s have been credited with mainstreaming gender violence as a social problem in America, evinced by the proliferation of government funding, policymaking, and criminal justice responses to the issue.[1] While state intervention is often cited as confirmation of the success of these advocacy efforts, feminist scholars argue that in practice these legal reforms have developed and are applied unevenly, underscored by hegemonic norms and power relations. This is, perhaps, unsurprising, considering the patriarchal, racist, and colonialist violence upon which our legal system is founded and the function of the law as a social control mechanism.[2] By turning to the state for redress, critics argue, feminist activism has ceded ground to a neoliberal carceral agenda, whereby the initial goals of ending violence against women have been replaced with an overemphasis on criminal justice intervention, increasing convictions, and punishment as justice.[3] Such policies have resulted in the heightened use of policing against poor, immigrant, and indigenous and people of color communities, as well as policing against queer/trans persons and the disproportionate incarceration of these groups.[4] Moreover, research suggests the efficacy of these legal reforms in reducing violence against women is ambivalent at best. Changes in the criminal justice system have not improved attrition or conviction rates or the treatment of survivors by the system, and they have failed to challenge rape culture and gender norms, which remain central to efforts to end gendered violence.[5] In fact, critical and abolitionist activists argue, the criminal legal system ends up harming the very communities it claims to protect.[6]

Considering the shortcomings of the criminal justice system, some feminist scholars have advocated for the need to explore alternative avenues of justice available to survivors, with an emphasis on victim participation. Work on restorative justice has identified a range of survivor justice needs and interests, including voice, participation, validation, recognition, and offender accountability.[7] Digital platforms have helped transform how victim-survivors address these needs, providing a particularly powerful medium for facilitating online counter-publics and political activism in response to sexual violence and harassment.[8] Scholars here theorize digital activism through Nancy Fraser's concept of "subaltern counter-publics," spaces in which culturally and discursively subordinated groups create and circulate resistant and/or critical speech that is ordinarily excluded from the public sphere.[9] In addition to providing victim-survivors with opportunities for resistive politics, Anastasia Powell further asserts that social media enable the development of new techno-social practices of informal justice that help survivors meet their justice needs outside of the criminal justice system.[10] How, then, might new technologies be used in ways that help meet these goals and facilitate rape justice? In this chapter I investigate what alternative paths for justice and accountability online spaces and social media platforms may offer victim-survivors. Following Clare McGlynn and colleagues, I approach justice as an ongoing and situated process and ask which justice needs can be met for whom, and in what circumstances.[11] In this way, this chapter also considers the challenges and complexities that digital technologies present for achieving rape justice, particularly in cases involving young and vulnerable victims.

ALTERNATIVE PATHWAYS TO JUSTICE

Voice, Recognition, Validation

Key aspects of victims' justice needs include having a voice and control over their narratives and their lives, and social media can go some way in helping meet these goals. Sexual assault survivors are not always able to express their experiences in a meaningful way in their own words; for young victims, in particular, it is often the state or their parents who take on this role, telling their stories and speaking on their behalf. Digital spaces provide a forum for survivors to disclose what happened in their own terms and to identify their experiences as unfair, allowing for forms of control and empowerment that can offer survivors a sense of justice. This is especially important in cases where the criminal legal system misrepresents a victim's experience or silences it altogether, and instances where the experience is defined by the perpetrator rather than the victim. In Maryville, for example, the county prosecutor did not consider Daisy Coleman's sexual assault allegations legitimate, deciding not to pursue a criminal investigation in the case. In addition to media appearances and Facebook postings, Daisy also wrote an account of her abuse for the website xoJane.com, where she was able to tell her story in her own terms.[12]

Survivors may also feel they lack a voice and control when their experiences of sexual violence are made public by others, like perpetrators or bystanders who share and circulate the abuse on social media, imposing their definitions and interpretations on the events. Both Jane Doe's and Audrie Pott's assaults are examples of this. In another high-profile case that occurred in 2014, Jada Smith, a 16-year-old Black girl from Texas, was drugged and raped at a party by at least one young man after passing out from drinking a spiked beverage. The assault was documented by both her attacker and bystanders at the party. Just as in Steubenville, in subsequent weeks the offender and Jada's classmates took to Twitter to circulate photos of her undressed and unconscious on the floor, ridiculing her and abusively calling her a "hoe" and a "fiend."[13] Jada reported the assault to the police, but she also went on Twitter to post a picture of herself in a pose of defiance and strength—her arm curled like Rose the Riveter—and holding a sign saying #IAmJada. The tweet enabled Jada to put a face to her story, to reclaim her humanity and her strength, while also allowing her to reframe the narrative surrounding her rape and her person.

By sharing their experiences online, some victim-survivors are able to fulfill the need to have their accounts of sexual violence be believed and for others to recognize that the behavior of the perpetrator(s) was wrong and unacceptable. In part, the cases discussed in this book went viral on social media because of public interest in, and sympathy for, the young victims.[14] By providing a means through which the incidents can be shared and circulated, digital technologies also increase the number of witnesses to a sex crime. When everyone bears witness through these platforms, sexual assault shifts from an abstract "he said/she said" to a hard, visual reality we watch and listen to and also become implicated in as bystanders. This imbrication makes it difficult to ignore that sexual violence is a problem and rape culture is real. The digital creates a "stark dilemma," useful for shaming people and institutions into taking strong action in a case and feeling responsible for doing so.[15]

Although broader audiences can and do result in online bullying and harassment, victim-survivors like Daisy Coleman and Jada Smith have also commented on the outpouring of support they received on social media following their allegations and the strength they gained from these responses.[16] We further saw expressions of this online solidary during the #MeToo campaign, as well as in the aftermath of Christine Blasey Ford's testimony that US Supreme Court nominee Brett Kavanaugh raped her when they were in college. When many people, including then president Donald Trump, questioned her veracity and her delay in reporting, the internet responded with the #IBelieveHer hashtag in support of Ford. In instances where victims are dismissed or disbelieved by the criminal justice system or by their peers and communities, it matters to find others in digital spaces who believe their accounts. The generally supportive nature of many of these sites can function as spaces of validation, where survivors' experiences, and the harm done to them, are taken seriously and believed, responses missing from formal institutions of justice. Moreover, such spaces enable women to connect and built community across identity lines, wherein they can support each other, resist self-blame narratives, and take important steps toward healing and recovery.[17] These online communities and support networks may be particularly helpful for young victim-survivors, who may fear not being believed or may not be able to disclose to adults in their lives.

Institutional Critique and Accountability

In some instances, new technologies can help victims and the broader public to criticize formal justice mechanisms and advocate for better institutional responses to sexual violence. This includes calls for believing victims and taking sexual assault allegations seriously, but also demands that offenders face appropriate consequences for their actions. In Steubenville, responses by local officials to Jane Doe's rape allegations were slow. Online discussion forums revealed some community members were concerned the football coaching staff, the high school, and even local police might cover up the complaint in an effort to protect the football stars and the town's winning Big Red football team.[18] In part, it was this concern that drove local blogger Alexandra Goddard to screenshot the social media postings from the night of the assault and attempt to bring attention to the case. Allegations of a cover-up also contributed to the *New York Times* reporting on the incident in December 2012 and the hacktivist collective Anonymous becoming involved in gathering and publishing information on the case to the greater public. Together, these efforts catapulted the Steubenville rape onto the national stage, and public outrage on social media toward the town and local officials was swift. It is difficult to say the exact impact this national attention had on the local investigation, but certainly the pressure was on for officials to take the allegations seriously and to increase the transparency of their response. According to Nemann, defense attorney for Trent Mays, it was following this publicity that any offer of a plea deal in the case was withdrawn, with prosecutors opting for a trial instead.

Anonymous also got involved in Maryville when Nodaway county prosecutor Robert Rice decided to drop the sexual assault charges in Daisy Coleman's case. This time there was concern that local politics had resulted in the charges being dismissed, since the alleged offender's grandfather was a former highway patrolman and had served four terms as state representative in the Missouri legislature.[19] "We demand an immediate investigation into the handling by local authorities of Daisy's case," Anonymous posted online. If the Maryville authorities will not "do their jobs," the statement read, "we will have to stand for them." Another member of the collective began publicizing the case on Twitter, and campaigns #OpMaryville and #Justice4Daisy quickly trended on the platform.[20] Within days the social media campaigns and mounting public pressure successfully resulted in the local prosecutor asking for a new investigation. Although the second investigation also failed to find sufficient evidence for a felony sexual assault charge, Matthew Barnett did plead guilty to misdemeanor child endangerment for leaving Coleman outside in freezing weather, and apologized to Daisy as part of his plea agreement.[21]

Sometimes it is the victim-survivors themselves who take to social media to protest against institutional actors who have attempted to silence them or have failed to ensure perpetrators of sexual violence are held accountable for their abuse. In a now famous case from 2011, 16-year-old Savannah Dietrich of Louisville, Kentucky, took to Facebook and Twitter to name the boys who sexually assaulted her. Savannah's actions were the result of frustration with the court's light punishment of the young men, a plea agreement made without her input. She was also angry about the gag order from the judge presiding over the proceedings, which prohibited her from speaking about the case with anyone.

Frustrated over her treatment by the court, Savannah tweeted the names of the boys, writing:

> There you go, lock me up. I'm not protecting anyone that made my life a living Hell.
>
> Protect rapist is more important than getting justice for the victim in Louisville.
>
> They said I can't talk about it or I'll be locked up. So I'm waiting for them to read this and lock me up. F--k justice.[22]

The court responded by charging her with contempt, but public opprobrium on social media was quick, with many expressing outrage that the court would silence (and revictimize) a survivor for speaking out about her assault. Many found the fact that Dietrich faced a potential jail sentence for violating the gag order, while the boys who assaulted her were facing only community service, particularly egregious. And while some consideration was given to the ethics of violating the court order, the predominant view expressed online was that Savannah was "brave" and "heroic" for speaking out and standing up for herself. Not only did the intense media attention and national backlash result in the contempt charges against Dietrich being dropped, but the court records of the case were unsealed, and the boys received a more appropriate sentence for the crime.[23] In addition, a few months after the incident made headlines, Kentucky legislators passed a bill that would allow victims in juvenile court cases to speak about them publicly once a case is decided.[24]

These examples illustrate the ways social media can help victims and their advocates reach sympathetic online counter-publics that acknowledge survivors' experiences and the wrongfulness of their victimization—whether by the perpetrators or the criminal justice system—and offer them validation and support. By criticizing local and institutional responses in such instances, online counter-publics are also situating these incidents within the broader context of sexual violence, condemning officials who abuse their power, the privileged position of male athletes in society, practices of victim-blaming and denigration, and a rape culture that accepts and sanctions violence against women. Furthermore, in advocating for transparency and offender accountability and providing survivors with spaces to tell their stories, online counter-publics also impose additional sanctions against perpetrators of abuse. Online searches of the Steubenville, Maryville, and Dietrich cases, for instance, result in articles, blog posts, and social media threads identifying the young offenders as rapists. This digital trail is likely to cause ongoing reputational damage to the boys for many years. Such extrajudicial punishment may offer some survivors the accountability and retribution they were seeking and were denied by formal legal systems. "Naming and shaming" has a long history in anti-rape activism, although in the digital age the practice does raise due process concerns over whether the right to presumptions of innocence as well as a fair and impartial trial are violated when alleged perpetrators are named and shamed on social media.[25] Given the persistence of the digital trail and the young age of juvenile offenders, it is also important to consider whether the reputational harm and secondary punishment meted out by digital publics is actually just or not, and what criteria we use to arrive at such an assessment.[26]

Challenging Rape Scripts, Challenging Rape Culture

There is a further argument to be made that by enabling survivors to tell their stories, digital platforms may create an opportunity to speak about sexual violence in ways that go beyond the traditional frameworks through which rape and sexual assault are articulated. Here, I borrow from Rachel Loney-Howes's nuanced analysis of how online anti-rape campaigns have the potential to challenge the hegemonic norms of rape and trauma testimony.[27] Since the 1970s, feminist activists have sought to break the silence surrounding women's experiences of rape by bringing the private into the public sphere. Decades of speak outs and activism have attempted to challenge the normative narrative tropes that govern and constrain the ways experiences of rape can be spoken about, to shift the rape script away from stranger rape toward marital and date and acquaintance rape as far more pervasive and needing recognition. Nevertheless, the myth of stranger rape as the most common and "authentic" experience of rape persists, as does the belief that rape is often accompanied by physical violence and visible signs of struggle. These are the stories that continuously receive public and media attention and recognition. Victims are expected to be deeply traumatized by the attack but still present a coherent and consistent account of events if they are to be believed.[28] Incidents that do not map neatly onto these discourses, such as date or acquaintance rape, or cases involving drugs or alcohol, are considered messy, and as we saw in previous chapters, often are culturally and institutionally dismissed as "just sex."[29]

In many ways, the sexual assaults discussed in this book do not fit neatly within the parameters of what sexual violence ought to look like. All of the young victims were violated by boys they knew, and the assaults were lacking in (visible) violence and coercion. Each girl was assaulted at a party after hours of socializing, drinking, and sometimes even flirting with her abusers. Further, the young women were heavily intoxicated and/or unconscious when they were assaulted and had little or no recollection of the rape, making it difficult to construct a coherent narrative of events. It is hard to imagine these girls and their allegations being taken seriously and their experiences being believed without judgment, and they certainly were not, as I detail later. But social media provided them with a platform to tell their stories in their own words and to reach sympathetic others who believed and supported them. In instances where a digital trail exists, such as in Steubenville, technologies also offer visual and textual proof of the assaults that can bolster survivors' claims and also challenge normative assumptions by exposing the everyday reality of sexual violence. As such, they have the potential to push the boundaries of "approved" rape testimonies, troubling myths and beliefs about "real rape" and notions of "ideal" victims.[30] By offering a platform to all types of survivors, digital media can broaden the horizons of what is culturally (and legally) conceived of and recognized as rape and the context in which sexual violence occurs, helping erode long-standing rape myths and victim-blaming discourses. Moreover, the support that survivors whose experiences do not reflect hegemonic norms garner in online spaces also opens up the capacity for other women to claim their experience as rape and to disclose online, further challenging the boundaries of what "counts" as sexual violence.

Perhaps new media technologies and their capacity to capture and circulate evidence of sexual abuse can most contribute to challenging and deconstructing rape culture.[31] Writing about the photos of the rape and their distribution on social media in the Steubenville case, Jordan Fairbairn and Dale Spencer observe that

> this secondary victimization was, for many, seen as an extension of the sexual assault, or an additional piece of sexual violence perpetrated by online publics. In this way, the meaning of the images of the assault came to represent not just the act of sexual assault, but the entitlement, misogyny, and normalization of sexual violence that surrounded this crime and the societal reactions it generates.[32]

Digital evidence and online platforms are important because they can help demonstrate rape culture writ large, not only among the young people who perpetrate or record these assaults, but also among the institutions and (international) publics who fail to react in these instances, or whose responses voice support for the perpetrators and/or blame for the victims. The commentary accompanying the images and videos shared online in such cases, the social media responses to the digital trail, expose the male peer-support networks that normalize and sanction such abuse, as well as the sexism, misogyny, and disregard for women that permeate our culture, including our youth.[33] Such digital activity also demonstrates these offenders are not acting in a vacuum, that their behavior is not pathological and aberrant but rather normal, indicative of the heteronormative and patriarchal culture surrounding them. It is a mirror, reflecting back on us.

In doing so, digital media also create the space for victim-survivors, advocates, and allies to present counter-narratives that challenge rape myths and hegemonic representations of rape and its causes, critique social and institutional responses to sexual violence, and help organize against sexism and misogyny. On these platforms, survivors have the possibility to actively challenge the blame and stigma historically attached to victims of sexual violence by telling their stories and reallocating attention to the perpetrator and their actions. Further, they can turn to digital spaces to identify and deconstruct rape myths and victim-blaming practices, as well as to engage in discussions of patriarchy and gender-based violence.[34] These are the contributions we see from feminist hashtag activist campaigns such as #EverydaySexism, #yesallwomen, #hollaback, #BeenRapedNeverReported, and most recently #MeToo—they help bring attention to larger issues surrounding gender and power while shifting the cultural discourse to support and believe rather than blame or deny victims.[35]

POWER AND DIGITAL PARTICIPATION

Digital activism may offer opportunities for resistance and critique for some survivors, but this is not guaranteed to many of them, especially if we consider intersections of race, sexuality, age, social status, and ability, among others. The publicity and participation social media make possible can be turned against survivors, exposing young victims of sexual violence to many of the same harms they face within formal justice mechanisms. Like the criminal legal system, the technological landscape also fails to account for the gendered power relations that shape online participation, and often the public sphere amplifies the suffering of young victim-survivors.

Vulnerable Victims and Online Harm

One aspect that social media compromise is the victim's anonymity, which the courts commonly protect from the public in sexual assault cases. Digital platforms make it easier than ever to reveal a survivor's identity, through the perpetrators' social media postings, the pictures and videos of the attacks, and any additional online discussions by bystanders or peers.[36] These reveals are often incredibly humiliating, exposing young women in their most compromised state to family and friends, but also to broad groups of people online. They also deeply undermine survivors' sense of control, as others (often their abusers) get to define their experience and decide when the incident becomes public, and for which audiences. This is even more acute for young women who, like the girls discussed in this book, are assaulted while heavily intoxicated and/or unconscious and often find out about their victimization online, through the digital activity of unsympathetic and abusive perpetrators and peers.[37]

Losing their anonymity means victims become more vulnerable to digital abuse and revictimization. Perpetrators can reach out to survivors through private messages as well as public posts, to further torment, bully, and humiliate them, and so can their friends and family.[38] Others can take to social media to publicly voice support for the offender(s). In Jada's case, for instance, her assault was turned into a meme. People mimicked the pose Jada was in when someone took a photo of her and shared it online—unconscious, sprawled out on the floor, partially unclothed—and then took pictures and tweeted them with the hashtag #JadaPose. The hashtag, which started in Houston, spread quickly and went viral. Jada's abuser also went on Twitter to harass her, bragging about the incident and directing slurs at her.[39] Audrie Pott faced similar harassment and shaming following her assault. On Facebook, messages appeared in Audrie's inbox, mocking her: "u were one horny mofo" one informed her, and "shit went down ahah jk i bet u already got enough ppl talking about it so ill keep it to myself haha" wrote another. "Do you know how people view me now?" Audrie messaged one of her friends on Facebook. "My life is over" she wrote to another, and within a week, Pott took her own life.[40]

Daisy Coleman, too, faced serious backlash and vitriol on social media, with classmates writing that she had been "asking for it," and Twitter messages exclaimed, "Fuck yea. That's what you get for bein a skank :)" following the dismissal of charges against her alleged perpetrator.[41] In the 2016 documentary *Audrie & Daisy*, she and her brother further discuss how kids at school called her a "liar" and a "slut."[42] The bullying took a toll on Daisy, who attempted suicide multiple times in the 18-month period following her original complaint. In an interview for a local radio station, she explains: "You're the s-word, you're the w-word, b-word. Just, after a while, you start to believe it"; "I really did start to hate myself," she observes in a later interview.[43] Coleman went on to cofound SafeBAE, a nonprofit organization aimed at ending sexual assaults in schools.[44] Despite her public activism and years of connecting with and advocating alongside other survivors of sexual violence, including Jada Smith, Coleman died by suicide in August 2020, at the age of 23.

Daisy's ongoing struggles and eventual suicide reveal the long-lasting trauma of sexual violence and of the backlash and abuse young victims are subjected to in online platforms. While cases like Jada's, Coleman's, and Pott's are somewhat rare, their occurrence is a reminder that the visibility and accessibility of digital media considerably augment the bullying and humiliation victims experience, exposing them to victim-blaming, slut-shaming, and racialized misogyny.[45] Photos, videos, and comments about the assaults extend the damage to survivors beyond the rape itself. The persistence of new technologies prolongs and intensifies the trauma and emotional duress of these negative experiences, potentially into an infinite future, which in turn makes it very difficult for sexual assault survivors to escape interpersonal harm or heal.[46]

Social media may further increase the possibility of revictimization survivors face by elevating incidents into high-profile events with national audiences, making the rapes go viral. Sometimes this attention results in victims being marginalized or silenced, as their stories are co-opted by others. In Steubenville, involvement by Anonymous initially focused on shaming the perpetrators, but their Twitter feed quickly became about seeking resignations from the police force, mayoral office, school board, and football team. Once sexual assault cases go viral, it is difficult to contain them; survivors have no control over where their stories go or who can use them, and there is a risk their narratives and needs will be hijacked by larger movements or used toward unexpected ends.[47] Feminist scholars in particular warn of the possibility of public rape stories being incorporated into criminal justice discourses that present the criminal legal system as the site of managing sexual violence.[48] In the Stanford rape case in California, for instance, online demands for harsher punishment for Brock Turner often overshadowed discussions of rape culture, culminating in a campaign to implement new mandatory minimum sentences for cases of sexual assault in the state.[49] We see aspects of this in some of the assaults discussed in this book, as well. In Steubenville, and in the Coleman and Dietrich cases, victim activism and public pressure resulted in harsher sentences for the young perpetrators. Calls for punitiveness and formal intervention to sexual assault can contribute to the uneasy alliance between law-and-order politics and carceral feminism. As decades of scholarship have shown, such responses do more harm than good for marginalized and vulnerable populations, as they disproportionately contribute to the incarceration of women and racial minorities.[50]

Additionally, increased attention in such instances can also expose survivors to increased scrutiny and further avenues of humiliating commentary and abuse. Even in cases where the digital evidence seems more clear-cut, as in the Steubenville rape, and aids in the investigation and successful prosecution of the offenders, the victory is not without a cost for the victim. As I detailed in chapter 2, Jane Doe was subject to serious backlash and harassment from digital audiences following the verdict in Steubenville. Responses on Twitter, Facebook, and Reddit repeatedly disparaged and blamed her, while expressing sympathy for the boys:

> Maybe if you don't want to get raped, don't get blackout drunk. Just a thought.

> I honestly feel sorry for the boys in the Steubenville trial. That whore was asking for it.

> Fuck that whore seriously. Bottom line she's a whore. She GOES. She would have fucked anyway because she got trained before SOBER.

> So you got drunk at a party and two people take advantage of you, that's not rape you're just a loose drunk slut.

> She doesn't remember what she did a couple weeks ago #Alcoholic #Whore.

> Disgusting outcome on #Steubenville trial. Remember kids if you're drunk/slutty at a party, and embarrassed later, just say you got raped!

> I'll stop tweeting about this when everyone stfu and understands #JaneDoe or ------ is a whore.

> That's a shame. The bitch got what she deserved.[51]

Two teen girls also threatened Jane on Twitter, posting: "You ripped my family apart. You made my cousin cry. So when I see you b---- it's going to be homicide"; they were later charged over the threats.[52]

It is hard to imagine most teenage girls, and most survivors, coping with this deluge of abuse without experiencing further harm or trauma, regardless of the support networks they might have in place. Dealing with victim-blaming, online threats, and revictimization by online publics can be extremely mentally and emotionally taxing for survivors, limiting the potential of digital technologies as avenues of extralegal justice. Importantly, the social media reactions in these cases highlight the gendered bind and ongoing stigmatization of female sexuality facing young women, which ultimately compromise their justice goals both within and outside of the legal system. However significant social media's contributions to digital advocacy and public discourse on gendered violence have been, these new possibilities coexist alongside traditional and misogynist notions of feminine modesty and propriety. As a result, despite the context in which the images of their bodies, and their abuse, were created—non-consensually, and during a criminal sex act—the boundaries are lost, and the photos become signifiers of "bad" public feminine behavior and sexuality on display.[53] In turn, online publics deploy these digital artifacts against survivors—and women in general—to police their sexuality and behavior and reinforce traditional gender norms.

Hierarchies of Victimhood

The bullying faced by Audrie, Daisy, and Jane is important not only for demonstrating the prevalence of rape myths and respectability politics informing public responses to victims of sexual violence, and particularly young women, but also for underscoring the fact that these girls were subject to such backlash *despite* what may be considered their status as ideal victims.[54] Rape literature has consistently shown that attractive, white, heterosexual, cis-gendered, middle-class survivors are more likely to be believed by both the public and the criminal justice system. Victim-survivors who may not necessarily meet these criteria, such as women of color or sexual minorities, face a higher possibility of disbelief, blame, and threat of digital harm.[55] The photo of Jada Smith's abuse becoming a Twitter meme, for example, is indicative of the ways sexism and racism intersect to dehumanize Jada and objectify her body for consumption and entertainment.[56] Additionally, women may find limited support in online publics when their victimization does not match traditional representations of rape (i.e., violence, coercion, trauma), or when they fail to meet appropriate representations of respectable (white) femininity (e.g., intoxicated, partying), as in the incidents discussed here.[57]

This means the capacity to weaponize the power of social media to garner support and be heard in a meaningful way is not equal for all young survivors. In many ways, Savannah Dietrich was able to speak out on social media because she is an attractive, white, middle-class, well-educated, and articulate young woman, who had the support of her family. Her activism was made easier by the court's validation of her complaint (the young men were found guilty) and the lack of a digital trail; with all evidence of her assault deleted, she faced a lower risk of public shaming. Further helping her to garner sympathy and credibility was the cultural capital and financial support provided by her family, who were able to pay for legal advice so Dietrich could strategically engage media in ways that could advance her case.[58] This is a high standard for most survivors to meet, considering such affordances are not always available to them. Digital spaces, then, do not necessarily overcome barriers women have encountered in the public sphere, and in fact may reproduce hierarchies of speaking, visibility, and victimhood based on race, class, gender, and sexual orientation.[59]

There is the further related danger that in addition to reproducing hierarchies of victimhood, online platforms simultaneously risk reifying hegemonic rape scripts and unintentionally narrowing representations of harm. Survivors who share their stories publicly regularly find themselves having to construct an account of their experiences that fits within a recognizable sociocultural and legal script in order to be rendered credible. As such, their testimonies often end up reproducing normative tropes about the experience of sexual violence and present rape as a deeply painful and traumatic experience, depictions that privilege a Western, white, middle-class worldview.[60] Moreover, Loney-Howes argues, in the neoliberal context, stories of sexual violence have to illustrate that a victim took steps to ensure her sexual safety, in addition to expressing severe levels of trauma.[61] Survivors whose stories of sexual victimization have been told by others, as in instances of assault where the victim is drunk or unconscious and their rape has gone viral on social media, are under particular pressure to reframe their experiences within accepted discourses so as to be believed.

Following the dismissal of her allegations by both the police and her community, Daisy Coleman wrote an essay for the website xoJane.com detailing her sexual assault. In her post she constructs a narrow and linear narrative of predatory boys who took advantage of her age and inexperience, getting her drunk with the express purpose of taking advantage of her. She mentions explicitly that she was not romantically attracted to her abuser, that she trusted him because he was one of her brother's friends, and that the boys should have known the effect that high alcohol consumption would have on her. She also describes the incident and its aftermath as profoundly traumatic, something that "will live with me forever," marked on her body by ugly "scars from self mutilation."[62] Public support and calls for justice resulting from narratives such as Daisy's can obscure other forms of sexual violence and risk marginalizing or silencing survivors whose storytelling and experiences do not fit within these parameters.[63] Because of the highly visual nature of these incidents (i.e., photos, video, etc.) and the age of the victims, digital activism is further in danger of reproducing stereotypical depictions of women as vulnerable, fearful, passive, and helpless, arguably perpetuating what Renee Heberle calls the "spectacle of women's sexual suffering."[64]

Seeking Justice through Unjust Platforms

While there are many examples of social media being used in creative and empowering ways to challenge and critique gendered violence, their potential for meeting the justice needs of survivors will always be limited by the functions and values built into technologies. Digital media scholars have documented men's monopoly of technology from the outset, developing platforms and products that reflect their values and protect their interests.[65] The internet emerged from male-dominated fields, spaces that were also overwhelmingly white, straight, and characterized by a culture of competition and masculine aggression.[66] These assumptions and prerogatives, about who the users will be and how they will interact online, have informed the design of social media, embedding inequality and systemic bias into its architecture.[67] Although social media are host to a more diverse user base, including a high percentage of female users, specific platforms, such as Twitter and Reddit, are characterized by highly combative and aggressive behavior norms that restrict women's engagement.[68] As both a product and a reproduction of gender and racial hierarchies, social media is also used by boys and men as a tool of power and control, exposing and attacking intimate aspects of women's lives online as a way to sanction women for violating traditional gender norms or participating in the public sphere.[69]

Further, it bears repeating that social media platforms not only reflect but also help foster the cultural and material conditions that enable and sanction misogyny and digital abuse.[70] Dependent on the traffic and commodification of private information for profit, digital media reward users for disclosure and for sharing attention-grabbing content, while simultaneously publicly comparing them to each other through the number of followers, "likes," and other indices of appreciation.[71] As previously discussed, these metrics promote an objectifying milieu that increasingly manifests itself in racist, misogynist, and homophobic abuse and harassment online.[72] It is a space that continues unregulated because of the libertarian ethos informing digital participation, whereby tech platforms present themselves as fierce defenders of individual freedom of expression, a position that enables them to minimize and delegitimize claims of harm and abuse caused by social media.[73] In actuality, what tech companies are defending is their profit margins. They require users to publicize their private lives yet fail to provide any of the safety features that would protect users from having these public intimacies used against them, because there is profit in misogyny and racism. There is value in the images of women and girls; value in high-profile cases that attract public attention; value in humiliating, inflammatory, and hateful content that users will like, comment, share, and organize around, all while increasing platform traffic. And if these digital platforms contribute to further marginalizing already disadvantaged groups, there is additional value in their capacity to maintain the status quo and male, white privilege.[74]

These materialities are important for the potential of extralegal justice and digital activism for young survivors of sexual violence. Informal justice and online feminist counter-publics may work to mitigate the effects of sexual assault, primarily by challenging the rape culture that underlies public and policy responses to the problem. We see evidence that such mass resistance is possible in campaigns like *Hollaback!* and #MeToo, among others. At the individual and local levels, however, this advocacy may not be possible for some victims, especially those belonging to disadvantaged and marginalized groups. Moreover, it may be harder for some survivors to contend with the threat of negative attention, harassment, racism, homophobia, and violent misogyny they may encounter in online spaces, restricting the liberatory potential of social media.[75] These platforms render women and girls more visible and accessible—and therefore more vulnerable to abuse than ever before, especially because of the lack of regulation of digital spaces.

The onus placed on victims to mobilize digital platforms, without much support from tech companies, also demands that we consider who is responsible for doing the work needed to get them that justice, as well as the emotional and physical toll of such labor.[76] The key for feminists going forward will be how to reconcile digital activism—and the larger conversations on rape culture, entitlement, and consent it helps foster—with survivors' individual justice needs and the cost for the more vulnerable victims.

6

Toward Harm Reduction
and Prevention

This book has detailed how the non-consensual recording and distribution of sexual assault by adolescents through mobile technologies and social media platforms is understood and responded to in the present socio-legal context. A central and recurring theme in my analysis is that current cultural and institutional responses treat sexual violence and its digital circulation as discrete events, often subsuming one phenomenon in the other. Where the criminal justice system is concerned, the digital evidence of the assaults discussed in this book is simply proof of a sex crime. For parents, the media, and the broader public, the incidents are examples of technological risk, of immature youth interacting with platforms whose features and consequences they do not fully understand. In the experiences of young people, however, the production, circulation, and interpretation of images of sexual abuse on digital platforms underscore the continuity between teens' online and offline behavior and the complexity of the gender, power, and technology nexus they are trying to navigate in their daily lives. Their insights suggest that a robust approach is needed to help address and prevent sexual violence and image-based sexual abuse, requiring a concerted combination of educational, technological, legal, and social interventions.

BEYOND TECHNOLOGICAL RISK

Because mainstream discourses surrounding the cases discussed in this book decouple the digital violence from the sexual assaults, the policy and educational solutions they offer for image-based sexual abuse are often limited and misguided. Much of this advice echoes the messages found in public educational campaigns on youth, sexting, and cyberbullying in countries like the United Kingdom, Canada, and Australia.[1] They center narrowly on personal risk, advising young women to protect themselves by limiting their digital engagement, and recommending parents safeguard their teens through increased monitoring and surveillance of their devices and online activity. Advising adolescents to abstain from engaging with social media, particularly as it relates to their sexuality and peer cultures, only contributes to a failure to provide them with the skills necessary to negotiate this shifting landscape. A focus on self-managing risk does not help teens navigate the deeply gendered contours of digital platforms and technological practice; issues of ethical consent; or the ongoing sexist norms and values that persist in the production, distribution and exchange of digital content, including intimate images and photos of sexual abuse.[2]

In my focus groups, young people reported that cyber-safety messages from their parents and schools were often superficial and counterproductive, ignoring the primacy of technology for their identity and relationships as well as the complexity of how gender and power relations shape teens' sexual and digital behaviors. Research on youth, technology, and sex consistently shows such narratives often end up policing young women's behavior and making them responsible for managing the risk of digital participation, resulting in a reinforcement of victim-blaming attitudes that excuses those who perpetrate digital abuse from any responsibility.[3] These approaches ignore situations in which individuals are coerced into sharing intimate images or, as in the cases discussed here, instances where images are taken without the knowledge or consent of the victim. They fail to account for the abuse and harassment survivors face once such images are shared online and the ways in which this abuse is often gendered and disproportionately harms young women. Most importantly, such responses fail to address the gender dynamics and sexual norms that inform young people's digital practices and the larger social contexts that make these practices meaningful.

EDUCATIONAL INTERVENTIONS FOR SEXUAL VIOLENCE IN THE DIGITAL AGE

Adopting a Sexual Ethics Framework

It is tempting to prioritize digital literacy interventions as the solution to preventing digital abuse. However, we cannot understand the recording and sharing of sexual assault as separate from the sex crime, as doing so fails to situate young people's digital activity in the context of male dominance, rape culture, and gender inequality and obscures the actions and responsibility of the perpetrators in such instances. The same gender inequalities and culture that sanction the sexual assault also enable its technological afterlife and ongoing digital abuse. If we want to introduce preventative measures that challenge the ethics that allow such digital praxis to occur, we first must address the sexual and gender norms informing young people's interactions and intimate relationships.

If we listen to teenagers, what we hear are deeply unequal and heteronormative dynamics informing many of their gendered relations and sexual norms. Adolescents construct women as passive, lacking in sexual agency and desire. Boys, meanwhile, are described as inherently sexual and aggressive, likely to exploit girls for sexual pleasure and in their pursuit for social status among peers. Heterosexuality and sexual conquest still matter among adolescent males for successfully performing masculinity and attaining peer approval. Such a heteronormative framework helps naturalize and promote unequal gender dynamics between the sexes, prioritizing young men's needs over young women's sexual desires. It is a privileging of male sexual desire that can lead boys to feel entitled to sex and to women's bodies, fostering women's objectification and treatment as currency in young men's (hetero)masculinity performances. The gendered binary of male dominance and female submission can also provide normative scripts that sometimes reconstruct rape as sex, allowing it to slip by as normal sexual behavior, especially when alcohol and drugs are involved. Rape myths that minimize and legitimate men's violation of sexual boundaries or shift blame onto women to justify and excuse such behavior further cement the reframing of rape as sex.

The prevalence of traditional gender attitudes, normative sex scripts, and rape myths in young people's understandings of sexual violence in my own and others' research underscores the poverty of our current models of sex education and "no means no" anti-rape campaigns, as well as the pressing need for educational intervention and sexual violence prevention at much younger stages in the education system and over sustained periods of time.[4] Scholarship shows effective prevention strategies often take into account the reality of young people's lives, including drinking and sexual behaviors; teach youth about the importance of consent, respect, and privacy; and involve adolescents in the development and implementation of initiatives.[5] Rather than individualized interventions, the focus should be on peer groups and norms, helping young people to identify the attitudes and norms that support gendered violence, discussing positive bystander intervention strategies, and engaging them in building knowledge and skills about ethical decision-making in their intimate encounters. Research also suggests prevention initiatives should pay more direct attention to the role of alcohol in sexual assault perpetration, particularly how intoxication impacts decision-making and the capacity to consent, as well as its effect on bystanders' perception of risk and willingness to intervene in certain situations.[6]

There is further a need to develop interventions that more directly address bodily autonomy and sexual expression among youth, considering their conflicting and problematic understandings and practices around consent and sexual harm. Such interventions have to include a sexual ethics framework that recognizes and respects the rights of each person, and legitimizes female desire and sexuality while also deconstructing masculinity models that celebrate sexual aggression and pressure young boys into sexually harmful sexual practices.[7] Additionally, educational efforts should help students develop verbal and non-verbal communications skills necessary to establish consent; negotiate conflicting desires and needs in their relationships; and address how power, gender, and cultural norms help shape understandings of consent.[8]

Programs on sex education and sexual violence prevention must also effectively engage with social media technologies and practices, considering their embeddedness in peer and intimate relationships, violence perpetration, and bystander intervention. These too must be grounded within adolescents' lived experiences, rather than on adult fears and anxieties. Educators and young people can work alongside each other to unpack how broader gender norms and sexual messaging inform adolescents' digital engagement and create spaces where youth can explore the dilemmas and tensions around issues like sexting, privacy violations, and the digital mediation of sexuality and bodily expression. Such efforts should aim to build an understanding of girls as sexual agents, destigmatizing their sexting practices, while also interrogating unethical and abusive digital practices and the unequal risks and harms young people face. These should be nonjudgmental spaces, fostering discussions of digital rights, ethics, and responsibility, with the goal of helping young people navigate risk and make informed choices to address harm.[9]

Finally, educational efforts need to account for pornography, especially in light of the increased access to porn that digital technologies make possible for teens, often before they have the chance to test and develop their own sexual boundaries and practices.[10] Presently, scholarship does not show a causal relationship in which viewing porn results in an increase in sexually risky and violent behavior. Nevertheless, studies find that exposure to sexually explicit media online can enhance young people's belief that women are sexual objects, can foster violence-supportive attitudes, and may influence young men's sexual behavior.[11] Content analyses of popular pornography films reveal that consent is portrayed as murky and nonverbal and is often assumed in the absence of explicit resistance or a verbal no.[12] Given the lack of standardized and quality formal sex education in the United States, it would not be surprising if online pornography has become a primary source of young people's sexual education, even if it is not designed to be so. Consequently, it is important for schools to teach about the potential effects of pornography use, including discussing expectations for real-life sexual activity, safer sex practice, sexual consent and healthy sexual norms, behavior and attitudes toward the opposite sex, and respect and informed decision-making when engaging in sexual activity. As previously noted, such interventions should be socially and culturally relevant, reflecting young people's experiences, and led by their peers. More than simply delivering information and warnings, their focus should be on skill development, and providing young people with a space to critically reflect on their practices and develop their own sexual ethics.[13]

Toward Ethical Digital Participation

To effectively address digital harm as it relates to sexual violence, school programs on sexual ethics and violence prevention must be developed and adopted alongside ethical digital citizenship initiatives. Incidents of youth capturing and sharing sexual abuse through new technologies exist on the extreme end of a disclosure spectrum in a culture where mediation and humiliation have become routine practice. They require us to consider the issue of consent more broadly given the shifting boundaries of privacy and ethical engagement in the digital age. However, because we continue to approach on- and offline activity as separate spheres, our educational and policy interventions remain siloed, limited, and individualistic. Most high school educational programs related to digital media are week-long initiatives focused on improving digital literacy and teaching youth about responsible digital citizenship, often defined as maintaining a clean digital footprint that will not compromise one's future.[14] This is a much narrower definition of digital participation than examining what it means to be an ethical digital citizen or addressing digital engagement in the context of inequality and violence.[15]

Adolescents, and I would argue children in much younger grades, need to engage with questions of identity, privacy, and consent in digital participation, as well as exercises and activities designed to teach them about intent, audiences, and different perspectives and responsibilities in their social media decision-making.[16] My suggestion here is that we use young people's digital practices, including the recording and dissemination of sexual assault and the digital shaming and cyberbullying of survivors, to open up critical discussions with youth about new media production and consumption and ethical digital citizenship. Such conversations must include the impact of attention economies and the cultural turn toward online disclosure and humiliation, as well as considerations of the logics of new media platforms, on young users' digital practices. These educational efforts can help broaden young people's capacity to consider the ethical implications of their digital activity and provide them with multiple strategies to negotiate technologically mediated relationships. As such, they are likely to be more effective in reducing harmful digital practices and abuse than responses that focus on limiting and/or surveilling young people's social media activity.[17]

School Culture

Successfully implementing any of these preventative and educational measures on sexual violence and digital abuse in the United States first requires that K–12 schools and administrators buy into the necessity of such initiatives and have the funding and resources available to successfully implement them. Yet many schools are reluctant to investigate cases of sexual assault, whether an incident occurs on or off campus.[18] This hesitation was also evident in the Steubenville and Audrie Pott cases (among others), where administrators failed to address the cyberbullying by their students in the aftermath of the incidents or to sanction the individuals perpetuating image-based sexual abuse in each case.

Recent stories by news sources and nonprofit organizations on sexual assault and image-based abuse in public schools indicate a systemic failure among them to recognize and address sexual violence. Allegations are typically handled by administrators with no specialized training, who often respond by either suspending or expelling the victims from school, especially victims who are young women of color.[19] Although less is known about how private schools handle this problem, studies find that a lack of training and institutional support for responding to sexual violence is widespread among K–12 schools. Middle and high school staff, for example, report being insufficiently trained on identifying peer-based sexual harassment between students and often unaware of the policies or skills needed to protect them from harmful experiences in education settings.[20] Recent scholarship from the United Kingdom shows school personnel lacking the necessary vocabularies of gender or nuanced understanding of consent to address online harassment.[21] Rather, as Carlene Firmin's research suggests, schools may be providing an environment that facilitates gendered abuse.[22] Her investigation found that harmful sexual practices among teens are both expected and normalized by school staff, in turn sanctioning such practices among students at the schools.

It is unclear how American schools are responding to the intersection of sexual violence and technology. The extent to which schools see themselves as sites where such abuse occurs or recognize the role of school cultures and staff responses in contributing to peer violence and harassment needs further investigation. There is an additional paucity of research on the digital knowledge and literacy skills of school personnel or their capacity to effectively address image-based sexual abuse perpetrated by students. The lack of federal or state-wide measures and funding to implement digital ethics and literacy courses as part of the regular educational and/or health curriculum suggests there may be serious deficiencies in how schools respond to digital abuse, as does scholarship showing the increasing use of new technologies to perpetuate dating violence and to threaten, harass, and control victims. A much needed update to sexual violence and harassment responses in K–12 schools, then, is specific policies to account for digital abuse. Such policies would require schools to train staff on the gendered nature of this harm as well as issues of privacy and consent relating to digital participation.[23]

By taking a more survivor-centered approach to complaints of technology-facilitated sexual violence, schools can also develop guidelines that take a more restorative response to such harms, rather than punitive disciplinary action or police involvement and criminalization. Emerging research suggests that disciplinary measures, such as suspension or expulsion, fail to account for the multiple sources of relational harm in cases of digital abuse.[24] Punishing the perpetrator(s) of the abuse does nothing to stop the spread of an image or video, address the harassment and shaming of the victim by peers and the wider community, or help the survivor cope with these harms.[25] Instead, scholars argue that schools should adopt restorative responses that can offer a space for perpetrators, survivors, and the school community to think deeply about why this harm occurred and how to address and prevent such harms in the future.[26] Restorative approaches in schools have been shown to be particularly effective for responding to bullying behaviors and discriminatory beliefs. Coupled with educational efforts to improve sex education, as well as digital ethics, they offer a promising avenue for addressing technology-facilitated sexual violence among youth.

LEGAL REFORM AND SURVIVOR-CENTERED RESPONSES

My findings indicate that it is not only parents, educators, and the media that engage with the creation and distribution of non-consensual images of sexual abuse as unrelated to sexual violence. Law enforcement and courtroom actors also treat the digital trail following a sexual assault as proof of the sex crime, as corroborating evidence, rather than as an extension of it. There is certainly potential in social media's evidentiary capacity and its ability to substantiate rape allegations and aid police investigations. Prosecutors, too, find the incriminating evidence the digital trail provides useful for pleading out cases, and during trials for challenging defense claims around consent and offenders' intent to harm the victim. How effectively this potential is realized, however, remains uneven across departments, courtrooms, and jurisdictions, due to a lack of training, resources, and cultural attitudes pertaining to the shifting digital terrain. Such ongoing challenges leave survivors of sexual violence who turn to the criminal legal system for help increasingly frustrated with long delays in processing cases and with the lack of successful prosecutions despite the volume of digital evidence turned over to the authorities. More importantly, it leaves victims whose sexual violation has been digitally documented without any criminal recourse because the law does not consistently or effectually recognize image-based sexual abuse as sexual violence. What avenues of accountability and justice are possible then, for young survivors who want to stop images of their abuse from being shared online?

A holistic response to sexual violence requires us to situate image-based sexual abuse on the continuum of gendered violence and update the law to recognize its harms.[27] Legislation is important for communicating disapproval and social condemnation for digital abuse, signaling that the state is serious about curbing its occurrence, and sanctioning its perpetuation. For survivors who want to turn to the criminal justice system for recourse, legal reform offers them an option to pursue accountability. Symbolically, the law can also operate to offer victim-survivors a level of acknowledgment of their abuse, signal to them that such harms are being taken seriously, and help restore and affirm their dignity.[28]

The debate over whether state intervention and legal change are the most effective interventions to image-based sexual abuse is ongoing. Criminalizing non-consensual pornography and the unauthorized distribution of intimate images and punishing offenders sends a message that such acts are harmful and unacceptable.[29] Despite recent laws to this effect, however, technology-facilitated sexual violence remains a growing social problem, and the harm following distribution remains unaddressed.[30] Research on image-based abuse among youth further suggests that criminal responses to these harms do not adequately address the needs of this group. Many young victim-survivors are less concerned with punishing perpetrators than they are with finding assistance in stopping the spread of images, addressing related bullying or harassment, and dealing with reactions from their family and peers.[31] Throughout this book, as well, I have detailed the many ways that criminal justice responses and the law continue to fail young victims of sexual violence and digital abuse. It is clear the criminal legal system is not the only solution to addressing technology-facilitated sexual violence, nor should it be seen as such. But it is equally apparent the law has not caught up to what young people are experiencing in the digital age, and as such, it needs updating.

If we want the criminal justice system to improve its responses to sexual assault and to take image-based abuse seriously, then the law has to intervene to ensure legal actors have the knowledge, training, and resources needed to tackle these issues. As it stands, there is need for improving law enforcement training on treating adolescents' complaints of sexual violence and image-based sexual abuse seriously. Legal recognition of digital harm as a form of gendered violence would require police officers, lawyers, and judges to improve their understanding of and attitudes toward new technologies and their consequences, as well as to increase efforts to build digital skills across the criminal legal system, aiding survivors of sexual and digital violence in their efforts to seek justice and redress. A better understanding of the capacities, features, and harms of digital platforms throughout the criminal justice system may also result in more robust and critical assessments of digital evidence by the courts and improved awareness and sensitivity to the ways the digital trail can be used to perpetuate racial and gendered stereotypes in the courtroom and blame survivors.

Thus far, legal approaches to image-based abuse in most jurisdictions have been inconsistent and piecemeal. Some states rely on recent nonconsensual porn laws that specifically target the unlawful dissemination or publication of an intimate image, while others use already existing laws for sexting, stalking, harassment, voyeurism, and cyberbullying to prosecute instances of digital abuse. Police are not always aware of all the relevant laws, lack the resources to use them, and often have difficulty enforcing them in practice.[32] Most image-based abuse offenses are classified as misdemeanors, and legal actors exercise wide discretion and caution in their sanctions. Yet juvenile offenders who record and distribute images of sexual assault, for example, can still be charged under existing child pornography statutes, as happened in Steubenville, which require them to register as sex offenders. Such inconsistencies in legal responses raise concerns about who is being criminalized in the response to digital harm and how these laws risk becoming overly punitive and may be unequally applied to young perpetrators.[33]

Legal reform is necessary if we are to recognize the harms of technology-facilitated sexual violence for survivors and protect young offenders from arbitrary and retributive punishment. Involvement with the law does not have to mean alignment with the carceral state or pursuing more punitive responses toward perpetrators.[34] Instead, we can develop solutions that offer victim-survivors and offenders multiple avenues toward accountability through a process that is meaningful and restorative for both parties.[35] Sanctions against offenders, rather than criminal sentences, should include restorative interventions, comprising diversionary programs such as counseling services, work with sexual violence and victim support organizations, participation in gender-based violence and/or ethical digital citizenship education-based initiatives, and restorative conferences with survivors.[36] Where victims are concerned, our reform efforts should be informed by their justice needs and focus on reducing the spread and prevalence of digital artifacts, ensuring that images of sexual abuse do not get circulated or distributed and that victims are not bullied and harassed when such digital dissemination occurs. Funding of such initiatives requires updating the law to recognize image-based sexual abuse and may also contribute to increased mandates for policies and programs designed to address factors correlated with sexual violence and digital harm.

If our approaches to technology-facilitated sexual violence are to be survivor-centered, then criminal law is but one avenue of redress available to victims. Survivors should have a range of legal options available to them to choose the course of action they deem most appropriate when addressing their experiences of violence and help them reclaim control of the situation.[37] Civil laws, for instance, such as sexual harassment, invasion of privacy, and copyright laws, enable victims to hold perpetrators and internet companies to account. As in the case of existing criminal interventions, such laws are inconsistently applied across states and jurisdictions and fail to adequately capture the harms associated with digital abuse. There are also significant costs associated with civil litigation for victims who may lack the necessary resources to bring civil action.[38] Nevertheless, civil rights laws also have the potential to contribute to the transformation of social attitudes by responding to the harms suffered by a group, as in the case of sexual harassment. Importantly, both civil and criminal law responses should work together to help address all the difficulties survivors face, while remaining flexible enough to meet the specific needs of each victim and the varying degrees to which they want to be involved with the law. The United States could also follow the examples of other countries and develop government-funded organizations tasked with helping survivors remove digital content from the internet.[39] Such responses offer some of the possibilities of progressive legal reform and of using the law's coercive power to encourage cultural and systemic change.

TECH INDUSTRY

Technology companies, social network service providers, search engines, and other intermediaries also have an important role to play in preventing digital harm from happening. There is a tendency to view digital platforms as neutral because they are not directly involved in perpetrating gender-based violence, but rather host content and facilitate its exchange between third parties.[40] As corporate actors, however, such intermediaries have the opportunity to shape and regulate how their services are accessed and used. Through their terms of services and algorithmic functioning, companies can determine the boundaries of what is acceptable digital content and behavior on their platforms, a crucial step in identifying and preventing digital harm.[41] Moreover, it is the underlying logics and values of digital platforms that help generate an objectifying environment in which abuse and harassment are likely outcomes.[42] Since digital harm is a byproduct of social media participation, then, digital platforms have a social responsibility to prevent online gendered violence and ensure equitable digital citizenship among users.

Technology companies based in the United States have enjoyed broad legal protection against liability for content posted by third parties through Section 230 of the Communications Decency Act of 1996. Nevertheless, in recent years social pressure from users and civil advocacy groups, as well as a desire to protect their reputations and profit margins, have led these companies to undertake a number of notable initiatives to address digital harm.[43] These include crafting specific community standards and policies on digital abuse and the non-consensual sharing of intimate photos and videos.[44] Various measures to tackle image-based sexual abuse have also been put in place, such as disabling or suspending accounts, providing survivors the means to report their experiences, easing the restrictions under which they can request content be deleted, and ensuring harmful content is taken down or excluded from internet searches.[45] Beyond prohibiting certain types of behavior, digital platforms are also using algorithms, automation, and machine learning to detect and censor image-based sexual abuse. For instance, several platforms use photo-matching, digital fingerprinting, and artificial intelligence tools to detect intimate and non-consensual images and prevent their distribution.[46]

Although these are welcome developments, the policies and tools designed to address and prevent image-based sexual abuse remain piecemeal and reactive. Inconsistent and ambiguous language in content policies across platforms, coupled with varying definitions of what constitutes image-based sexual abuse, can make it difficult and confusing for victim-survivors to report abuse or to inform platform users of the rules of acceptable behavior. Current reporting systems also continue to predominantly place the onus on survivors (and other users) to find and report abusive content, essentially making them responsible for minimizing their chances of victimization.[47] This risks placing additional burdens on already vulnerable individuals, rather than requiring tech companies to proactively develop solutions that reduce harm and ensure the safety of users. Further, in the process of reporting, reviewing, and responding to flagged content or users, companies ultimately still reserve the right to make decisions on whether something qualifies as abuse, what content has violated their terms of service, and whether action should be taken against the claim, since there is no law to protect victims.[48] The issue is made worse by the facts that removing non-consensual images and video is often a slow and complicated process, unevenly (and unequally) enforced, and that companies tend to be non-transparent about decisions on whether content has violated their terms of service.[49] In criminal cases, platforms tend to comply with law enforcement requests to take down harmful material, but this requires survivors to engage with the criminal justice system, an avenue many of them are reluctant to pursue.

I do not mean to suggest here that moderating abusive content on social media is easy, and the numerous challenges facing tech companies are well documented in the literature.[50] But digital platforms need to engage more proactively to address digital harm; otherwise they risk failing survivors and implicating themselves in the perpetration of image-based sexual abuse. Scholars working at the intersection of technology and gendered violence have outlined several steps the industry can take to better address digital harm. These include clear policies that specifically prohibit image-based sexual abuse content; more resources invested in content moderation and AI tools for detecting and removing content; increased transparency and accountability over how platforms respond to abuse; and greater collaboration between platforms, survivors, civil advocacy groups, and the government to achieve common goals, among others.[51]

Due to the significant harms of image-based sexual abuse, some researchers also argue that tech companies should be held accountable for providing legal services for victim-survivors to help combat abuse, as well as funding organizations that provide them with the support and resources they need to remove content from the web and deal with the emotional and psychological consequences of their experiences.[52] Universal among these solutions is the request for effective regulatory governance for digital platforms. Left to their own devices, tech companies will continue to be governed by the libertarian values of freedom of expression and free market informing their industry. As scholars and activists have pointed out, hate, humiliation, and abuse online trigger traffic and participation, which translate into material gains for platforms, disincentivizing them from curbing such practices.[53] It is difficult to imagine platforms built toward capital reorienting themselves toward human ends and counteracting gendered violence without legislative change and state-based regulation to incentivize the industry.

Ultimately, addressing image-based abuse and the interrelated problem of sexual violence requires a flexible and multifaceted approach that includes education; legal, technological, and social interventions; and the collaboration of actors across institutions and social spheres. Gendered violence and digital harassment and abuse are the consequence of broader structural inequalities and sexist, racist, homophobic, and misogynistic attitudes that educational and prevention efforts should aim to identify and disrupt. At the same time, the criminal legal system and tech industry need to listen to and collaborate with survivors and civil advocacy groups to develop more robust responses to digital harm, improve efforts to support victim-survivors, and hopefully engender a broader cultural shift in attitudes toward sexual violence and digital abuse. Finally, we must also recognize that social media offer opportunities to critique existing responses to sexual violence, even as we demand better of these platforms. We should take further advantage of their capacity to empower survivors, challenge rape myths and rape culture, and better inform publics on the problem of gendered violence, to galvanize further support for change. There is power in public recognition and discourse, and digital platforms offer victimized individuals and marginalized groups the spaces and opportunities to voice their experiences and invite the larger public to participate in debating and formulating potential solutions. But these discussions and activism must translate into institutional practices and initiatives to effect real change and advance the movement toward gender justice.

Conclusion

My students often ask me what my research is about. When I tell them I am interested in sexual violence, youth, and technology, and describe for them the incidents of sexual and image-based abuse that my work examines, they typically and casually reply, "Oh, yeah, that's high school." Then they proceed to regale me with stories of "messy" sexual experiences and privacy violations, of intimate photos and videos being (non-consensually) circulated among private social media groups and text chains, of embarrassing leaks that destroyed girls' reputations or resulted in boys being suspended from school. I am repeatedly struck by how much their experiences echo the stories and perspectives of the teens I interviewed for this book. I am also reminded anew of all the ways we continue to fail our youth and the ongoing salience of the cases discussed in this book and the lessons they offer us.

A decade ago, the Steubenville, Pott, and Coleman incidents grabbed our attention because they were novel in their use of technology to capture, share, and perpetuate sexual violence. We all seemed to share an understanding that the cases had something significant to tell us about young people, technology, and the implications of the digital turn for our society. They opened questions about how teens are engaging with digital media. What reasons do young people have to record and publicly share instances of sexual assault? How do they understand and assess technological risk? What social and cultural conditions have enabled such events, have normalized the sharing of this type of abuse across social media platforms? Because the behaviors documented through digital media also depicted a sex crime, the cases raised further questions about peer cultures and sexual norms among youth, as well as concerns over their understandings of sexual violence and consent. Moreover, the assaults provided an early opportunity for examining the consequences of digital technologies for institutional responses to sexual violence. What would the digital trail mean for young victim-survivors and perpetrators of sexual assault, and for the problem of sexual violence?

In the intervening years, such questions have only become more pressing. Social media and mobile technologies are now an integral part of our world and of young people's lives, their identities and daily practices embedded in and dependent on these platforms. How we define privacy, perform identity, and negotiate our relationships; how we seek status, consume, participate in the public sphere, and measure value, have all been fundamentally altered, our social dynamics and inequalities digitally enhanced. This digital turn has also been accompanied by an increase in technology-facilitated harm, including image-based sexual abuse. While we know more now about the prevalence and harms of digital abuse, the questions raised by the cases at the center of this research remain mostly unanswered, the causes of image-based sexual abuse among youth undertheorized.

In this book, I have argued that the digital recording and distribution of sexual assault is the result of multiple interacting factors between the interpersonal and the structural. Specifically, individual gender goals and peer culture norms intersect with objectifying and attention-seeking behaviors informed by unequal gender relations, technological affordances, and online cultures of humiliation. In many ways, the underlying issues these instances of juvenile sexual assault and image-based abuse help expose are by no means new. Hegemonic gender norms and unequal power dynamics continue to inform adolescent peer cultures and relations between the sexes, including their sexual behaviors. And heterosexuality and peer validation still matter for boys' masculinity performances. Young men sharing their sexual conquests (consensual or otherwise) on social media is the latest iteration of these identity and peer dynamics in the digital realm. As the young participants in this study inform us, the production and circulation of images of sexual abuse have value-generating potential for young men's social status and their enactments of gender and (hetero)sexuality. Identifying the gendered motivations for capturing and disseminating sexual assault helps us recognize the relationship between sexual and digital violence and conceptualize image-based abuse as a form of sexual violence.

That some teens find it acceptable to publicly brag about sexual violence and generally seem resigned to the inherently gendered and exploitative nature of their interactions and digital exchanges reveals the unequal power relations informing adolescents' sexual practices and digital norms. Their behaviors and ways of thinking are reflective of broader patterns of rape culture, patriarchy, and heterosexism. Many of the attitudes expressed by parents, communities, and the media following the sexual assault cases discussed in this book were sympathetic to the perpetrators, minimizing their culpability while blaming the young women for their victimization. During our interviews it became apparent youth have internalized many of the misconceptions and myths circulated by rape culture and, alongside sex scripts, rely on them to help interpret instances of sexual assault. When discussing the Steubenville case, for example, despite initially recognizing the incident as problematic, they invoked rape myths and narratives of male aggression and sexual need to justify the violence, placing responsibility on the girls to "say no" and manage risk in such situations. While recognizing the harm victims encounter, many of the male participants also ended up blaming the young women for engaging in risky behavior in a gendered social and sexual context where inequality is assumed to be the norm.

At the same time, the cases discussed throughout this book demonstrate the role of digital cultures and social media logics in facilitating and engendering an abusive and unequal milieu in which technology-facilitated sexual violence is possible. Driven by profit, digital platforms actively encourage users to publicize every aspect of their lives, commodifying every interaction, while undermining concerns over ethics and responsible digital engagement. They reward abusive and demeaning content because it generates traffic and platform participation. Young people have grown up in a culture where individuals promoting hate, racism, and misogyny become overnight celebrities, with hundreds of millions of online followers and millions of dollars in ad revenue. Attention, status, and social validation also drive their digital praxis. Teens recording and sharing sexually abusive content exists on the extreme end of the disclosure spectrum in a culture where mediation and humiliation have become routine practice. My goal in highlighting such patterns is to encourage us to think more deeply and critically about how our engagement with technology is impacting our relationship with ethics, consent, and empathy. We cannot continue to turn a blind eye to the material harms of digital abuse, failing to legally recognize it as a social problem, minimizing the harms victims experience, and ignoring the growing practices of humiliation among youth as a means of attaining status. Digital technologies are here to stay, and our involvement with them will only increase, as will the potential for harm.

In making explicit the connections between gender goals, sexual violence, and digital abuse, I hope this book provides key insights and a framework from which scholars, educators, and practitioners can create targeted and effective educational and prevention interventions for youth. Addressing technology-facilitated sexual violence means developing responses that speak to sexual violence and image-based sexual abuse as interrelated occurrences. Young people need adults and institutions who will look out for them, providing them with the skills, support, and resources they need to navigate adolescence, including gender and sexuality, and the shifting terrain of digital technology. We have to educate our youth to respect sexual autonomy, privacy, and bodily integrity, to treat others with dignity, and we have to teach them how to engage with social media platforms ethically. Our institutions and technologies also need to reflect these values.

Understanding the dynamics of technology-facilitated sexual violence further matters for institutional responses to sexual violence and image-based abuse. I have investigated the consequences of the digital trail for young victims and perpetrators of sexual assault to show that our legal and criminal justice systems need to account for the harms that technologies enable. Our social and institutional responses need to take digital abuse seriously and treat it as an extension of gendered violence. We must improve our responses to recognize the damage done to victim-survivors and provide them with a range of options for redress and justice, empowering them to choose a course of action they deem most appropriate when addressing their experiences of violence. At the same time, we need to develop rehabilitative interventions for perpetrators that are oriented toward empathy, dignity, and respect, rather than retribution. As a society, we are increasingly relying on digital tools and surveillance to improve responses to crime. It is my further hope that criminal justice professionals and technology companies learn from my discussion of the potentials and harms the digital trail makes possible, to better engage with digital evidence in sexual assault investigations and work toward reducing barriers and inequalities in responses to sexual violence and digital abuse.

Legal reform is needed if we want to effectively involve multiple stakeholders to address technology-facilitated violence. State intervention cannot be the only solution to this problem, as the state is itself a site where violence is enacted and reproduced, and turning to it does not engage the root causes of sexual violence, such as patriarchy and gender inequality. Yet without legal reform, digital harm will continue unfettered as a private and immaterial issue, and its relationship to the systemic nature of sexual violence (and its causes) is similarly obscured. Importantly, technology-facilitated sexual violence involves technical infrastructures, corporate and law enforcement policies, education, and awareness, in addition to social structures like misogyny. If we want to affect change across these sectors, if we want resources to help set up alternatives to incarceration, to fund organizations that support victims of digital abuse, to hold digital platforms accountable, and to change culture through education, then regulatory intervention is necessary. While not a cure-all, such efforts are part of a holistic approach to successfully combating digital abuse and gender-based violence.

Researchers, too, have a role to play in the efforts to reduce digital harm, in helping improve and nuance educational, community, and policy responses to technology-facilitated violence through their scholarship. This book is my contribution toward increasing our understanding of image-based sexual abuse among youth, but I hope it is also a starting point for more localized and sensitized research in the field. Interest in technology-facilitated sexual violence is growing; however, a lack of empirical evidence about the nature, extent, and consequences of this behavior remains. Most scholarship to date investigates a broad spectrum of harassing and harmful practices online rather than the unique dynamics or impact of specific types of abuse. Few studies have gathered information directly from survivors or offenders or examined the various motives of perpetrators who engage in online gendered violence. More research with racial and sexual minorities is also needed, to tease out what the rates, causes, and consequences of digital harassment and abuse look like across population groups facing interlocking oppressions. As noted in the last chapter, there is a dearth of knowledge on the digital literacy skills of school personnel or how schools respond to instances of image-based abuse, and scholarly inquiries on these topics are crucial.

Presently, little is known about how digital evidence is used in sexual assault investigations and trials, the value of the digital trail for victim-survivors, or how the criminal justice system treats cases in which sexual violence or intimate partner violence occur alongside digital abuse, especially in the US context. Such research must also engage with questions of intersectionality, to tease out differences in experiences and treatment by the criminal legal system based on factors such as race, class, sexuality, age, ability, or immigration status, among others. Further, scholarship should examine the effectiveness of recent legal reforms and measures taken by digital platforms to address image-based sexual abuse, domestically and globally, to help identify best practices for prevention and harm reduction. The rapidly evolving nature of technology means scholars, educators, practitioners, policy makers, and the law will always be playing catch-up to new platforms and the changing ways we use them to perpetuate harm. Our advocacy efforts, our demands for accountability and reform in the fight to end gendered and racialized violence in all its manifestations, must likewise be ongoing.

Methods

The methodological approach for this book is primarily qualitative. My project follows the phenomenon of adolescents recording and disseminating sexual assault through digital media as it moves across different spheres, involving various persons and institutions, and as such it has required a mixed methods approach to investigate its central questions. Mixed methods research can permit researchers to "address more complicated research questions and collect a richer and stronger array of evidence than can be accomplished by any single method alone."[1] Throughout, I rely on in-depth analysis of high-profile juvenile sexual assault cases, group interviews with teens, and interviews with criminal justice professionals and reporters, as well as critical analysis of news media coverage, to investigate how crime, gender, and status intersect with technology for young people growing up digital. The processes, data management, and analysis for each of these methods are detailed in the following sections.

CASE STUDIES

Robert Yin defines the case study method as "an empirical inquiry that investigates a contemporary phenomenon within its real-life context, especially when the boundaries between phenomenon and context are not clearly evident."[2] Case study research is relevant when seeking to understand a complex social phenomenon and particularly well suited to exploring "why" and "how" questions about an event. This is because the approach allows the researcher the use of multiple sources of evidence and to develop converging lines of inquiry in their study, contributing to more accurate and convincing findings.[3] An additional strength of the method is that case studies allow the researcher to examine instances of the same phenomenon with the aim of developing or testing theory regarding the causes of similarities or differences among them. The goal of case study research, then, is not to extrapolate findings onto populations (statistical generalization), but to explore causal mechanisms and to expand and generalize theories about an issue or phenomenon.[4]

This research study investigates three cases of juvenile sexual assault occurring in the United States in 2012. All cases feature the assault of an intoxicated underage girl by one or more adolescent male perpetrators and the use of mobile technologies to record and/or circulate images of the assault by the offenders and/or bystander witnesses of the incidents, including sharing and discussing the assaults on social media platforms. I categorize these incidents as multi-perpetrator assaults because of their group settings; even in instances when there is only one sexual offender, there are bystanders witnessing and recording the abuse. The selected assaults are also similar in that new technologies feature heavily in the aftermath of each case, used to cyberbully and publicly shame the young victims, but also providing survivors, hackers and the criminal justice system with a powerful tool to investigate the assault allegations and seek justice.

The Jane Doe, Daisy Coleman, and Audrie Pott cases were selected from a pool of a dozen similar multi-offender assaults occurring across the country between 2010 and 2015. They were narrowed down based on similarity of case details, their occurrence in the same year (2012), and the parallel level of media attention each received. The three assaults dominated headlines in 2013, appearing on local, national, and international media outlets and online news platforms within weeks of each other. The news media discussed the three incidents together in their reporting and presented them as instances of the same theme. Related incidents involving Black, Latino, and/or working-class youth, social media, and cyberbullying were ignored or did not receive similar coverage in the press, making it difficult to include them for in-depth analysis. The existence of such occurrences, however, alongside research showing that youth of color use social media at the same or higher rates than white teens, suggests the peer cultures and digital practices displayed in the selected cases are generalizable to other adolescent populations.[5] A last point of consideration in selecting these three assaults was their representation of a variety of outcomes in technology-facilitated sexual violence, including convictions, dismissal of charges, and victim suicide. It should be noted that while the analysis focuses primarily on the three incidents, parallel cases occurring from 2013 onward are also discussed in some of the chapters as more recent variations on a theme, typically to offer more support for a specific argument or observation.

While extreme on the spectrum of how youth engage with social media, the Doe, Pott, and Coleman cases are paradigmatic of the problem and prevalence of sexual violence in our culture, including the rise of image-based sexual abuse, and social and institutional responses in such instances. Moreover, at the time of occurrence they were novel in their use of new media technologies and thus important for the insights they can provide on the intersections of digital media with adolescents' gender and sexuality performances and the desire for status and recognition in an increasingly mediated society. Despite centering on white victim-survivors and primarily white perpetrators, the incidents nevertheless offer an opportunity to examine the role of new technologies in reporting, investigating, and prosecuting juvenile sex crimes and to assess their implications for institutional responses to sexual violence.

FOCUS GROUPS

Most of the discussions and explanations following public awareness and media coverage of the selected assaults came from adults and experts talking about adolescents rather than including their perspectives on the issue. Instead, I wanted to rely on and draw from young people's voices and perceptions to identify the motives that may be driving some of their peers to digitally capture and disseminate sexual abuse. I decided to conduct focus groups rather than individual interviews with young people in part because they offered the best approach for reproducing the dynamics my research sought to understand. The assaults discussed in this study all occurred in group situations and involved multiple offenders and/or bystanders, as did the digital distribution and commentary following each incident. Focus groups offer a rich platform to reproduce this setting and help capture some of the identity work and peer dynamics that emerged in these circumstances, including gender and sexuality performances among respondents.[6] They also provide an interview structure most closely reflecting young people's digital praxis, which is heavily performative and peer-oriented. As a method, focus groups enable researchers to identify a range of views within a group, document how group members respond to each other's perspectives and beliefs, and ascertain the reasons underpinning the beliefs held by group members.[7]

During 2016 I conducted four group interviews with 35 adolescents between 16 and 18 years old. The sample included 18 girls and 17 boys, all high school students from Long Island, Queens, and Westchester County in New York. The age bracket reflects that of the individuals typically involved in the assault cases discussed in this book. All efforts were made to select schools from towns approximating the demographic patterns of the communities where the sexual assaults occurred. While studies find that geographic location is not a factor impacting adolescent uses of social media, my goal here was to capture data on patterns of gender inequality and sexual violence among middle- and upper-middle-class youth.[8] This is a subgroup that is often underrepresented in youth and sexual violence scholarship, but is also the category to which most of the young perpetrators discussed in this study belong. As participants were adolescents, class was assessed based on family of origin, including parents' highest level of education, occupation, and annual income (if known). Of the 35 respondents, 48.6 percent (n = 17) were identified as upper-middle class families, having one or both parents employed in professions that require an advanced degree (or who owned their own business), and had an average household income of $75,000 or higher; 34 percent of participants (n = 12) were defined as middle class, in which one or both parents were employed in positions that required a bachelor's degree and typically had a household income averaging $50,000–$75,000 per year; and 17 percent of teens (n = 6) came from households in which one or both parents were employed in blue or pink collar occupations that do not require a bachelor's degree and estimated annual income was less than $50,000. The sample was also racially diverse, with 41 percent of respondents identifying as white, 32 percent as Latino/a, 14 percent as Black/African American, 11 percent as Asian, and 3 percent as belonging to another ethnic or racial group.

Participants were recruited through contacts at various schools in these areas. This was a long and often difficult process. While teachers were typically enthusiastic about participating in the research, school principals and superintendents were wary of working with me and denied me access to their student body. One school allowed me access to all of their senior classes on condition of anonymity and in exchange for offering educational workshops about social media and identity during their digital citizenship week. Following these workshops, I would speak to students about my research and ask for participants. Teachers agreed to give volunteer students credit for one hour of community service (required at the school) in exchange for participating in the study. A robust number of students signed up to participate and received approval from their parents; however, scheduling conflicts and simple attrition resulted in only 10 participants (all female) being recruited from this site. A similar agreement was set up with another school, where I would gain access to the senior student body in exchange for guest lecturing in the school's sociology courses. The day before scheduled interviews with students were to take place, the district superintendent withdrew the school from participation. Some of these students contacted me and offered to meet at a nearby coffee shop after school to be interviewed. This group of young men (6 total) resulted in my second focus group; they were each given a $10 iTunes gift card for their participation. Respondents for the other two focus groups were recruited from a third high school and volunteered for the study in exchange for extra credit for one of their classes.

Prior to their being interviewed, consent forms were distributed to each student and required both the participant's and a parent's signature to be enrolled in the study. All subjects were informed that their participation in the study would remain anonymous when the research was written up. Respondents were also given a survey to complete prior to the focus groups that captured demographic information, as well as social media usage. To qualify for the study, participants were required to be at least somewhat active users of mobile technologies and social media platforms. The average female participant identified as active to very active on social media (4.3 on an increasing activity scale of 1 to 5); the average male participant identified as somewhat active to active (3.7) on social media.

When doing qualitative research with children and youth, researchers must be aware of how their structural position as adults makes them outsiders as well as authority figures in young people's worlds and must actively take strategies to reduce this power differential.[9] To navigate these power dynamics, I undertook a number of strategies to help minimize differentials in my interactions with the teen participants. Three of the four focus group interviews took place on school grounds, after school hours, to ensure students felt safe and comfortable in their environment. The fourth focus group occurred at a coffee shop near school grounds; the participants selected the location and time of meeting, again to ensure their comfort and safety during the interview. The focus groups consisted of 6–10 participants and lasted between 60 and 75 minutes each. Respondents were given the option of having the digital recorder turned off or leaving the interview at any point without needing to provide an explanation, although no participants exercised this right. The ethical dimensions of the interviews were discussed with respondents, who agreed to ground rules around keeping any sensitive aspects of the discussion within the groups.

To further aid in minimizing power differentials between the researcher and the teen respondents, I introduced my role during the interview as a "student," wanting to learn from the participants about their worlds and social media practices, positioning them as "experts" in these areas. The focus groups started with a general overview of young people's digital profiles, including which applications they used and why, to facilitate further comfort and commonality among participants. Participants were then asked to discuss their own engagement with and practices on social media platforms, as well as that of their friends and peers, and to detail some of the norms and ethics guiding young people's digital behavior and sharing practices. These conversations organically resulted in discussing risky or problematic behavior captured and shared on social media, such as sexting or substance use.

At this point in the interview, I circulated a handout with the Steubenville case study (with all identifying information removed) for the participants to read. Using the actual incident as a case study facilitates more direct and relevant consideration of such events and gives young people the chance to speak for themselves and articulate their own motives and ethics of behavior. In the second half of the focus group, then, participants were asked to examine the actions of the involved parties and offer their perspectives on the incident. The discussion included hypothetical responses to the scenario by respondents, reasons the sexual assault occurred, and their thoughts on why the offenders and bystanders had digitally recorded and circulated the assault or commented about it online. The focus groups also sought to ascertain how teens understand and define sexual assault, rape, and cyberbullying, as well as to gauge their knowledge of the technical features of digital media and the consequences of non-consensually sharing sexually explicit or violent material. After each focus group, I typically spent 15–30 minutes jotting down my impressions and observations in a notebook or speaking them into the digital recorder. These notes included observations about both the participants and the gender dynamics of the focus groups; reflections on issues of race, gender, and ethnicity that arose during the data collection; and observations on the effects of my social location as a researcher on participant dynamics and responses. Revisiting these notes after my data coding and analysis helped to refine my conclusions and remind me of the limitations of my research.

Given that sexual violence is a sensitive and gendered experience, and that digital practices are also gendered, I decided it would be easier for participants to discuss these topics in groups comprising people of the same sex with whom they were familiar.[10] One of the strengths of focus groups is that they encourage participants to share their thoughts, impressions, and experiences in a permissive and nonthreatening environment.[11] Keeping teens in same-sex groups was more likely to ensure their comfort and foster an honest discussion around the norms and ethics informing their digital practices, including interactions with the opposite sex, the creation and sharing of risky and/or sexually explicit behavior on social media, and their perceptions of the recording and distribution of sexual assault on these platforms. All the participants in each focus group knew each other, although they did not necessarily have close friendships. Familiarity among participants was important to foster disclosure and help balance power dynamics between them and the researcher. I noticed that for both female and male participants, having friends and peers in the room helped them gain confidence and minimized my presence in the room, allowing for more disclosure and honest discussion during the interview. Having friends in the room also helped some of the quieter or shy young women speak up and share some of their digital practices, something that would not necessarily have occurred in a space full of unknown peers. The young men who participated in this study were similarly more forthcoming in a group setting. Especially when discussing their social media practices and the sharing of sexually explicit and/ or risky behavior on these platforms, the familiarity among the male participants worked to encourage disclosure, as they were often aware of each other's digital practices and told on their friends during the course of the interview. This structure also worked as a corrective to some less than honest answers provided by participants, or instances in which young men gave responses they thought I wanted to hear (i.e., performances of positive masculinity). Instead, laughter or vocal protest by their friends led to the participants' admitting to more honest views and/or practices.

This is not to say the focus group format was completely able to neutralize my presence as a white, heterosexual, middle-class female. Just as being an adult interviewing young people informs the power dynamics within the space of the interview, so too does the social location of the researcher, in terms of race, gender, and class positioning.[12] For the young women respondents in this study, my identity was often a positive attribute, helping them feel more comfortable during the interview and motivating them to participate in the discussion. With the male participants, on the other hand, there were certainly moments when my gender inhibited disclosure, especially when asking them to discuss risky or problematic social media usage they thought I might not approve of (e.g., use of 4chan and Reddit, which often feature racist and misogynist content). One group of male participants was also more cautious in their response to the case study, either expressing very strong negative reactions to the sexual assault or demurring when asked if the victim in the case was to blame for the assault; they often took a few beats before answering to try to ascertain what type of response I would deem appropriate and acceptable.

The focus groups were digitally recorded and then transcribed. All identifying information was removed from transcripts, including names and places. Pseudonyms are used for teen participants throughout this book. Transcripts were imported into Atlas.ti software for coding. Analysis was guided by the principles of grounded theory in that it was sensitive to the participants' frameworks of experience and understanding, which aligns with the epistemological and ethical commitments of feminist and pro-feminist research.[13]

TABLE 1   NEWS COVERAGE BY SOURCE AND ARTICLE TYPE

	Doe	Pott	Coleman
	News articles		
Yahoo! News	13	4	6
Huffington Post	23	3	7
CNN.com	14	2	5
New York Times	7	0	3
Los Angeles Times	10	11	4
Subtotal	67	20	25
	Op-eds		
Yahoo! News	0	0	0
Huffington Post	21	0	2
CNN.com	7	1	1
New York Times	1	0	0
Los Angeles Times	1	0	0
Subtotal	30	1	3
Total per case	97	21	28
Total articles = 146			

MEDIA COVERAGE ANALYSIS

Throughout the book, my discussions of the media's reporting on the selected sexual assaults are based on findings from my doctoral research and those I have published in a separate article in the journal *Crime, Media, Culture*.[14] I reviewed a total of 146 unique articles on the three cases, published by the top most-widely read mainstream online and print national news sources in the country. These included Yahoo!, the *Huffington Post*, CNN, the *New York Times*, and the *Los Angeles Times*. Table 1 provides a breakdown of the stories by source and type. The articles were examined through thematic analysis, with the goal of identifying and reporting common trends on the various presentations of technology in the stories.[15]

JOURNALIST INTERVIEWS

I also interviewed 10 journalists and editors who produced stories on the Steubenville, Pott, and Coleman cases to supplement my thematic analysis of the reporting on these incidents. Research has shown news frames reflect how journalists naturalize constructions of reality, using routines and practices developed over time to accommodate journalistic traditions, news values, and organizational pressures and constraints, as well as the political and/or ideological orientations of journalists and media organizations.[16] In the interviews, reporters and editors detail the major elements drawing them to each case, discussing both the individual interests and cultural (and market) forces influencing their story selection and focus. Their words provide richer context and deeper insight into the news values and media frames relevant in the Steubenville, Maryville, and Pott reporting, while also further validating and strengthening the findings of my thematic analysis.

I contacted many of these reporters in early 2015 through the email address listed under their byline or provided on their news organization's website. This initial email outlined the broad scope of my research and my interest in speaking to them to gain a better understanding of their selection of these stories for coverage, as well as the content and focus of their reporting over the course of the story. Ten journalists, and two of their editors, initially agreed to be interviewed for the study. Two reporters dropped out due to scheduling issues, resulting in a final sample of eight reporters and two editors, six of whom wrote for national media outlets and the remaining four from local news organizations. All participants agreed to have the interviews recorded; six reporters consented to being identified in the study, with the remaining four opting to remain anonymous. Of the final ten interviews, nine were conducted via the phone and one was done in person, and they lasted between 30 and 60 minutes each.

Participants were asked to generally elaborate on the reasons contributing to their decision to report on the Doe, Pott, or Coleman cases and the major themes highlighted in their coverage. Interview questions also probed more specifically whether new media technologies impacted the tone and content of how the incidents were reported, explained, and discussed by both the news media and the public, and expanded to include a discussion of the effect of these platforms for reporting of sexual violence more generally. Journalists were also asked to reflect on the potential of new technologies to challenge or complicate traditional discourses and coverage of sex crimes and criminal justice responses to the issue, as well as to increase social awareness and debate on the problem. The interviews were digitally recorded, transcribed, and then coded using Atlas.ti software. Main categories were developed alongside the new media coverage analysis and included reasons for story selection, key themes in reporting, the role of technology, and opinion (e.g., the impact of digital evidence on reporting of sexual violence).

ATTORNEY INTERVIEWS

I conducted interviews with 12 prosecuting, defense, and civil attorneys. This sample included the defense attorneys from the Steubenville rape case, the civil attorneys representing the victims in the Steubenville and Pott cases, and a prosecutor from the Santa Clara County District Attorney's office, which handled Audrie Pott's case. The names of these attorneys were publicized in the media coverage of each incident; a web search directed me to their law firms or the local district attorney's office and their contact information. I emailed each attorney detailing the scope of my research and my interest in speaking to them to gain a better understanding of the role of digital evidence in each case. Everyone I contacted agreed to participate in this study, except the district attorney's offices involved in investigating and prosecuting the Steubenville and Maryville (Coleman) cases. As an alternative, I reached out to the juvenile sex crimes prosecutor in Louisville, Kentucky, where the Savannah Dietrich case had been handled. The Dietrich case was one of the dozen incidents initially considered for selection in this study and featured many of the same details as the selected assaults; insights offered by the attorneys involved in the case are relevant for this analysis. Both that prosecutor and Dietrich's civil attorney agreed to participate in the research. These interviews were conducted via phone, lasted approximately 35–60 minutes each, and were completed in early 2015. All participants agreed to have their names be used for this project.

The interviews helped fill in important gaps in the media's reporting of the selected incidents, including insights into why the defendants in these cases may have recorded the assaults, the specific role of digital media in investigating and prosecuting the three cases, and how defense and prosecuting attorneys handled the digital trail in each instance. Community and public reactions to the cases on social media, and how these may have impacted responses by the criminal justice system, were also discussed. Finally, the interviews addressed the ability of the law to effectively respond to emerging technologies and the issues arising from the intersections of sexual violence and digital media, particularly among youth.

As my analysis moved from the specifics of the cases to larger patterns relating to technology, juvenile sex crimes, and the law, I recruited a second round of interview participants from New York City for comparison and to improve the generalizability of my findings. Contacted between late 2015 and early 2016, this second group of participants included two prosecuting attorneys from the New York County District Attorney's Office (one now a judge) and two civil attorneys working with adolescent victims of sexual violence. These attorneys were recruited through snowball sampling; one participant was initially contacted through a mutual acquaintance, and following our interview connected me with the next attorney in the sample. The final group of interviews were all conducted in person and centered on the second half of the interview questions used with the case attorneys. Just like the first round of interviews, they lasted 45–60 minutes; the two prosecuting attorneys participated on condition of anonymity, while the civil attorneys consented to have their names used for the study. All the attorney interviews were digitally recorded, transcribed and then coded using Atlas.ti software. As the purpose of these interviews was informational, codes were constructed to capture the different roles of technology during the life of the case, such as uses of digital evidence, challenges, impact on the investigation, impact on the victims, youth and technology, and law and technology.

I did not interview any of the victim-survivors or perpetrators from the sexual assault cases included in this study. The underage status of both victims and offenders and the intense media scrutiny they had already experienced ethically prevented me from reaching out to these individuals. Also, some of the cases, tragically, do not have surviving victims. Instead, where possible I have relied on public interviews, social media postings, courtroom transcripts, and media coverage of the incidents to include their words and voices in this project. I have further tried to present their perspectives and experiences of the events through interviews with the legal experts responsible for representing them and advocating on their behalf.

Notes

INTRODUCTION

1. Macur and Schweber, "Rape Case Unfolds Online."

2. Arnett, "Nightmare in Maryville."

3. The three young men who assaulted Audrie were minors at the time of the incident, and their names were not disclosed to the press. Although their identities have since become publicly available, I will continue to keep them anonymous in this book and protect their right to move on beyond their juvenile records.

4. Burleigh, "Sexting, Shame, and Suicide."

5. Gjika, "New Media, Old Paradigms." See also Armstrong, Hull, and Saunders, "Victimized on Plain Sites"; and Pennington and Birthisel, "New Media Make News."

6. See, for example, McGlynn, Rackley, and Houghton, "Beyond 'Revenge Porn'"; Oliver, "Rape as Spectator Sport"; Phillips, *Beyond Blurred Lines*; and Powell and Henry, *Sexual Violence*.

7. For example, Dodge, "Trading Nudes"; Dragiewicz et al., "Tech Facilitated Coercive Control"; and Henry et al., *Image-Based Sexual Abuse*.

8. While there was only one perpetrator of sexual assault in the Daisy Coleman case, I include this incident as an example of multi-offender rape because there was another young man in the room who witnessed the abuse and recorded it on his phone. See the appendix for a further discussion of my methodology.

9. Holley, "Chicago Police 'No Suspects.'"

10. DiTirro, "3 Accused of Raping Teen."

11. Harris, "3 Charged for Raping Teen."

12. Varandani, "Girl's Assault Livestreamed."

13. Griffith, "Facebook Video of Assault."

14. Vogels, Gelles-Watnick, and Massarat, *Teens, Social Media, Technology*.

15. Crofts et al., *Sexting and Young People*; Hasinoff, *Sexting Panic*; Ringrose et al., "Teen Girls, Double Standards"; and Setty, *Youth Sexting*.

16. Crawford and Goggin, "Generation Disconnections"; Critcher, *Moral Panics*; and Buckingham, *Youth and Digital Media*.

17. boyd, *It's Complicated*; and Sturken and Thomas, "Introduction: Technological Visions."

18. James, Jenks, and Prout, *Theorizing Childhood*.

19. Cohen, *Folk Devils*; Savage, *Teenage*; and Valentine, *Culture of Childhood*.

20. Ayman-Nolley and Taira, "Dark Side of Adolescence"; Jackson and Scott, "Sexual Antinomies"; and Thiel-Stern, *Dance Hall to Facebook*.

21. Chmielewski, Tolman, and Kincaid, "Constructing Risk"; Killias, "Emergence of New Taboo"; and Thiel-Stern, *Dance Hall to Facebook*.

22. boyd, *It's Complicated*; and Burke, *Young People*.

23. Crawford and Goggin, "Generation Disconnections"; and Albury, Hasinoff, and Senft, "Media Abstinence to Production."

24. Thorne, *Gender Play*.

25. See also James, *Disconnected*.

26. See Salter, *Crime, Justice and Social Media*, for a full discussion of instrumental accounts of technology in the social sciences.

27. boyd, *It's Complicated*; and van Dijck, *Culture of Connectivity*.

28. Hessick, "Limits of Child Pornography"; Kushner, "Sexting Law Reform"; Judge, "'Sexting' among U.S. Adolescents"; and Salter, Crofts, and Lee, "Beyond Criminalisation."

29. Williams, *Television*; and Wajcman, "Feminist Theories of Technology."

30. Baym, *Personal Connections*; and Sassen, "Sociology of Information Technology."

31. Wajcman, "Feminist Theories of Technology," 149.

32. Sloan and Quan-Haase, *Social Media Research Methods*; and van Dijck, *Culture of Connectivity*.

33. Powell and Henry, *Sexual Violence*, 5.

34. McGlynn and Rackley, "Image-Based Sexual Abuse," 536.

35. Kelly, *Surviving Sexual Violence*; Kelly, "Standing Test of Time?"; and Henry and Powell, "Embodied Harms."

36. Freedman, *No Turning Back*; and Regehr, Birze, and Regehr, "Technology Facilitated Re-victimization."

37. See also Maier, *Rape, Victims, and Investigations*, on the significance of using *victim* when discussing sexual violence.

CHAPTER 1: UNDERSTANDING THE YOUTH, IDENTITY, AND TECHNOLOGY NEXUS

1. Harkinson, "Exclusive: Anonymous' Anti-rape Operations."

2. Collins, "Exclusive: Steubenville Rape Victim"; Harkinson, "Exclusive: Anonymous' Anti-rape Operations"; and Levy, "Trial by Twitter."

3. Ley, "She Is So Raped."

4. Gjika, "New Media, Old Paradigms."

5. ABC News, "Steubenville Social Media."

6. Albury, "Just Because It's Public"; Chmielewski, Tolman, and Kincaid, "Constructing Risk"; Crofts et al., *Sexting and Young People*; Draper, "Teen at Risk?"; and McGovern et al., "Discourses around Sexting."

7. Gjika, "New Media, Old Paradigms."

8. Macur and Schweber, "Rape Case Unfolds Online."

9. Mendoza, "Lawyer: Teen Had Drawings"; and Noveck, "Social Media."

10. Noveck, "Social Media"; and Oppel, "Ohio Teenagers Guilty."

11. Susman, "Ohio Teens Guilty."

12. Draper, "Mo. Man Accused"; and Mendoza, "Lawyer: Teen Had Drawings."

13. Goff, "Prevent Another Steubenville"; Simon, "Prevent Another Steubenville"; and Wallis, "Boys Behaving Badly."

14. Boteach, "American Tragedy in Steubenville"; and Pecsenye, "Letter to My Sons."

15. Lang, "Talk about Steubenville"; and Leavy, "Participate in Rape Culture."

16. Draper, "Teen at risk?," 232.

17. Cooley, *Human Nature*; Mead, *Mind, Self, and Society*; and Goffman, *Presentation of Self.*

18. Hogan, "Presentation of Self"; and Robinson, "Cyberself."

19. Marshall, *Celebrity and Power*; Thompson, "New Visibility"; Turner, "Mass Production of Celebrity"; and Van Doorn, "Ties That Bind."

20. Yar, "Will-to-Representation," 250.

21. boyd, *It's Complicated*; and Weinstein and James, *Behind Their Screens.*

22. Hargittai and Marwick, "What Can I Do?"; Keen, "Apathy, Convenience or Irrelevance?"; and Weinstein and James, *Behind Their Screens.*

23. boyd, *It's Complicated*; De Ridder, "Young People's Sexualities"; Harvey, Ringrose, and Gill, "Ratings and Masculinity"; and Taddicken and Jers, "Uses of Privacy Online."

24. In offering this data, I do no mean to suggest the interviewees I cite represent *all* young people. Rather, their voices are presented as a sample of how gender, sexuality, peer cultures, and digital technologies intersect for young people; how teens try to navigate these dynamics; and the implications of these insights for our responses to risky and unethical digital participation.

25. boyd, *It's Complicated.*

26. Livingstone and Brake, "Rise of Social Networking Sites," 76. See also Weinstein and James, *Behind Their Screens.*

27. De Ridder, "Young People's Sexualities"; Hasinoff, *Sexting Panic*; Henry et al, *Image-Based Sexual Abuse*; and Setty, *Youth Sexting.*

28. Madigan et al., "Sexting Behavior among Youth."

29. Burén and Lunde, "Sexting among Adolescents"; Madigan et al., "Sexting Behavior among Youth"; and Setty, *Youth Sexting.*

30. Barrense-Dias et al., "Non-consensual Sexting"; Burén and Lunde, "Sexting among Adolescents"; Clancy, Klettke, and Hallford, "Dark Side of Sexting"; Hinduja and Patchin, "Digital Dating Abuse"; Reed et al., "'It Was a Joke'"; Ringrose, Regehr, and Whitehead, "'Wanna Trade?'"; Stonard, "'Technology Designed for This'"; and Walker and Sleath, "Review of Revenge Pornography."

31. Dobson and Ringrose, "Sext Education"; Naezer and van Oosterhout, "Only Sluts Love Sexting"; Ringrose et al., "Teen Girls, Double Standards"; Ringrose, Regehr, and Whitehead, "'Wanna Trade?'"; Salter, "Privates in Online Public"; and Setty, *Youth Sexting*.

32. Barrense-Dias et al., "Non-consensual Sexting"; Burén and Lunde, "Sexting among Adolescents"; Clancy et al., "Sext Dissemination"; Ravn, Coffey, and Roberts, "Currency of Images"; Ringrose et al., "Teen Girls, Double Standards"; Salter, *Crime and Social Media*; and Setty, *Youth Sexting*.

33. Also De Ridder, "Young People's Sexualities"; Ringrose et al., "Teen Girls, Double Standards"; Ringrose, Regehr, and Whitehead, "'Wanna Trade?'"; and Salter, *Crime and Social Media*.

34. Amundsen, "'Price of Admission.'" For a discussion of how some youth perceive this as a violation of privacy rather than as image-based sexual abuse, see Meehan, "'It's Like Mental Rape.'"

35. Ravn, Coffey, and Roberts, "Currency of Images"; and Naezer and van Oosterhout, "Only Sluts Love Sexting."

36. DeKeseredy and Schwartz, *Male Peer Support*.

37. Flood, "Men and Homosociality"; Kimmel, *Gender of Desire*; and Messner, *Taking the Field*.

38. I rely on Connell's definition (in *Masculinities*) of hegemonic masculinity here, as the category of masculinity considered most legitimate and desirable in a society. In the West, this is a category constructed as white, middle class, and represented by dominance, aggression, competition, and heterosexual desire (see also Butler, *Gender Trouble*, and Messner, *Taking the Field*). Hegemonic masculinity is not a fixed category and can take multiple forms, responding to changing historical and cultural ideals, although currently it continues to include heteronormativity, homophobia, and misogyny (Connell and Messerschmidt, "Hegemonic Masculinity"; Kimmel, *Gender of Desire*; Messerschmidt, *Gender and Heterosexuality*; and Robinson, "Referencing Hegemonic Masculinities").

39. Connell and Messerschmidt, "Hegemonic Masculinity"; Duckworth and Trautner, "Gender Goals"; Franklin, "Enacting Masculinity"; Robinson, "Referencing Hegemonic Masculinities"; and Schippers, "Recovering the Feminine Other."

40. Duckworth and Trautner, "Gender Goals"; Hlavka, "Normalizing Sexual Violence"; Kimmel, *Gender of Desire*; Lamb et al., "Voices of the Mind"; Messerschmidt, "Hegemonic Masculinity"; Ringrose et al., "Teen Girls, Double Standards"; Rogers, Scott, and Way, "Racial and Gender Identity"; Skinner et al., "Gender Typicality"; and Widman et al., "Susceptibility to Peer Influence."

41. Lim et al., "Facework on Facebook"; Moreno et al., "'Real Cool'"; and Pyrooz, Decker, and Moule, "Activities in Online Settings."

42. Casey and Masters, "Sexual Violence Risk"; DeKeseredy and Schwartz, *Male Peer Support*; and Mandau, "'Directly in Your Face.'"

43. Davel, "Phone as Extension of Self"; and Park and Kaye, "Smartphone and Self-Extension."

44. Keen, "Apathy, Convenience or Irrelevance?"; Nagy and Neff, "Imagined Affordance"; Pangrazio and Selwyn, "'It's Not Life or Death'"; and Weinstein and James, *Behind Their Screens*.

45. Filipovic, "Degrading Women"; Oliver, "Rape as Spectator Sport"; and Powell and Henry, *Sexual Violence*.

46. Oliver, "Rape as Spectator Sport."

47. Lefkowitz, *Our Guys*; and Sanday, *Fraternity Gang Rape*. See also Franklin, "Enacting Masculinity"; Da Silva, Woodhams, and Harkins, "Multiple Perpetrator Rape"; and Sutton, "Athlete Multiple Perpetrator Rape."

48. For a full literature review of homosocial masculinities and trading nudes, see Ringrose, Regehr, and Whitehead, "'Wanna Trade?'"

49. See also Flood, "Men and Homosociality"; and Messner, *Taking the Field*.

50. DeKeseredy and Schwartz, *Male Peer Support*; Franklin, "Enacting Masculinity"; Ringrose et al., "Teen Girls, Double Standards"; and Sanday, *Fraternity Gang Rape*.

51. Flood, "Men and Homosociality," 341.

52. Schambelan, "Everybody Knows."

53. Carpenter, "Text Messages in Steubenville."

54. DeKeseredy and Schwartz, *Male Peer Support*.

55. Brooms, *Being Black on Campus*; Grundy, "Lifting the Veil"; Hirsch and Khan, *Sexual Citizens*; and Marwick, Fontaine, and boyd, "'Nobody Sees It.'"

CHAPTER 2: MISSING CULTURES OF CONSENT

1. Susman, "Ohio Teens Guilty."

2. Macur and Schweber, "Rape Case Unfolds Online"; and In the Matter of, preliminary hearing transcript.

3. Willis et al., "Sexual consent in K-12."

4. Coy et al., *Sex without Consent*; and Hirsch and Khan, *Sexual Citizens*.

5. Levy, "Trial by Twitter."

6. *Audrie & Daisy*.

7. In "Sexual Assault as Spectacle," Sambor also suggests that by speaking of Jane Doe as if she were dead, the young men implicitly mitigate the emotional impact of the sexually violent actions they have participated in.

8. Franklin, "Enacting Masculinity"; and Sanday, *Fraternity Gang Rape*.

9. Sambor, "Sexual Assault as Spectacle"; and Schrock and Schwalbe, "Manhood Acts."

10. Gavey, *Just Sex?*; and Hlavka, "Normalizing Sexual Violence."

11. Rich, "Compulsory Heterosexuality." While Rich was originally writing about women, in *Masculinities*, Connell expanded this analysis of compulsory heterosexuality to also include men.

12. Connell, *Masculinities*; Rich, "Compulsory Heterosexuality"; and Tolman et al., "Seeds of Violence." Of course, compulsory heterosexuality is not a monolithic privileging of all men at the same kind of expense for all women, as gender intersects with factors like race and class to create hierarchies of privilege and oppression within compulsory heterosexuality.

13. Butler, *Gender Trouble*; and Schilt and Westbrook, "Doing Gender."

14. Dunn and Orchowski, "Boys Garner Sexual Consent"; Gavey, *Just Sex?*; Jozkowski, Marcantonio, and Hunt, "Sexual Consent Communication"; and Righi et al., "Beliefs about Consent."

15. Hirsch and Khan, *Sexual Citizens*; and Hirsch et al., "Social Dimensions of Consent."

16. Gavey, *Just Sex?*; Messerschmidt, *Gender and Heterosexuality*; Stanko, *Intimate Intrusions*; and Tolman et al., "Seeds of Violence."

17. See also Fine, "Sexuality, Schooling, Adolescent Females"; Hlavka, "Normalizing Sexual Violence"; and Tolman et al., "Just How It Is."

18. Amin et al., "Masculinity Norms"; Hirsch and Khan, *Sexual Citizens*; Tolman et al., "Just How It Is"; and Willis et al., "Sexual Consent in K–12."

19. Bohner et al., "Rape Myths"; and Burt, "Cultural Myths."

20. Cossins, *Closing the Justice Gap*; Gavey, *Just Sex?*; and Phillips, *Beyond Blurred Lines*.

21. Gavey, *Just Sex?*, 148.

22. Ybarra et al., "Prevalence of Sexual Violence." See also Cossins, *Closing the Justice Gap*; Hockett et al. "Rape Myth Consistency"; and Lichty and Gowen, "Youth Response to Rape."

23. Cowley, "'Let's Get Drunk'"; Hockett et al., "Rape Myth Consistency"; Hoxmeier, O'Connor, and McMahon, "'She Wasn't Resisting'"; and Lichty and Gowen, "Youth Response to Rape."

24. Barca, "Agency Factor"; and Dines, "Defanging of Feminism."

25. For further literature, see Lichty and Gowen, "Youth Response to Rape."

26. Levy, "Trial by Twitter" (emphasis in original).

27. Coy et al., *Sex without Consent*; and Lichty and Gowen, "Youth Response to Rape."

28. boyd, *It's Complicated*.

29. Katz and Aakhus, *Perpetual Contact*; Schrock, "Communicative Affordances"; and Trottier, "Policing Social Media."

30. Deuze, "Media Life"; and Sandberg and Ugelvik, "Offenders Tape Their Crimes."

31. Marshall, *Celebrity and Power*; Serazio, "Shooting for Fame"; Turner, "Mass Production of Celebrity"; and Yar, "Will-to-Representation". By celebrity culture I mean the process by which people turn into a commodity (see Turner).

32. Andrejevic, "Privacy, Exploitation"; boyd, *It's Complicated*; Salter, *Crime and Social Media*; and van Dijck, *Culture of Connectivity*.

33. Kohm, "Shaming and Criminal Justice"; and Sandberg and Ugelvik, "Offenders Tape Their Crimes."

34. Carrabine, "Just Images"; Pugliese, "Abu Ghraib"; and Sandberg and Ugelvik, "Offenders Tape Their Crimes."

35. Lumsden and Harmer, *Online Othering*; Powell and Henry, *Sexual Violence*; and Segrave and Vitis, *Gender, Technology and Violence*.

36. Loughnan et al., "Objectification."

37. Hirsh and Glowinski, *Surveillance and Spectacle*; Samuel, "Hard to Be Moral"; and Thorkelson, "Phones Stunt Bravery."

38. Dodge, "Digitizing Rape Culture"; Gavey, *Just Sex?*; Penny, "This Is Rape Culture."

39. Oppel, "Ohio Teenagers Guilty."

40. Levy, "Trial by Twitter"; and Macur and Schweber, "Rape Case Unfolds Online."

41. Wade, "Responses to Steubenville."

42. Wade, "Responses to Steubenville."

43. Burleigh, "Sexting, Shame and Suicide."

44. Arnett, "Nightmare in Maryville."

45. ABC News, "Video Steubenville."

46. Thacker, "Rape Culture."

47. Draper, "Mo. Man Accused"; and Oppel, "Ohio Teenagers Guilty." For a full discussion of media coverage of the cases and stories that focused on teen drinking, see Gjika, "New Media, Old Paradigms."

48. For a review of this literature, see Cossins, *Closing the Justice Gap*.

49. Oliver, "Rape as Spectator Sport."

50. Bidisha, "Rape Shame"; Birdsell, "Reevaluating Gag Orders"; and Das, "Andrew Tate."

51. Ash et al., "Tear Men Down."

52. Ferré-Sadurní, "Teenager Deserves Leniency."

CHAPTER 3: A GOLD MINE OF INFORMATION?

1. Susman, "Ohio Teens Guilty."

2. Wetzel, "Football Players Found Guilty."

3. Oppel, "Ohio Teenagers Guilty."

4. Susman, "Ohio Teens Guilty"; and Carter, "Teen Rape Trial."

5. Boux and Daum, "Social Media and Rape"; Dodge et al., "Your Father's Police Force"; Ramirez, "Digital Divide"; and Watson and Huey, "Technology and SVU."

6. Arnes, *Digital Forensics*; Fontecilla, "Social Media as Evidence"; and Goodison, Davis, and Jackson, *Digital Evidence*.

7. Dodge et al., "Your Father's Police Force"; Rumney and McPhee, "Electronic Communications in Rape"; and Watson and Huey, "Technology and SVU."

8. Corrigan, *Up against a Wall*; Estrich, *Real Rape*; Konradi, *Taking the Stand*; and Spohn and Tellis, "Response to Sexual Violence."

9. See note 8. See also Cossins, *Closing the Justice Gap*; Henry, Powell, and Flynn, *Rape Justice*; and Hlavka and Mulla, *Bodies in Evidence*.

10. For a review of this literature, see Cossins, *Closing the Justice Gap*.

11. Estrich, *Real Rape*; and Sleath and Bull, "Police Perceptions of Rape."

12. Belknap, "Rape"; Cossins, *Closing the Justice Gap*; and Sleath and Bull, "Police Perceptions of Rape."

13. Lisak et al., "False Allegations"; and Smith and Skinner, "Rape Myths in Trials."

14. Lisak et al., "False Allegations"; and Hohl and Stanko, "Complaints of Rape."

15. Estrich, *Real Rape*; and Holh and Stanko, "Complaints of Rape."

16. Lisak et al., "False Allegations."

17. For a review of the literature, see Boux and Daum, "Social Media and Rape"; and Smith and Skinner, "Rape Myths in Trials."

18. Alderden and Ullman, "More Complete Picture"; McMillan, "Perceptions of False Allegations"; and Spohn and Tellis, "Justice Denied?"

19. Brodsky, Griffin, and Cramer, "Witness Credibility Scale"; Corrigan, *Up against a Wall*; Estrich, *Real Rape*; Konradi, *Taking the Stand*; Nagel et al., "Attitudes toward Victims"; and Taslitz, *Rape and the Courtroom*.

20. Moore and Singh, "Seeing Crime."

21. Macur and Schweber, "Rape Case Unfolds Online."

22. ABC News, "Steubenville Social Media."

23. See notes 3 and 19.

24. Moore and Singh, "Seeing Crime," 126.

25. Naffine, *Feminism and Criminology*; and Smart, *Feminism and Law*.

26. Carrabine, "Just Images"; and Young, "From Object to Encounter."

27. Biber, *Captive Images*; Edmond et al., "Law's Looking Glass"; Feigenson "Visual in Law"; and Mnookin, "Image of Truth."

28. Dubrofsky and Magnet, *Feminist Surveillance Studies*; and Young, "From Object to Encounter."

29. Larcombe, "Falling Rape Conviction Rates."

30. Carpenter, "Convictions in Steubenville Trial."

31. Burleigh, "Sexting, Shame and Suicide."

32. Sulek, "San Jose: Boys Apologize."

33. Diss, "Whether You 'Like' It"; Frieden and Murray, "Admissibility of Electronic Evidence"; and Janzen, "Amending Rape Shield Laws."

34. Bluett-Boyd et al., "Communication Technologies in Sexual Violence"; Dodge et al., "Your Father's Police Force"; Vincze, "Challenges in Digital Forensics"; and Watson and Huey, "Technology and SVU."

35. Dodge et al., "Your Father's Police Force"; Losavio et al., "Why Digital Forensics"; and Stanton, "Victims Say NYPD Fails."

36. Novak, "Collection of Digital Evidence."

37. Bluett-Boyd et al., "Communication Technologies in Sexual Violence"; Bond and Tyrrell, "Understanding Revenge Pornography"; Dodge et al., "Your Father's Police Force"; and Watson and Huey, "Technology and SVU."

38. Gogolin, "Digital Crime Tsunami"; and Goodison et al., *Digital Evidence*.

39. Dodge et al., "Your Father's Police Force"; Khan, "Four Year Wait"; Watson and Huey, "Technology and SVU."

40. Lane, Ramirez, and Patton, "Defending against Social Media."

41. Kessler, "Judges' Awareness."

42. Kessler, "Judges' Awareness"; and Uncel, "Facebook Friends with Court."

43. Susman, "Ohio Teens Guilty".

44. Mateescu et al., "Social Media Surveillance"; and Ramirez et al., "'Her Age Not Given.'"

45. Hill, "Imagine Being on Trial"; and Ramirez, "Digital Divide."

46. Bond and Tyrrell, "Understanding Revenge Pornography"; Safronova and Halleck, "Rape Victims Sue"; and Wang, "NYPD Mishandling of Rape."

47. Dodge et al., "Your Father's Police Force."

48. Black, Lumsden, and Hadlington, "Block Them"; Killean, McAlinden, and Dowds, "Sexual Violence"; and Kinlaw, "Snap of Justice."

49. Brayne, "Big Data Surveillance"; Mateescu et al., "Social Media Surveillance"; and Ramirez, "Digital Divide."

50. Ballotpedia, "Revenge Porn Laws."

51. This has also been an issue with several high-profile sexting cases involving youth in the last decade. See Kushner, "Sexting Law Reform."

52. Eaton and McGlynn, "Nonconsensual Porn"; Hasinoff, *Sexting Panic*; Powell and Henry, *Sexual Violence*; and Shariff and DiMartini, "Defining the Legal Lines."

53. Brayne, "Big Data Surveillance"; Joh, "Automated Policing"; Lane, Ramirez, and Pearce, "Guilty by Visible Association"; and Mateescu et al., "Social Media Surveillance."

54. Lane, Ramirez, and Patton, "Defending against Social Media"; and Ramirez, "Digital Divide."

55. Buckwalter-Poza, "Making Justice Equal."

56. See note 45.

57. Dodge and Spencer, "Online Sexual Violence." See also Broll and Huey, "Just Being Mean."

58. Pearson, "Steubenville Not Done Yet."

59. Burleigh, "Sexting, Shame and Suicide."

60. Brodsky, Griffin, and Cramer, "Witness Credibility Scale"; Flood, *Rape in Chicago*; Frohmann, "Discrediting Victims' Allegations"; Nagel et al., "Attitudes toward Victims"; and Tillman et al., "Shattering Silence."

61. Buckwalter-Poza, "Making Justice Equal."

CHAPTER 4: NAVIGATING JUSTICE

1. Macur and Schweber, "Rape Case Unfolds Online."

2. Oppel, "Ohio Teenagers Guilty."

3. Susman, "Ohio Teens Guilty."

4. Burleigh, "Sexting, Shame and Suicide."

5. Morgan and Thompson, *Criminal Victimization 2020*. BJS data indicates reporting rates over the last five years usually hover between the 20 to 35 percent range.

6. CDC, "Youth Risk Behavior Survey"; Finkelhor et al., "Child Sexual Abuse."

7. Finkelhor et al. "Child Sexual Abuse"; and Gewirtz-Meydan and Finkelhor, "Sexual abuse and Adolescents."

8. Estrich, *Real Rape*; Hohl and Stanko, "Complaints of Rape"; RAINN, "Victims of Sexual Violence"; and Spohn and Tellis, "Response to Sexual Violence."

9. Campbell et al., "Pathways to Help."

10. Alaggia et al., "Child Sexual Abuse Disclosures"; Bicanic et al., "Delayed Disclosure of Rape"; and Manay and Collin-Vézina, "Disclosures of Childhood Sexual Abuse."

11. Young et al., "Alcohol-Related Sexual Assault."

12. Edinburgh et al., "Multiple Perpetrator Rape." See also Ullman, "Gang and Individual Rapes."

13. Alderden and Ullman, "More Complete Picture"; Clark, "Fair Way to Go"; and Spohn and Tellis, "Response to Sexual Violence."

14. Alderden and Ullman, "More Complete Picture"; Cossins, *Closing the Justice Gap*; Dodge et al., "Your Father's Police Force"; Maier, *Rape, Victims,*

and Investigations; Sleath and Bull, "Police Perceptions of Rape"; and Spohn and Tellis, "Response to Sexual Violence."

15. Alderden and Ullman, "More Complete Picture"; Clark, "Fair Way to Go"; Daly, "Sexual Violence and Justice"; Hohl and Stanko, "Complaints of Rape"; and Ransom, "'Nobody Believed Me.'"

16. Corrigan, *Up against a Wall*; Konradi, *Taking the Stand*; and Randall, "Sexual Assault Law."

17. Powell, "Seeking Rape Justice"; and Spencer at al., "Re-Victimizing Victims."

18. Konradi, *Taking the Stand*; Smart, *Feminism and Law*; Spencer et al., "Re-victimizing Victims"; and Thacker, "Rape Culture."

19. Cossins, *Closing the Justice Gap*; Hlavka and Mulla, *Bodies in Evidence*; and Randall, "Sexual Assault Law."

20. Oppel, "Ohio Teenagers Guilty."

21. La Ganga and Mather, "Audrie Pott Case."

22. Alexander, *New Jim Crow*; Pfaff, *Locked In*; and Lynch, *Hard Bargains*.

23. Gross, Possley, and Stephens, *Race and Wrongful Convictions*; and Smith and Hattery, "Wrongful Conviction & Exoneration."

24. Hymes et al., "Acquaintance Rape"; and Sommers, "Race and Juries."

25. I draw here on McGlynn and Westmarland's notion of "kaleidoscopic justice," meaning that survivors interpret justice in a myriad of different ways and that the practice of justice takes on multiple forms, both legal and extralegal.

26. Dunn, "Is It Actually Violence?"; Henry et al., *Image-Based Sexual Abuse*; and McGlynn et al., "'Torture for the Soul.'"

27. Bailey, Flynn, and Henry, *Emerald International Handbook*; Eaton and McGlynn, "Psychology of Nonconsensual Porn"; Henry et al., *Image-Based Sexual Abuse*; and Rackley et al., "Seeking Justice."

28. Citron, *Hate Crimes in Cyberspace*; Jane, "Gendered Cyberhate"; Powell and Henry, *Sexual Violence*; and Rackley et al., "Seeking Justice." See also note 27.

29. Meehan, "'It's Like Mental Rape'"; and Salter, Crofts, and Lee, "Beyond Criminalisation."

30. Henry and Powell, "Embodied Harms"; Mathen, "Crowdsourcing Sexual Objectification"; and McGlynn et al., "'Torture for the Soul.'"

31. See also Marques, "Intimate Image Dissemination"; and Regehr, Birze, and Regehr, "Technology Facilitated Re-victimization."

32. Oliver, "Rape as Spectator Sport."

33. Hasinoff, *Sexting Panic*; Ringrose et al., "Teen Girls, Double Standards"; Salter, *Crime and Social Media*; and Setty, *Youth Sexting*.

34. Henry et al., *Image-Based Sexual Abuse*, 53. Also Regehr, Birze, and Regehr, "Technology Facilitated Re-victimization"; and McGlynn et al., "Torture for the Soul."

35. Clevenger and Navarro, "'Third-Victimization.'"

36. Salter, "Privates in Online Public," 2728.

37. Dodge and Lockhart, "'Young People Resolve It'"; Dodge and Spencer, "Online Sexual Violence"; and Marques, "Intimate Image Dissemination."

38. Burleigh, "Sexting, Shame and Suicide."

39. Burkell, "Remembering Me."

40. McGlynn et al., "Torture for the Soul"; and Marques, "Intimate Image Dissemination."

41. Dodge, "Digitizing Rape Culture"; and Powell and Henry, *Sexual Violence*.

42. See also Birdsell, "Reevaluating Gag Orders."

43. Black, Lumsden, and Hadlington, "Block Them"; Kinlaw, "Snap of Justice"; and Regehr, Birze, and Regehr, "Technology Facilitated Re-victimization."

44. Moore and Singh, "Seeing Crime, Feeling Crime"; Regehr, Birze, and Regehr, "Technology Facilitated Re-victimization"; and Spencer et al., "'Re-victimizing Victims.'"

45. Regehr, Birze, and Regehr, "Technology Facilitated Re-victimization," 11.

46. Biber, *In Crime's Archive*; Regehr, Birze, and Regehr, "Technology Facilitated Re-victimization"; and Zanobini, "Protecting Victims."

47. Browning, "Digital Dirt"; and Smith and Skinner, "Rape Myths in Trials."

48. Busby, "Sexual Assault Cases."

49. Dearden, "Victims Stop Reporting"; and Martin, "Prosecution of Sexual Assault."

50. Dearden, "Victims Stop Reporting"; Killean, McAlinden, and Dowds, "Sexual Violence"; and Rumney and McPhee, "Electronic Communications in Rape."

51. Ramirez et al., "'Her Age Not Given.'" See also the study done by Bottoms, Davis, and Epstein, "Race in Sexual Abuse Cases," in which they discuss how Black girls are often perceived as older than their ages, which works to make them more responsible for the sexual violence perpetrated against them.

52. Hlavka and Mulla, "'That's How She Talks'"; and Urbina, "Trove of Clues."

53. Sexual history evidence is admitted when the victim has previously been intimate with the defendant, when the defendant claims he held a reasonable but mistaken belief as to her consent, or when the complainant has previously engaged in a pattern of prostitution or other promiscuity. For a fuller discussion see Anderson, "Chastity Requirement"; Loewen, "Rejecting Purity Myth"; and Janzen, "Amending Rape Shield Laws."

54. Davis, "Social Media under Rape Shield"; Loewen, "Rejecting the Purity Myth"; and Martin, "Prosecution of Sexual Assault."

55. Macur and Schweber, "Rape Case Unfolds Online."

56. Wang and Weinstock, "Yale Student Not Guilty."

57. See Loewen, "Rejecting the Purity Myth," for a longer discussion of cases in which social media profiles were used by defense attorneys to suggest a survivor's sexual promiscuity and dismiss cases against the accused.

58. Glasbeek, "He Said, She Said."

59. Dodge, "Digitizing Rape Culture."

60. Segal, *Rehtaeh Parson's Case*, 79.

61. Boux and Daum, "Social Media and Rape." See also Killean, McAlinden, and Dowds, "Sexual Violence," for a full review of the literature on hierarchies of victimhood and the ways these are raced, classed, and gendered, among other factors.

62. Hlvaka and Mulla, "'That's How She Talks.'" See also Cossins, *Closing the Justice Gap*.

63. Jones, "Protests in Spain."

64. Baker, "Sent Home from School." See Keierleber, "Sexual-Violence Victims," for similar responses across the country.

65. Dubrofsky and Magnet, *Feminist Surveillance Studies*; Mnookin, "Image of Truth"; and Young, "From Object to Encounter."

66. Gavey, *Just Sex?* See also Flood, *Rape in Chicago*; Frohmann, "Convictability and Discordant Locales"; Hlavka and Mulla, *Bodies in Evidence*; and Taslitz, *Rape and the Courtroom*.

67. Curry et al., "Barriers to Disclosing Abuse"; McClennen, Summers, and Vaughan, "Gay Men's Domestic Violence"; and Tillman et al., "Shattering Silence."

68. Bottoms, Davis, and Epstein, "Race in Sexual Abuse Cases"; and Hlavka and Mulla, *Bodies in Evidence*.

69. Clark, "Fair Way to Go"; Daly, "Sexual Violence and Justice"; and McGlynn and Westmarland, "Kaleidoscopic Justice."

CHAPTER 5: BEYOND THE LAW

1. Loney-Howes, *Anti-rape Activism*; and Richie et al., "Resisting the State."

2. Davis, *Women, Race, & Class*; Smart, *Feminism and Law*; and Sokoloff and Dupont, "Domestic Violence at Intersections."

3. Bumiller, *In an Abusive State*; Gotell, "Reassessing Criminal Law Reform"; and Kim, "Carceral Creep."

4. Goodmark, "Reimagining VAWA"; INCITE!, *Color of Violence*; Thuma, "Lessons in Self-Defense"; and Whittier, "Carceral Feminism."

5. Corrigan, *Up against a Wall*; Goodmark, "Reimagining VAWA"; Henry, Powell, and Flynn, *Rape Justice*; and Larcombe, "Falling Rape Conviction Rates."

6. Bumiller, *In an Abusive State*; Goodmark, "Reimagining VAWA"; and Richie, *Arrested Justice*.

7. Clark, "Fair Way to Go"; Daly, "Sexual Violence and Justice"; Koss, "Restoring Rape Survivors"; and McGlynn and Westmarland, "Kaleidoscopic Justice."

8. Salter, "Online Counter-Publics"; Fileborn, "Justice 2.0"; Powell, "Seeking Rape Justice"; and Loney-Howes, *Online Anti-rape Activism*.

9. Fraser, "Rethinking the Public Sphere."

10. Powell, "Seeking Rape Justice."

11. Fileborn, "Justice 2.0"; Loney-Howes, *Online Anti-rape Activism*; and McGlynn, Downes, and Westmarland, "Seeking Justice for Survivors."

12. Vingiano, "Coleman Essay."

13. Daum, "Social Media Become Enemy"; and Lezon, "#jadapose Rape Case."

14. Gjika, "New Media, Old Paradigms."

15. Banyard, "Prosocial Bystander Behavior"; and Fairbairn and Spencer, "Virtualized Violence."

16. McNamara, "This Is Why"; and Stewart, "#IamJada."

17. Loney-Howes, *Online Anti-rape Activism*; Mendes, Ringrose, and Keller, "Digital Feminist Activism"; and O'Neill, "'Today I Speak.'"

18. Macur and Schweber, , "Rape Case Unfolds Online."

19. Arnett, "Nightmare in Maryville."

20. Stuart, "Anonymous Focuses on Maryville."

21. Draper, "Mo. Man Accused."

22. Pesta, "Ruining My Life."

23. Baker, "Value of Speaking Out"; Bartkewicz, "Court Records Opened"; and Salter, "Online Counter-Publics."

24. Alter, "Bill Passed."

25. Powell, "Seeking Rape Justice"; and Salter, "Online Counter-Publics."

26. Hess and Waller, "Digital Pillory"; and Salter, "Online Counter-Publics."

27. Loney-Howes, *Online Anti-rape Activism*.

28. Loney-Howes, *Online Anti-rape Activism*; and Serisier, *Speaking Out*.

29. Gavey, *Just Sex?*; and Kelly, "Standing Test of Time?"

30. Boux and Daum, "Social Media and Rape"; Keller, Mendes, and Ringrose, "Speaking 'Unspeakable Things'"; Mendes, Ringrose, and Keller, "Digital Feminist Activism."

31. Loney-Howes, *Online Anti-rape Activism*; and Segrave and Vitis, *Gender, Technology and Violence*.

32. Fairbairn and Spencer, "Virtualized Violence," 489.

33. DeKeseredy and Schwartz, *Male Peer Support*.

34. Keller, Mendes, and Ringrose, "Speaking 'Unspeakable Things'"; Loney-Howes, *Online Anti-rape Activism*; Mendes, Ringrose, and Keller, "Digital Feminist Activism"; Rentschler, "Feminist Politics"; Sills et al., "Rape Culture and Social Media"; Powell and Henry, *Sexual Violence*; and Wood, Rose, and Thompson, "Viral Justice?"

35. Loney-Howes, *Online Anti-rape Activism*; Serisier, *Speaking Out*; and Tambe, "Silences of #MeToo."

36. Birdsell, "Reevaluating Gag Orders"; and Sills et al., "Rape Culture and Social Media."

37. Oliver, "Rape as Spectator Sport."

38. See Birdsell, "Reevaluating Gag Orders," for a discussion of multiple cases in which survivors were bullied and threatened online by perpetrators and classmates via private messages on social media platforms.

39. See note 16.

40. Burleigh, "Sexting, Shame and Suicide."

41. Arnett, "Nightmare in Maryville."

42. *Audrie & Daisy*

43. Arnett, "Daisy Suicide Attempt."

44. McNamara, "This Is Why."

45. Birdsell, "Reevaluating Gag Orders"; Curtis, Karlsen, and Anderson, "Transmuting Girls into Women"; Hasinoff, *Sexting Panic*; Marques, "Intimate Image Dissemination"; Ringrose et al., "Teen Girls, Double Standards"; and Salter, "Privates in Online Public."

46. Henry and Powell, "Embodied Harms"; Oliver, "Rape as Spectator Sport"; Ullman and Peter-Hagene, "Reactions to Disclosure"; and Wolak et al. "Sextortion of Minors."

47. Powell, "Seeking Rape Justice"; Vitis and Naegler, "Online Resistance"; and Wood, Rose, and Thompson, "Viral Justice?"

48. Bumiller, *In an Abusive State*; Gotell, "Reassessing Criminal Law Reform"; Gottschalk, *Prison and the Gallows*; and Thuma, "Lessons in Self-Defense."

49. Phillips and Chagnon, "'Six Months a Joke.'"

50. Bernstein, "Carceral Politics"; and Richie, *Arrested Justice*.

51. Wade, "Responses to Steubenville."

52. Dewey, "Girls Threatening Steubenville Victim."

53. Salter, "Privates in Online Public."

54. Killean, McAlinden, and Dowds, "Sexual Violence"; Salter, "Online Counter-Publics"; and Tilly, *Credit and Blame*.

55. Burke, "#MeToo Was Started"; Hackworth, "Limitations of 'Just Gender'"; Jewkes, *Media and Crime*; Mack and McCann, "State and Gendered Violence"; and Serisier, *Speaking Out*.

56. For a longer discussion on the gendered and racialized vulnerabilities women of color face in online platforms, see Curtis, Karlsen, and Anderson, "Transmuting Girls into Women"; and Lawson, "Platform Vulnerabilities."

57. Salter, "Online Counter-Publics"; and Wood, Rose, and Thompson, "Viral Justice?"

58. See also Salter, "Online Counter-Publics."

59. Easteal, Holland, and Judd, "Enduring Themes"; Jewkes, *Media and Crime*; Killean, McAlinden, and Dowds, "Sexual Violence"; Lawson, "Platform Vulnerabilities"; and Wood, Rose, and Thompson, "Viral Justice?"

60. Loney-Howes, *Online Anti-rape Activism*; Roeder, "'You Have to Confess'"; and Serisier, *Speaking Out*.

61. Loney-Howes, *Online Anti-rape Activism*. See also Gotell, "Reassessing Criminal Law Reform."

62. Vingiano, "Coleman Essay."

63. Mainstream second wave anti-rape activism all the way through to the #MeToo movement has been heavily criticized for the ways it fails to capture and acknowledge the multiple intersections of violence experienced by women of color. See hooks, *Feminist Theory*; Bevacqua, *Rape on Public Agenda*; Crenshaw, "Mapping the Margins"; Davis, *Women, Race, & Class*; Fileborn and Loney-Howes, *#MeToo and Social Change*.

64. Heberle, "Deconstructive Strategies," 64; Jewkes, *Media and Crime*; Loney-Howes, *Online Anti-rape Activism*; and Wood, Rose, and Thompson, "Viral Justice?"

65. Citron, "Law's Expressive Value"; Harris and Vitis, "Digital Intrusions"; and Wajcman, *TechnoFeminism*.

66. Chang, *Brotopia*; Harris and Vitis, "Digital Intrusions"; and Reed, *Digitized Lives*.

67. Bivens, "Under the Hood"; Jemielniak, "Breaking the Glass Ceiling"; Suzor et al., "Human Rights by Design"; and van Dijck, *Culture of Connectivity*.

68. Bear and Collier, "Where Are the Women"; Jane, "Gendered Cyberhate"; and Massanari, "#Gamergate and The Fappening."

69. Jane, "Gendered Cyberhate"; Nagle, *Kill All Normies*; and Salter, "Publicising Privacy."

70. Burgess and Matomoros-Fernández, "Mapping Sociocultural Controversies"; and Salter, "Publicising Privacy."

71. Salter, *Crime and Social Media*; and van Dijck, *Culture of Connectivity.*

72. Banet-Weiser and Mitner, "#MasculinitySoFragile"; Lawson, "Platform Vulnerabilities"; Matamoros-Fernández, "Platformed Racism"; Nagle, *Kill All Normies*; and Salter, "Publicising Privacy."

73. Herring, "Gender Harassment On-Line"; and Suzor et al., "Human Rights by Design."

74. Also Harris, "Technology and Violence"; and Salter, "Publicising Privacy."

75. Also Curtis, Karlsen, and Anderson, "Transmuting Girls into Women"; and Jane, "Gendered Cyberhate."

76. Loney-Howes, *Online Anti-rape Activism*; and Mendes et al., Ringrose, and Keller, "Digital Feminist Activism."

CHAPTER 6: TOWARD HARM REDUCTION AND PREVENTION

1. For a full discussion of these campaigns, see Henry et al., *Image-Based Sexual Abuse.*

2. Fairbairn, Bivens, and Dawson, *Sexual Violence*; Salter, "Privates in Online Public"; and Shariff and DeMartini, "Defining the Legal Lines."

3. Albury, "Just Because It's Public"; Crofts et al., *Sexting and Young People*; Dobson and Ringrose, "Sext Education"; Salter, Crofts, and Lee, "Beyond Criminalization"; and Setty, *Youth Sexting.*

4. Coker et al., "Bystander Training"; DeGue et al., "Effects of Dating Matters"; Edwards at al., "Evaluation of Bystander Program"; and Miller et al., "Middle School Violence Prevention."

5. Angelides, "'Technology, Hormones and Stupidity'"; Bluett-Boyd et al., "Communication Technologies in Sexual Violence"; Carmody, "Young Men, Sexual Ethics"; and Fairbairn, Bivens, and Dawson, *Sexual Violence.*

6. Cowley, "Let's Get Drunk"; Hoxmeier, O'Connor, and McMahon, "'She Wasn't Resisting'"; and Young et al., "Alcohol-Related Sexual Assault."

7. Crofts et al., *Sexting and Young People*; Gavey, *Just Sex?*; Henry et al., *Image-Based Sexual Abuse*; and Setty, *Youth Sexting.*

8. Bolger, "Bystander Intervention"; Carmody, "Young Men, Sexual Ethics"; and Dobson, "Intimate Media Practices."

9. Dobson, "Intimate Media Practices"; Jorgensen et al., "Views on Sexting Education"; and Setty, *Youth Sexting.*

10. Baker, "Teaching Young People Risks"; Martellozo et al., "Affects Online Pornography Has"; and Rodriguez-Castro et al., "Intimate Partner Cyberstalking."

11. Baker, "Teaching Young People Risks"; Lim, Carrotte, and Hellard, "Impact of Pornography"; Peter and Valkenburg, "Adolescents and Pornography"; Rodriguez-Castro et al., "Intimate Partner Cyberstalking"; and Rostad et al. "Teen Dating Violence."

12. Willis et al., "Sexual Consent Communication."

13. Carmody, "Young Men, Sexual Ethics"; Jorgensen et al., "Views on Sexting Education"; and Setty, *Youth Sexting.*

14. Garcia et al., "Council of Youth Research"; Hobbs and Jensen, "Media Literacy Education"; and Tyner, *Literacy in Digital World.*

15. James, *Disconnected*; Jones and Mitchell, "Youth Digital Citizenship"; Lim et al., "Digital Citizenship in Primary Schools"; and Powell and Henry, *Sexual Violence*.

16. Albury, Hasinoff, and Senft, "Media Abstinence to Production"; and Weinstein and James, *Behind Their Screens*.

17. See also Dobson and Ringrose, "Sext Education"; Hasinoff, *Sexting Panic*; and Setty, *Youth Sexting*.

18. Brown, "Sexual Violence"; and Kingkade, "High Schools Failing Girls."

19. Brown, "Reporting School Sexual Assault"; Hauch, "Mishandled Sex Abuse Claims"; Kingkade, "High Schools Failing Girls"; Kingkade, "Schools Keep Punishing Girls"; Kingkade, "Mishandled Sexual Assault Cases"; Legal Services NYC, "NYC Schools Pay Survivors"; and Pollack, "Student Survivors of Violence."

20. Charmaraman et al., "Is It Bullying?"; Keierleber, "Sexual-Violence Victims"; Meyer and Somoza-Norton, "Addressing Sex Discrimination"; and Pollack, "Student Survivors of Violence."

21. Horeck, Mendes, and Ringrose, "Digital Defence in Classroom"; and Meehan, "'It's Like Mental Rape.'"

22. Firmin, *Abuse between Young People*. See also Lloyd, "Image Sharing in Schools."

23. For further detail on what such policy intervention might look like, see the recent online sexual harassment policy resources developed by scholars at the School of Sexuality Education in England, available at https://schoolofsexed .org/guidance-for-schools.

24. Russell and Crocker, "Restorative Justice in Schools."

25. Dodge and Spencer, "Online Sexual Violence"; Henry, Flynn, and Powell, "Policing Image-Based Abuse"; Segal, *Rehtaeh Parson's Case*; and Shariff and DeMartini, "Defining the Legal Lines".

26. Dodge, "Restorative Responses"; Hamilton, "Justice Best Served Cold"; and Russell and Crocker, "Restorative Justice in Schools."

27. See also Henry and Powell, "Embodied Harms"; Kelly, "Standing Test of Time?"; and McGlynn, Rackley, and Houghton, 'Beyond 'Revenge Porn.'"

28. Gotell, "Reassessing Criminal Law Reform"; McGlynn and Rackley, "Image-Based Sexual Abuse"; Powell and Henry, *Sexual Violence*; and Smart, *Feminism and Law*.

29. Citron, "Law's Expressive Value"; Flynn et al., *Shattering Lives and Myths*; and Powell and Henry, *Sexual Violence*.

30. See Henry and Witt, "Governing Image-Based Abuse," for a review of the literature. See also Rackley et al., "Seeking Justice and Redress."

31. Dodge and Lockhart, "'Young People Resolve It'"; Dodge and Spencer, "Online Sexual Violence"; Segal, *Rehtaeh Parson's Case*; Shariff and DeMartini, "Defining the Legal Lines."

32. Citron, "Sexual Privacy"; Eaton and McGlynn, "Psychology of Nonconsensual Porn"; and Rackley et al., "Seeking Justice and Redress."

33. As of the writing of this book, the Stopping Harmful Image Exploitation and Limiting Distribution (SHIELD) Act, which would establish narrow federal criminal liability for the non-consensual distribution of private, explicit

images, has been introduced to Congress with bipartisan support. This act does not speak specifically to image-based sexual abuse among teens and it is unclear how such legislation may impact them. One of the act's provisions aims to ensure those who share explicit photos of children (i.e., under 18 years old) are held accountable to the fullest extent of the law, which may result in harsher punishment for juveniles.

34. Gotell, "Reassessing Criminal Law Reform"; Larcombe, "Falling Rape Conviction Rates"; McGlynn, Downes, and Westmarland, "Seeking Justice for Survivors."

35. Daly, "Sexual Violence and Justice"; and McGlynn and Westmarland, "Kaleidoscopic Justice."

36. Coburn, Connolly, and Roesch, "Cyberbullying"; Fairbairn, Bivens, and Dawson, *Sexual Violence*; Koss, "RESTORE Program"; and Shariff and DiMartini, "Defining the Legal Lines."

37. Hrick, "Technology-Facilitated Violence"; and Eaton and McGlynn, "Psychology of Nonconsensual Porn."

38. Powell and Henry, *Sexual Violence*; and Rackley et al., "Seeking Justice and Redress."

39. See Yar and Drew, "Image-Based Abuse, Non-Consensual Pornography, Revenge Porn," for a full discussion of such initiatives in Australia, England, and Wales.

40. Gillespie, *Custodians of the Internet*; and Klonick, "New Governors."

41. Pavan, "Internet Intermediaries"; and Shaikh, "Violence against Women Online."

42. Pavan, "Internet Intermediaries"; Salter, *Crime and Social Media*; and Yar, "Will-to-Representation."

43. See Henry and Witt, "Governing Image-Based Sexual Abuse," for a thorough discussion of such initiatives on a global scale.

44. See Henry et al., *Image-Based Sexual Abuse* (esp. ch. 8) for a review of these measures.

45. Henry and Witt, "Governing Image-Based Sexual Abuse"; Powell and Henry, *Sexual Violence*; and Salter, *Crime and Social Media*.

46. Davis, "Detecting Non-Consensual Images"; Henry and Witt, "Governing Image-Based Sexual Abuse"; Langston, "PhotoDNA for Video"; and Salinas, "Facebook A.I. Tool."

47. Dragiewicz et al., "Technology Facilitated Coercive Control"; Henry and Witt, "Governing Image-Based Sexual Abuse"; and Rackley et al., "Seeking Justice and Redress."

48. Dunn, "Is It Actually Violence?"; Goldberg, "Revenge Porn Victims"; Henry et al., *Image-Based Sexual Abuse*; Henry and Witt, "Governing Image-Based Sexual Abuse."

49. Gillespie, *Custodians of the Internet*; Harper, "Putting Out Twitter Trashfire"; Henry and Witt, "Governing Image-Based Sexual Abuse"; Rackley et al., "Seeking Justice and Redress"; and Suzor, *Lawless*.

50. These include difficulties differentiating between consensual and non-consensual sexual content; differing cultural standards for what constitutes a "nude" or "sexual" image; the limitations of AI in identifying abusive content;

the precarity of content moderators; and the viral nature of technology, which makes it impossible to control where content has been downloaded or shared. See Dickson, "Facebook Revenge Porn"; Henry et al., *Image-Based Sexual Abuse*; Pavan, "Internet Intermediaries"; and Roberts, *Behind the Screen*.

51. Dragiewicz et al., "Technology Facilitated Coercive Control"; Henry and Witt, "Governing Image-Based Sexual Abuse"; and Suzor et al., "Human Rights by Design."

52. Salter, *Crime and Social Media*; and Rackley et al., "Seeking Justice and Redress."

53. Henry and Witt, "Governing Image-Based Sexual Abuse"; Langlois and Slane, "Economies of Reputation"; Massanari, "#Gamergate and The Fappening"; Salter, "Publicising Privacy"; and Shepherd et al., "Histories of Hating."

APPENDIX: METHODS

1. Yin, *Case Study Research*, 66.

2. Yin, *Case Study Research*, 23.

3. Yin, *Case Study Research*.

4. George and Bennett, *Case Studies*.

5. Vogels, Gelles-Watnick, and Massarat, *Teens, Social Media, Technology*.

6. Allen, "Managing Masculinity."

7. Bryman, *Social Research Methods*.

8. Vogels, Gelles-Watnick, and Massarat, *Teens, Social Media, Technology*.

9. Greig, Taylor, and Mackay, *Research with Children*.

10. See also Lippman and Campbell, "Damned If You Do"; and Mandau, "'Directly in Your Face.'"

11. Barbour, *Doing Focus Groups*; and Krueger and Casey, *Focus Groups*.

12. Miller, *Getting Played*.

13. Strauss and Corbin, *Qualitative Research*.

14. Gjika, "New Media, Old Paradigms."

15. Braun and Clarke, "Using Thematic Analysis." Please see Gjika for a fuller discussion of the qualitative methods used in the article.

16. Tuchman, *Making News*.

Bibliography

ABC News. "Steubenville Social Media: By the Numbers." March 21, 2013. http://abcnews.go.com/blogs/technology/2013/03/steubenville-social-media -by-the-numbers.

———. "Video Steubenville: After the Party's Over." March 22, 2013. https:// abcnews.go.com/2020/video/steubenville-partys-18795344.

Alaggia, Ramona, Delphine Collin-Vézina, and Rusan Lateef. "Facilitators and Barriers to Child Sexual Abuse (CSA) Disclosures: A Research Update (2000–2016)." *Trauma, Violence, & Abuse* 20, no. 2 (2019): 260–83. https:// doi.org/10.1177/1524838017697312.

Albury, Kath. "Just Because It's Public Doesn't Mean It's Any of Your Business: Adults' and Children's Sexual Rights in Digitally Mediated Spaces." *New Media & Society* 19, no. 5 (2017): 713–25.

Albury, Kath, Amy Adele Hasinoff, and Theresa Senft. "From Media Abstinence to Media Production: Sexting, Young People and Education." In *The Palgrave Handbook of Sexuality Education*, edited by Louisa Allen and Mary Lou Rasmussen, 527–45. London: Palgrave Macmillan UK, 2017.

Alderden, Megan A., and Sarah E. Ullman. "Creating a More Complete and Current Picture: Examining Police and Prosecutor Decision-Making When Processing Sexual Assault Cases." *Violence against Women* 18, no. 5 (2012): 525–51. https://doi.org/10.1177/1077801212453867.

Alexander, Michelle. *The New Jim Crow: Mass Incarceration in the Age of Colorblindness*. New York: The New Press, 2012.

Allen, Louisa. "Managing Masculinity: Young Men's Identity Work in Focus Groups." *Qualitative Research* 5, no. 1 (2005): 35–57. https://doi.org/10 .1177/1468794105048650.

Alter, Marissa. "Bill Passed to Allow Juvenile Case Victims to Speak Publicly." *WLKY* (blog), March 28, 2013. www.wlky.com/article/bill-passed-to-allow -juvenile-case-victims-to-speak-publicly-1/3743073.

Amin, Avni, Anna Kågesten, Emmanuel Adebayo, and Venkatraman Chandra-Mouli. "Addressing Gender Socialization and Masculinity Norms among Adolescent Boys: Policy and Programmatic Implications." *Journal of Adolescent Health* 62, no. 3 (2018): S3–5. https://doi.org/10.1016/j.jadohealth .2017.06.022.

Amundsen, Rikke. "'The Price of Admission': On Notions of Risk and Responsibility in Women's Sexting Practices." In *Online Othering: Exploring Digital Violence and Discrimination on the Web*, edited by Karen Lumsden and Emily Harmer, 145–64. Palgrave Studies in Cybercrime and Cybersecurity. Cham: Springer International, 2019.

Anderson, Michelle J. "From Chastity Requirement to Sexuality License: Sexual Consent and a New Rape Shield Law." SSRN Scholarly Paper, Social Science Research Network, Rochester, NY, September 1, 2002. https://doi.org /10.2139/ssrn.326260.

Andrejevic, Mark. "Privacy, Exploitation and the Digital Enclosure." *Amsterdam Law Forum* 1, no. 4 (2009): 47–62. https://doi.org/10.37974/ALF.86.

Angelides, Steven. "'Technology, Hormones, and Stupidity': The Affective Politics of Teenage Sexting." *Sexualities* 16, nos. 5–6 (2013): 665–89. https://doi .org/10.1177/1363460713487289.

Armstrong, Cory L., Kevin Hull, and Lynsey Saunders. "Victimized on Plain Sites." *Digital Journalism* 4, no. 2 (2016): 247–65. https://doi.org/10.1080 /21670811.2015.1040043.

Arnes, Andre. *Digital Forensics*. Hoboken, NJ: John Wiley, 2018.

Arnett, Dugan. "Daisy Coleman, Teen at Center of Maryville Sexual Assault Case, Is Recovering after Suicide Attempt." *Kansas City Star*, January 7, 2014. www.kansas.com/news/article1131034.html.

———. "Nightmare in Maryville: Teens' Sexual Encounter Ignites a Firestorm against Family." *Kansas City Star*, October 12, 2013. www.kansascity.com /news/special-reports/maryville/article329412.html.

Ash, Erin, Jimmy Sanderson, Chenjerai Kumanyika, and Kelly Gramlich. "'Just Goes to Show How These Hoes Try to Tear Men Down': Investigating Twitter and Cultural Conversations on Athletic Ability, Race, and Sexual Assault." *Journal of Sports Media* 12, no. 1 (2017): 65–87. https://doi.org/10 .1353/jsm.2017.0003.

Audrie & Daisy. Documentary. Accessed May 19, 2022. www.audrieanddaisy .com/.

Ayman-Nolley, Saba, and Lora Taira. "Obsession with the Dark Side of Adolescence: A Decade of Psychological Studies." *Journal of Youth Studies* 3, no. 1 (2000): 35–48. https://doi.org/10.1080/136762600113022.

Bailey, Jane, Asher Flynn, and Nicola Henry. *The Emerald International Handbook of Technology-Facilitated Violence and Abuse*. Bingley, UK: Emerald Group, 2021.

Baker, Karen Elizabeth. "Online Pornography—Should Schools Be Teaching Young People about the Risks? An Exploration of the Views of Young

People and Teaching Professionals." *Sex Education* 16, no. 2 (2016): 213–28. https://doi.org/10.1080/14681811.2015.1090968.

Baker, Katie J. M. "Sent Home from Middle School after Reporting a Rape." *BuzzFeed News*, March 14, 2016. www.buzzfeednews.com/article/katiejm baker/sent-home-from-middle-school-after-reporting-a-rape.

———. "Teenage Girl Demonstrates Value of Speaking Out About Sexual Assault." Jezebel, December 10, 2012. https://jezebel.com/teenage-girl -demonstrates-value-of-speaking-out-about-s-5967151.

Ballotpedia. "Nonconsensual Pornography (Revenge Porn) Laws in the United States." Ballotpedia. Accessed January 17, 2023. https://ballotpedia.org /Nonconsensual_pornography_(revenge_porn)_laws_in_the_United_States.

Banet-Weiser, Sarah, and Kate M. Miltner. "#MasculinitySoFragile: Culture, Structure, and Networked Misogyny." *Feminist Media Studies* 16, no. 1 (2016): 171–74. https://doi.org/10.1080/14680777.2016.1120490.

Banyard, Victoria L. "Measurement and Correlates of Prosocial Bystander Behavior: The Case of Interpersonal Violence." *Violence and Victims* 23, no. 1 (2008): 83–97.

Barbour, Rosaline. *Doing Focus Groups.* Thousand Oaks, CA: Sage, 2007.

Barca, Lisa A. "The Agency Factor: Neoliberal Configurations of Risk in News Discourse on the Steubenville, Ohio Rape Case." *Critical Discourse Studies* 15, no. 3 (2018): 265–84. https://doi.org/10.1080/17405904.2017.1408476.

Barrense-Dias, Yara, Christina Akre, Diane Auderset, Brigitte Leeners, Davide Morselli, and Joan-Carles Surís. "Non-Consensual Sexting: Characteristics and Motives of Youths Who Share Received-Intimate Content without Consent." *Sexual Health* 17 (2020): 270–78. https://doi.org/10.1071/SH19201.

Bartkewicz, Anthony. "Court Records to Be Opened in Case of Kentucky Teen Who Named Abusers on Twitter." *NY Daily News*, August 29, 2012. www .nydailynews.com/news/national/court-records-opened-case-kentucky-teen -named-abusers-twitter-article-1.1146900.

Baym, Nancy K. *Personal Connections in the Digital Age.* Cambridge, UK: Polity, 2010.

Bear, Julia B., and Benjamin Collier. "Where Are the Women in Wikipedia? Understanding the Different Psychological Experiences of Men and Women in Wikipedia." *Sex Roles* 74, no. 5 (2016): 254–65. https://doi.org/10.1007 /s11199-015-0573-y.

Belknap, Joanne. "Rape: Too Hard to Report and Too Easy to Discredit Victims." *Violence against Women* 16, no. 12 (2010): 1335–44. https://doi.org /10.1177/1077801210387749.

Bernstein, Elizabeth. "Carceral Politics as Gender Justice? The 'Traffic in Women' and Neoliberal Circuits of Crime, Sex, and Rights." *Theory and Society* 41, no. 3 (2012): 233–59. https://doi.org/10.1007/s11186-012-9165-9.

Bevacqua, Maria. *Rape on the Public Agenda.* Boston: Northeastern University Press, 2000.

Biber, Katherine. *Captive Images: Race, Crime, Photography.* New York: GlassHouse, 2007.

———. *In Crime's Archive: The Cultural Afterlife of Evidence.* London: Routledge, 2018.

Bicanic, Iva A. E., Lieve M. Hehenkamp, Elise M. van de Putte, Arjen J. van Wijk, and Ad de Jongh. "Predictors of Delayed Disclosure of Rape in Female Adolescents and Young Adults." *European Journal of Psychotraumatology* 6, no.1 (2015). https://doi.org/10.3402/ejpt.v6.25883.

Bidisha. "The Rape Shame of Social Media." *Guardian*, September 22, 2011, www.theguardian.com/lifeandstyle/2011/sep/22/rape-shame-social-media.

Birdsell, Bonnie. "Reevaluating Gag Orders and Rape Shield Laws in the Internet Age: How Can We Better Protect Victims?" *Seton Hall Legislative Journal* 38, no. 1 (2014): 71–96. https://scholarship.shu.edu/shlj/vol38/iss1/4.

Bivens, Rena. "Under the Hood: The Software in Your Feminist Approach." *Feminist Media Studies* 15, no. 4 (2015): 714–17. https://doi.org/10.1080/14680777.2015.1053717.

Black, Alex, Karen Lumsden, and Lee Hadlington. "'Why Don't You Block Them?' Police Officers' Constructions of the Ideal Victim When Responding to Reports of Interpersonal Cybercrime." In *Online Othering: Exploring Digital Violence and Discrimination on the Web*, edited by Karen Lumsden and Emily Harmer, 355–78. Palgrave Studies in Cybercrime and Cybersecurity. Cham: Springer International, 2019.

Bluett-Boyd, Nicole, Bianca Fileborn, Antonia Quadara, and Sharnee Moore. *The Role of Emerging Communication Technologies in Experiences of Sexual Violence: A New Legal Frontier?* Australian Institute of Family Studies, February 2013. https://aifs.gov.au/sites/default/files/publication-documents/rr23_0.pdf.

Bohner, Gerd, Marc-André Reinhard, Stefanie Rutz, Sabine Sturm, Bernd Kerschbaum, and Dagmar Effler. "Rape Myths as Neutralizing Cognitions: Evidence for a Causal Impact of Anti-Victim Attitudes on Men's Self-Reported Likelihood of Raping." *European Journal of Social Psychology* 28 (1998): 257–68. https://doi.org/10.1002/(SICI)1099-0992(199803/04)28:2<257::AID-EJSP871>3.0.CO;2-1.

Bolger, Dana. "Why Do We Love Bystander Intervention and Fear Community Consequences for Rape?" *Feministing* (blog), January 14, 2015. http://feministing.com/2015/01/14/why-do-we-love-bystander-intervention-and-fear-community-consequences-for-rape/.

Bond, Emma, and Katie Tyrrell. "Understanding Revenge Pornography: A National Survey of Police Officers and Staff in England and Wales." *Journal of Interpersonal Violence* 36, nos. 5–6 (2018): 2166–81. https://doi.org/10.1177/0886260518760011.

Boteach, Shmuley. "An American Tragedy in Steubenville." *Huffington Post* (blog), March 18, 2013. www.huffingtonpost.com/rabbi-shmuley-boteach/steubenville-case_b_2898254.html.

Bottoms, Bette L., Suzanne L. Davis, and Michelle A. Epstein. "Effects of Victim and Defendant Race on Jurors' Decisions in Child Sexual Abuse Cases." *Journal of Applied Social Psychology* 34, no. 1 (2004): 1–33. https://doi.org/10.1111/j.1559-1816.2004.tb02535.x.

Boux, Holly Jeanine, and C. Daum. "At the Intersection of Social Media and Rape Culture: How Facebook Postings, Texting, and Other Personal

Communications Challenge the 'Real' Rape Myth in the Criminal Justice System." *Journal of Law, Technology & Policy* 2015, no.1 (2015): 149–86.

boyd, danah. *It's Complicated*. New Haven, CT: Yale University Press, 2014.

Braun, Virginia, and Victoria Clarke. "Using Thematic Analysis in Psychology." *Qualitative Research in Psychology* 3, no. 2 (2006): 77–101. https://doi.org/10.1191/1478088706qp063oa.

Brayne, Sarah. "Big Data Surveillance: The Case of Policing." *American Sociological Review* 82, no. 5 (2017): 977–1008. https://doi.org/10.1177/0003122417725865.

Brodsky, Stanley, Michael Griffin, and Robert Cramer. "The Witness Credibility Scale: An Outcome Measure for Expert Witness Research." *Behavioral Sciences and the Law* 28, no. 6 (2010): 892–907.

Broll, Ryan, and Laura Huey. "'Just Being Mean to Somebody Isn't a Police Matter': Police Perspectives on Policing Cyberbullying." *Journal of School Violence* 14, no. 2 (2015): 155–76. https://doi.org/10.1080/15388220.2013.879367.

Brooms, Derrick R. *Being Black, Being Male on Campus: Understanding and Confronting Black Male Collegiate Experiences*. Albany: State University of New York Press, 2018.

Brown, Emma. "Reporting a School Sexual Assault Can Increase a Victim's Risk of Punishment." *Washington Post*, January 17, 2016. www.washingtonpost.com/news/education/wp/2016/01/17/reporting-a-school-sexual-assault-can-increase-a-victims-risk-of-punishment/.

———. "Sexual Violence Isn't Just a College Problem: It Happens in K–12 Schools, Too." *Washington Post*, January 17, 2016. www.washingtonpost.com/local/education/sexual-violence-isnt-just-a-college-problem-it-happens-in-k-12-schools-too/2016/01/17/a4a91074-ba2c-11e5-99f3-184bc379b12d_story.html.

Browning, John G. "Digging for the Digital Dirt: Discovery and Use of Evidence from Social Media Sites." *Science and Technology Law Review* 14, no. 3 (2011): 465–96.

Bryman, Alan. *Social Research Methods*. 4th ed. Oxford: Oxford University Press, 2012.

Buckingham, David, ed. *Youth, Identity, and Digital Media*. The John D. and Catherine T. MacArthur Foundation Series on Digital Media and Learning. Cambridge, MA: The MIT Press, 2008.

Buckwalter-Poza, Rebecca. "Making Justice Equal." American Progress, December 8, 2016. www.americanprogress.org/article/making-justice-equal/.

Bumiller, Kristen. *In an Abusive State: How Neoliberalism Appropriated the Feminist Movement Against Sexual Violence*. Durham, NC: Duke University Press, 2008.

Burén, Jonas, and Carolina Lunde. "Sexting among Adolescents: A Nuanced and Gendered Online Challenge for Young People." *Computers in Human Behavior* 85 (2018): 210–17. https://doi.org/10.1016/j.chb.2018.02.003.

Burgess, Jean, and Ariadna Matamoros-Fernández. "Mapping Sociocultural Controversies across Digital Media Platforms: One Week of #gamergate on

Twitter, YouTube, and Tumblr." *Communication Research and Practice* 2, no. 1 (2016): 79–96. https://doi.org/10.1080/22041451.2016.1155338.

Burke, Roger Hopkins. *Young People, Crime and Justice*. Cullompton, Devon, UK: Willan Publishing, 2008.

Burke, Tarana. "#MeToo Was Started for Black and Brown Women and Girls: They're Still Being Ignored." *Washington Post*, November 9, 2017. www .washingtonpost.com/news/post-nation/wp/2017/11/09/the-waitress-who -works-in-the-diner-needs-to-know-that-the-issue-of-sexual-harassment-is -about-her-too/.

Burkell, Jacquelyn Ann. "Remembering Me: Big Data, Individual Identity, and the Psychological Necessity of Forgetting." *Ethics and Information Technology* 18, no. 1 (2016): 17–23. https://doi.org/10.1007/s10676-016-9393-1.

Burleigh, Nina. "Sexting, Shame and Suicide: A Shocking Tale of Sexual Assault in the Digital Age." *Rolling Stone Magazine*, September 17, 2013. www .rollingstone.com/culture/culture-news/sexting-shame-and-suicide-72148/.

Burt, M. R. "Cultural Myths and Supports for Rape." *Journal of Personality and Social Psychology* 38, no. 2 (1980): 217–30. https://doi.org/10.1037//0022 -3514.38.2.217.

Busby, Karen. "How to Keep Sexual Assault Cases on Track." *Canadian Lawyer*, March 20, 2017. www.canadianlawyermag.com/news/opinion/how-to -keep-sexual-assault-cases-on-track/270433.

Butler, Judith. *Gender Trouble*. New York: Routledge, 1999.

Campbell, Rebecca, Megan R. Greeson, Giannina Fehler-Cabral, and Angie C. Kennedy. "Pathways to Help: Adolescent Sexual Assault Victims' Disclosure and Help-Seeking Experiences." *Violence against Women* 21, no. 7 (2015): 824–47. https://doi.org/10.1177/1077801215584071.

Carmody, Moira. "Young Men, Sexual Ethics and Sexual Negotiation." *Sociological Research Online* 18, no. 2 (2013): 90–102. https://doi.org/10.5153 /sro.2932.

Carpenter, Don. "Text Messages That Led to Convictions in the Steubenville Rape Trial." *Mobile Broadcast News* (blog), March 17, 2013. www .mobilebroadcastnews.com/NewsRoom/Don-Carpenter/Text-Messages-led -convictions-Steubenville-Rape-Trial.

Carrabine, Eamonn. "Just Images: Aesthetics, Ethics and Visual Criminology." *British Journal of Criminology* 52 (2012): 463–89.

Carter, Chelsea J. "Teen Rape Trial Shines Unwelcome Spotlight on Ohio Town, Football Team." *CNN*, March 12, 2013. www.cnn.com/2013/03/12/justice /ohio-steubenville-case/index.html.

Casey, Erin A., and Tatiana Masters. *Sexual Violence Risk and Protective Factors: A Systematic Review of the Literature*. Washington State Department of Health, 2017. https://doh.wa.gov/sites/default/files/legacy/Documents/Pubs/ /140-164-SexualViolenceRiskProtectiveFactors.pdf.

Chang, Emily. *Brotopia: Breaking Up the Boys' Club of Silicon Valley*. New York: Portfolio/Penguin, 2019.

Charmaraman, Linda, Ashleigh E. Jones, Nan Stein, and Dorothy L. Espelage. "Is It Bullying or Sexual Harassment? Knowledge, Attitudes, and Professional

Development Experiences of Middle School Staff." *Journal of School Health* 83, no. 6 (2013): 438–44. https://doi.org/10.1111/josh.12048.

Chmielewski, Jennifer, Deborah Tolman, and Hunter Kincaid. "Constructing Risk and Responsibility: A Gender, Race, and Class Analysis of News Representations of Adolescent Sexuality." *Feminist Media Studies* 17, no. 3 (2017): 412–25. https://doi.org/10.1080/14680777.2017.1283348.

Citron, Danielle Keats. *Hate Crimes in Cyberspace.* Cambridge, MA: Harvard University Press, 2014.

———. "Law's Expressive Value in Combating Cyber Gender Harassment." *Michigan Law Review* 108, no. 3 (2009): 373–415. https://doi.org/10.3316/agispt.20191217021731.

———. "Sexual Privacy." *Yale Law Journal* 128, no. 7 (2019): 1870–1960.

Clancy, Elizabeth M., Bianca Klettke, Angela M. Crossman, David J. Hallford, Dominika Howard, and John W. Toumbourou. "Sext Dissemination: Differences across Nations in Motivations and Associations." *International Journal of Environmental Research and Public Health* 18, no. 5 (2021): 2429. https://doi.org/10.3390/ijerph18052429.

Clancy, Elizabeth M., Bianca Klettke, and David J. Hallford. "The Dark Side of Sexting—Factors Predicting the Dissemination of Sexts." *Computers in Human Behavior* 92 (2019): 266–72. https://doi.org/10.1016/j.chb.2018.11.023.

Clark, Haley. "A Fair Way to Go: Justice for Victim-Survivors of Sexual Violence." In *Rape Justice: Beyond the Criminal Law*, edited by Anastasia Powell, Nicola Henry, and Asher Flynn, 18–35. London: Palgrave Macmillan, 2015.

Clevenger, Shelly, and Jordana Navarro. "The 'Third-Victimization': The Cyber-victimization of Sexual Assault Survivors and Their Families." *Journal of Contemporary Criminal Justice* 37, no. 3 (2021): 356–78. https://doi.org/10.1177/10439862211001616.

Coburn, Patricia, Deborah Connolly, and Ron Roesch. "Cyberbullying: Is Federal Criminal Legislation the Solution?" *Canadian Journal of Criminology and Criminal Justice* 57, no. 4 (2015): 566–79. https://doi.org/10.3138/cjccj.2014.E43.

Cohen, Stanley. *Folk Devils and Moral Panics: The Creation of the Mods and Rockers.* London: MacGibbon and Kee, 1972.

Coker, Ann L., Heather M. Bush, Zhengyan Huang, Candace J. Brancato, Emily R. Clear, and Diane R. Follingstad. "How Does Green Dot Bystander Training in High School and Beyond Impact Attitudes toward Violence and Sexism in a Prospective Cohort?" *Journal of Interpersonal Violence* 37, nos. 15–16 (2021). https://doi.org/10.1177/08862605211006354.

Collins, Laura. "EXCLUSIVE: Steubenville Rape Victim Wants Role in Pitt's Movie of Case." *Daily Mail Online*, April 4, 2014. www.dailymail.co.uk/news/article-2596371/EXCLUSIVE-Steubenville-rape-victim-asks-input-Brad-Pitts-movie-ordeal-Anonymous-hacker-inspired-film-breaks-silence.html.

Connell, R. W. *Masculinities.* Cambridge, UK: Polity Press, 1995.

Connell, R. W., and James W. Messerschmidt. "Hegemonic Masculinity: Rethinking the Concept." *Gender and Society* 19, no. 6 (2005): 829–59.

Cooley, Charles Horton. *Human Nature and the Social Order*. New Brunswick, NJ: Transaction, 1902.

Corrigan, Rose. *Up Against a Wall: Rape Reform and the Failure of Success*. New York: NYU Press, 2013.

Cossins, Anne. *Closing the Justice Gap for Adult and Child Sexual Assault: Rethinking the Adversarial Trial*. London: Palgrave Macmillan UK, 2020.

Cowley, Amanda D. "'Let's Get Drunk and Have Sex': The Complex Relationship of Alcohol, Gender, and Sexual Victimization." *Journal of Interpersonal Violence* 29, no. 7 (2014): 1258–78.

Coy, Maddy, Liz Kelly, Fiona Elvines, Maria Garner, and Ava Kanyeredzi. "*Sex without Consent, I Suppose That Is Rape*": How Young People in England Understand Sexual Consent. Inquiry into Child Sexual Exploitation in Gangs and Groups. Office of the Children's Commissioner, 2013.

Crawford, Kate, and Gerard Goggin. "Generation Disconnections: Youth Culture & Mobile Media." In *Mobile Communication: Bringing Us Together or Tearing Us Apart?*, edited by Rich Ling and Scott Campbell. Piscataway, NJ: Transaction Publishers, 2011.

Crenshaw, Kimberle. "Mapping the Margins: Intersectionality, Identity Politics, and Violence against Women of Color." *Stanford Law Review* 43, no. 6 (1991): 1241–99. https://doi.org/10.2307/1229039.

Critcher, Chas. *Moral Panics and the Media*. Buckingham, UK: Open University Press, 2003.

Crofts, Thomas, M. Lee, A. McGovern, and S. Milivojevic. *Sexting and Young People*. London: Palgrave Macmillan, 2015.

Curry, Mary Ann, Paula Renker, Susan Robinson-Whelen, Rosemary B. Hughes, Paul Swank, Mary Oschwald, and Laurie E. Powers. "Facilitators and Barriers to Disclosing Abuse among Women with Disabilities." *Violence and Victims* 26, no. 4 (2011): 430–44. https://doi.org/10.1891/0886-6708.26.4.430.

Curtis, Michael G., Annika S. Karlsen, and Leslie A. Anderson. "Transmuting Girls into Women: Examining the Adultification of Black Female Sexual Assault Survivors through Twitter Feedback." *Violence against Women* 29, no. 2 (2022): 321–46. https://doi.org/10.1177/10778012221083334.

Da Silva, Teresa, Jessica Woodhams, and Leigh Harkins. "Multiple Perpetrator Rape: A Critical Review of Existing Explanatory Theories." *Aggression and Violent Behavior* 25 (2015): 150–58. https://doi.org/10.1016/j.avb.2015.07.017.

Daly, Kathleen. "Sexual Violence and Justice." In *Rape Justice: Beyond the Criminal Law*, edited by Anastasia Powell, Nicola Henry, and Asher Flynn, 36–52. London: Palgrave Macmillan UK, 2015.

Das, Shanti. "Inside the Violent, Misogynistic World of TikTok's New Star, Andrew Tate." *Observer*, August 6, 2022. www.theguardian.com/technology/2022/aug/06/andrew-tate-violent-misogynistic-world-of-tiktok-new-star.

Daum, Meghan. "When Cellphones and Social Media Become the Enemy." *Los Angeles Times*, July 16, 2014. www.latimes.com/opinion/op-ed/la-oe-daum-jada-rape-culture-20140717-column.html.

Davel, Coriena. "The Mobile Phone as an Extension of the Self: A Study among Adolescents in a Secondary School." PhD diss., University of South Africa, 2017.

Davis, Angela Y. *Women, Race, & Class*. New York: Knopf Doubleday, 2011.

Davis, Antigone. "Detecting Non-Consensual Intimate Images and Supporting Victims." *Meta* (blog), March 15, 2019. https://about.fb.com/news/2019/03/detecting-non-consensual-intimate-images/.

Davis, Kelly. "New Bill Would Bring Social Media Posts under the Rape Shield." *Voice of San Diego*, March 26, 2021. http://voiceofsandiego.org/2021/03/26/new-bill-would-bring-social-media-posts-under-the-rape-shield/.

De Ridder, Sander. "Social Media and Young People's Sexualities: Values, Norms, and Battlegrounds." *Social Media + Society* 3, no. 4 (2017): 1–11.

Dearden, Lizzie. "Victims May Stop Reporting Rape over Fears Phone Evidence Will Be Used against Them, Official Warns." *Independent*, August 8, 2018. www.independent.co.uk/news/uk/crime/rape-women-reporting-police-disclosure-evidence-phone-victims-commissioner-a8483411.html.

DeGue, Sarah, Phyllis Holditch Niolon, Lianne Fuino Estefan, Allison J. Tracy, Vi D. Le, Alana M. Vivolo-Kantor, Todd D. Little, et al. "Effects of Dating Matters® on Sexual Violence and Sexual Harassment Outcomes among Middle School Youth: A Cluster-Randomized Controlled Trial." *Prevention Science* 22, no. 2 (2021): 175–85. https://doi.org/10.1007/s11121-020-01152-0.

DeKeseredy, Walter S., and Martin D. Schwartz. *Male Peer Support and Violence against Women: The History and Verification of a Theory*. Boston: Northeastern University Press, 2013.

Deuze, Mark. "Media Life." *Media, Culture & Society* 33, no. 1 (2011): 137–48.

Dewey, Caitlin. "Two Teenage Girls Charged with Threatening Steubenville Rape Victim on Twitter." *Washington Post*, March 19, 2013. www.washingtonpost.com/national/two-teenage-girls-charged-with-threatening-steubenville-rape-victim-on-twitter/2013/03/19/2e41ae82-90d6-11e2-9abd-e4c5c9dc5e90_story.html.

Dickson, E. J. "Facebook Says It Has an AI Tool to Get Rid of Revenge Porn Once and for All: But Like . . . How?" *Rolling Stone Magazine*, March 15, 2019. www.rollingstone.com/culture/culture-news/facebook-revenge-porn-ai-software-808867/.

Dines, Gail. "Neo-Liberalism and the Defanging of Feminism." October 2, 2012. YouTube video. www.youtube.com/watch?v=kDcTtoemXhE.

Diss, Laura E. "Whether You 'Like' It or Not: The Inclusions of Social Media Evidence in Sexual Harassment Cases and How Courts Can Effectively Control It." *Boston College Law Review* 54, no. 4 (2013): 1841–80.

DiTirro, Tessa. "3 Accused of Raping Unconscious Teen at Mason Inn, Posting Video on Snapchat." *WKRC Local 12*, November 18, 2019. https://local12.com/news/local/3-accused-of-raping-unconscious-teen-at-mason-inn-posting-video-on-snapchat.

Dobson, Amy Shields. "Sexting, Intimate and Sexual Media Practices, and Social Justice." In *Digital Intimate Publics and Social Media*, edited by Amy Shields Dobson, Brady Robards, and Nicholas Carah, 93–110. Palgrave Studies in Communication for Social Change. Cham: Springer International, 2018.

Dobson, Amy Shields, and Jessica Ringrose. "Sext Education: Pedagogies of Sex, Gender and Shame in the Schoolyards of Tagged and Exposed." *Sex Education* 16, no. 1 (2016): 8–21. https://doi.org/10.1080/14681811.2015.1050486.

Dodge, Alexa. "Digitizing Rape Culture: Online Sexual Violence and the Power of the Digital Photograph." *Crime, Media, Culture* 12, no. 1 (2016): 65–82.

———. "Restorative Responses to the Rhizomatic Harm of Nonconsensual Pornography." In *The Palgrave Handbook of Gendered Violence and Technology*, edited by Anastasia Powell, Asher Flynn, and Lisa Suguira, 565–82. Cham: Springer International, 2021.

———. "Trading Nudes Like Hockey Cards: Exploring the Diversity of 'Revenge Porn' Cases Responded to in Law." *Social & Legal Studies* 30, no. 3 (2021): 448–68. https://doi.org/10.1177/0964663920935155.

Dodge, Alexa, and Emily Lockhart. "'Young People Just Resolve It in Their Own Group': Young People's Perspectives on Responses to Non-Consensual Intimate Image Distribution." *Youth Justice* 22, no.3 (2021): 304–19. https://doi.org/10.1177/14732254211030570.

Dodge, Alexa, and Dale C. Spencer. "Online Sexual Violence, Child Pornography or Something Else Entirely? Police Responses to Non-Consensual Intimate Image Sharing among Youth." *Social & Legal Studies* 27, no. 5 (2018): 636–57. https://doi.org/10.1177/0964663917724866.

Dodge, Alexa, Dale Spencer, Rose Ricciardelli, and Dale Ballucci. "'This Isn't Your Father's Police Force': Digital Evidence in Sexual Assault Investigations." *Australian & New Zealand Journal of Criminology* 52, no. 4 (2019): 499–515. https://doi.org/10.1177/0004865819851544.

Dragiewicz, Molly, Jean Burgess, Ariadna Matamoros-Fernández, Michael Salter, Nicolas P. Suzor, Delanie Woodlock, and Bridget Harris. "Technology Facilitated Coercive Control: Domestic Violence and the Competing Roles of Digital Media Platforms." *Feminist Media Studies* 18, no. 4 (2018): 609–25. https://doi.org/10.1080/14680777.2018.1447341.

Draper, Bill. "Mo. Man Accused of Rape Pleads to Lesser Charge." *Yahoo*, January 10, 2014. http://news.yahoo.com/mo-man-accused-rape-pleads-lesser-charge-203847769.html.

Draper, Nora R. A. "Is Your Teen at Risk? Discourses of Adolescent Sexting in United States Television News." *Journal of Children and Media* 6, no. 2 (2012): 221–36. https://doi.org/10.1080/17482798.2011.587147.

Dubrofsky, Rachel E., and Shoshana Amielle Magnet. *Feminist Surveillance Studies*. Durham, NC: Duke University Press, 2015.

Duckworth, Kiera D., and Mary Nell Trautner. "Gender Goals: Defining Masculinity and Navigating Peer Pressure to Engage in Sexual Activity." *Gender & Society* 33, no. 5 (2019): 795–817. https://doi.org/10.1177/0891243219863031.

Dunn, Hailee K., and Lindsay M. Orchowski. "Correlates of High School Boys' Intention to Garner Sexual Consent." *Journal of Interpersonal Violence* 37, nos. 21–22 (2021). https://doi.org/10.1177/08862605211042623.

Dunn, Suzie. "Is It Actually Violence? Framing Technology-Facilitated Abuse as Violence." In *The Emerald International Handbook of Technology-Facilitated*

Violence and Abuse, edited by Jane Bailey, Asher Flynn, and Nicola Henry, 25–45. Emerald Studies in Digital Crime, Technology and Social Harms. Bingley, UK: Emerald Publishing, 2021.

Easteal, Patricia L., Kate Holland, and Keziah Judd. "Enduring Themes and Silences in Media Portrayals of Violence against Women." *Women's Studies International Forum* 48 (2015): 103–13.

Eaton, Asia A., and Clare McGlynn. "The Psychology of Nonconsensual Porn: Understanding and Addressing a Growing Form of Sexual Violence." *Policy Insights from the Behavioral and Brain Sciences* 7, no. 2 (2020): 190–97. https://doi.org/10.1177/2372732220941534.

Edinburgh, Laurel, Julie Pape-Blabolil, Scott Harpin, and Elizabeth Saewyc. "Multiple Perpetrator Rape among Girls Evaluated at a Hospital-Based Child Advocacy Center: Seven Years of Reviewed Cases." *Child Abuse & Neglect* 38 (2014). https://doi.org/10.1016/j.chiabu.2014.05.008.

Edmond, Gary, Katherine Biber, Richard Kemp, and Glenn Porter. "Law's Looking Glass: Expert Identification Evidence Derived from Photographic and Video Images." *Current Issues in Criminal Justice* 20, no. 3 (2009): 337–77. https://doi.org/10.1080/10345329.2009.12035817.

Edwards, Katie M., Victoria L. Banyard, Stephanie N. Sessarego, Emily A. Waterman, Kimberly J. Mitchell, and Hong Chang. "Evaluation of a Bystander-Focused Interpersonal Violence Prevention Program with High School Students." *Prevention Science* 20, no. 4 (2019): 488–98. https://doi.org/10.1007/s11121-019-01000-w.

Estrich, Susan. *Real Rape: How the Legal System Victimizes Women Who Say No*. Cambridge, MA: Harvard University Press, 1987.

Fairbairn, Jordan, Rena Bivens, and Myrna Dawson. *Sexual Violence and Social Media: Building a Framework for Prevention*. Crime Prevention Ottawa, 2013.

Fairbairn, Jordan, and Dale Spencer. "Virtualized Violence and Anonymous Juries: Unpacking Steubenville's 'Big Red' Sexual Assault Case and the Role of Social Media." *Feminist Criminology* 13, no. 5 (2018): 477–97. https://doi.org/10.1177/1557085116687032.

Feigenson, Neal. "The Visual in Law: Some Problems for Legal Theory." *Law, Culture and the Humanities* 10, no. 1 (2014): 13–23. https://doi.org/10.1177/1743872111421126.

Ferré-Sadurní, Luis. "Teenager Accused of Rape Deserves Leniency Because He's from a 'Good Family,' Judge Says." *New York Times*, July 2, 2019. www.nytimes.com/2019/07/02/nyregion/judge-james-troiano-rape.html.

Fileborn, Bianca. "Justice 2.0: Street Harassment Victims' Use of Social Media and Online Activism as Sites of Informal Justice." *British Journal of Criminology* 57, no. 6 (2017): 1482–1501. https://doi.org/10.1093/bjc/azw093.

Fileborn, Bianca, and Rachel Loney-Howes. *#MeToo and the Politics of Social Change*. Cham: Springer International, 2019.

Filipovic, Jill. "'Revenge Porn' Is about Degrading Women Sexually and Professionally." *Guardian*, January 28, 2013. www.theguardian.com/commentisfree/2013/jan/28/revenge-porn-degrades-women.

Fine, Michelle. "Sexuality, Schooling, and Adolescent Females: The Missing Discourse of Desire." *Harvard Educational Review* 58, no. 1 (1988): 29–53. https://doi.org/10.17763/haer.58.1.u0468k1v2n2n8242.

Finkelhor, David, Anne Shattuck, Heather A. Turner, and Sherry L. Hamby. "The Lifetime Prevalence of Child Sexual Abuse and Sexual Assault Assessed in Late Adolescence." *Journal of Adolescent Health: Official Publication of the Society for Adolescent Medicine* 55, no. 3 (2014): 329–33. https://doi.org /10.1016/j.jadohealth.2013.12.026.

Firmin, Carlene. *Abuse between Young People: A Contextual Account.* New York: Routledge, 2017.

Flood, Dawn Rae. *Rape in Chicago: Race, Myth and the Courts.* Champaign: University of Illinois Press, 2012.

Flood, Michael. "Men, Sex, and Homosociality: How Bonds between Men Shape Their Sexual Relations with Women." *Men and Masculinities* 10, no. 3 (2008): 339–59.

Flynn, Asher, Nicola Henry, Anastasia Powell, Adrian Scott, Clare McGlynn, Erika Rackley, and Nicola Gavey. *Shattering Lives and Myths: Report on Image-Based Sexual Abuse.* June 2019. https://research.monash.edu /en/publications/shattering-lives-and-myths-report-on-image-based-sexual -abuse.

Fontecilla, Adrian. "The Ascendance of Social Media as Evidence." *Criminal Justice: Chicago* 28, no. 1 (2013): 55–56.

Franklin, Karen. "Enacting Masculinity: Antigay Violence and Group Rape as Participatory Theater." *Sexuality Research & Social Policy* 1, no. 2 (2004): 25–40. https://doi.org/10.1525/srsp.2004.1.2.25.

Fraser, Nancy. "Rethinking the Public Sphere: A Contribution to the Critique of Actually Existing Democracy." *Social Text*, nos. 25–26 (1990): 56–80. https://doi.org/10.2307/466240.

Freedman, Estelle. *No Turning Back: The History of Feminism and the Future of Women.* New York: Random House, 2007.

Frieden, Jonathan D., and Leigh M. Murray. "The Admissibility of Electronic Evidence under the Federal Rules of Evidence." *Review of Litigation* 29 (2011): 1–64.

Frohmann, Lisa. "Convictability and Discordant Locales: Reproducing Race, Class, and Gender Ideologies in Prosecutorial Decisionmaking." *Law & Society Review* 31, no. 3 (1997): 531–56.

———. "Discrediting Victims' Allegations of Sexual Assault: Prosecutorial Accounts of Case Rejections." *Social Problems* 38, no. 2 (1991): 213–26.

Garcia, Antero, Nicole Mirra, Ernest Morrell, Antonio Nieves Martinez, and D'Artagnan Scorza. "The Council of Youth Research: Critical Literacy and Civic Agency in the Digital Age." *Reading & Writing Quarterly* 31, no. 2 (2015): 151–67. https://doi.org/10.1080/10573569.2014.962203.

Gavey, Nicola. *Just Sex? The Cultural Scaffolding of Rape.* New York: Routledge, 2005.

George, Alexander L., and Andrew Bennett. *Case Studies and Theory Development in the Social Sciences.* Cambridge, MA: MIT Press, 2005.

Gewirtz-Meydan, Ateret, and David Finkelhor. "Sexual Abuse and Assault in a Large National Sample of Children and Adolescents." *Child Maltreatment* 25, no. 2 (2020): 203–14. https://doi.org/10.1177/1077559519873975.

Gillespie, Tarleton. *Custodians of the Internet: Platforms, Content Moderation, and the Hidden Decisions That Shape Social Media*. New Haven, CT: Yale University Press, 2018.

Gjika, Anna. "New Media, Old Paradigms: News Representations of Technology in Adolescent Sexual Assault." *Crime, Media, Culture* 16, no. 3 (2020): 415–30. https://doi.org/10.1177/1741659019873758.

Glasbeek, Amanda. "He Said, She Said, We Watched: Video Evidence in Sexual Assault Trials." In *The Palgrave Handbook of Gendered Violence and Technology*, edited by Anastasia Powell, Asher Flynn, and Lisa Sugiura, 441–59. Cham: Springer International, 2021.

Goff, Keli. "How We Can Prevent Another Steubenville." *Huffington Post* (blog), March 18, 2013. www.huffingtonpost.com/keli-goff/steubenville-trial_b_28 98152.html.

Goffman, Erving. *The Presentation of Self in Everyday Life*. New York: Anchor Books, 1959.

Gogolin, Greg. "The Digital Crime Tsunami." *Digital Investigation* 7 (2010): 3–8.

Goldberg, Carrie. "How Google Has Destroyed the Lives of Revenge Porn Victims." *New York Post*, August 17, 2019. https://nypost.com/2019/08/17/how -google-has-destroyed-the-lives-of-revenge-porn-victims/.

Goodison, Sean E., Robert C. Davis, and Brian A. Jackson. *Digital Evidence and the U.S. Criminal Justice System: Identifying Technology and Other Needs to More Effectively Acquire and Utilize Digital Evidence*. RAND Corporation, 2015. www.rand.org/pubs/research_reports/RR890.html.

Goodmark, Leigh. "Reimagining VAWA: Why Criminalization Is a Failed Policy and What a Non-Carceral VAWA Could Look Like." *Violence against Women* 27, no. 1 (2021): 84–101. https://doi.org/10.1177/1077801220949686.

Gotell, Lise. "Reassessing the Place of Criminal Law Reform in the Struggle Against Sexual Violence." In *Rape Justice: Beyond the Criminal Law*, edited by Anastasia Powell, Nicola Henry, and Asher Flynn, 53–71. London: Palgrave Macmillan UK, 2015.

Gottschalk, Marie. *The Prison and the Gallows: The Politics of Mass Incarceration in America*. Cambridge: Cambridge University Press, 2006.

Greig, Anne D., Jayne Taylor, and Tommy Mackay. *Doing Research with Children*. London: Sage, 2007.

Griffith, Janelle. "Facebook Video of Sexual Assault Found by Teenage Victim's Mother Leads to 7 Arrests." *NBC News*, September 3, 2020. www.nbcnews .com/news/us-news/facebook-video-sexual-assault-found-teenage-victim-s -mother-leads-n1239204.

Gross, Samuel R., Maurice Possley, and Klara Stephens. *Race and Wrongful Convictions in the United States*. The National Registry of Exonerations, Newkirk Center for Science and Society, 2017.

Grundy, Saida. "Lifting the Veil on Campus Sexual Assault: Morehouse College, Hegemonic Masculinity, and Revealing Racialized Rape Culture through the

Du Boisian Lens." *Social Problems* 68, no. 2 (2021): 226–49. https://doi.org/10.1093/socpro/spab001.

Hackworth, Lucy. "Limitations of 'Just Gender': The Need for an Intersectional Reframing of Online Harassment Discourse and Research." In *Mediating Misogyny: Gender, Technology, and Harassment*, edited by Jacqueline Ryan Vickery and Tracy Everbach, 51–70. Cham: Springer International, 2018.

Hamilton, Ashlee. "Is Justice Best Served Cold? A Transformative Approach to Revenge Porn." *UCLA Journal of Gender and Law* 25, no. 1 (2018). https://doi.org/10.5070/L3251040881.

Hargittai, Eszter, and Alice Marwick. "'What Can I Really Do?' Explaining the Privacy Paradox with Online Apathy." *International Journal of Communication* 10 (2016): 21.

Harkinson, Josh. "Exclusive: Meet the Woman Who Kicked Off Anonymous' Anti-Rape Operations." *Mother Jones* (blog), May 13, 2013. www.motherjones.com/politics/2013/05/anonymous-rape-steubenville-rehtaeh-parsons-oprollredroll-opjustice4rehtaeh/.

Harper, Randi Lee. "Putting out the Twitter Trashfire." *Medium* (blog), February 13, 2016. https://artplusmarketing.com/putting-out-the-twitter-trashfire-3ac6cb1af3e.

Harris, Bridget, and Laura Vitis. "Digital Intrusions: Technology, Spatiality and Violence against Women." *Journal of Gender-Based Violence* 4, no. 3 (2020): 325–41. https://doi.org/10.1332/239868020X15986402363663.

Harris, Bridget A. "Technology and Violence against Women." In *The Emerald Handbook of Feminism, Criminology and Social Change*, edited by Sandra Walklate, Kate Fitz-Gibbon, JaneMaree Maher, and Jude McCulloch, 317–36. Emerald Studies in Criminology, Feminism and Social Change. Bingley, UK: Emerald Publishing, 2020.

Harris, Chris. "3 People Charged for Allegedly Raping Teen Girl and Posting Video on Snapchat." *People*, July 8, 2020. https://people.com/crime/3-people-charged-allegedly-raping-teen-girl-and-posting-video-on-snapchat/.

Harvey, Laura, Jessica Ringrose, and Rosalind Gill. "Swagger, Ratings and Masculinity: Theorising the Circulation of Social and Cultural Value in Teenage Boys' Digital Peer Networks." *Sociological Research Online* 18, no. 4 (2013): 9.

Hasinoff, Amy Adele. *Sexting Panic: Rethinking Criminalization, Privacy, and Consent*. Champaign: University of Illinois Press, 2015.

Hauch, Grace. "Chicago Schools Mishandled Sex Abuse Claims, Violated Title IX: Probe." *USA Today*, September 12, 2019. www.usatoday.com/story/news/nation/2019/09/12/chicago-schools-mishandled-sex-abuse-claims-violated-title-ix-probe/2300861001/.

Heberle, Renee. "Deconstructive Strategies and the Movement against Sexual Violence." *Hypatia* 11, no. 4 (1996): 63–76. https://doi.org/10.1111/j.1527-2001.1996.tb01035.x.

Henry, Nicola, Asher Flynn, and Anastasia Powell. "Policing Image-Based Sexual Abuse: Stakeholder Perspectives." *Police Practice and Research* 19, no. 6 (2018): 565–81. https://doi.org/10.1080/15614263.2018.1507892.

Henry, Nicola, Clare McGlynn, Asher Flynn, Anastasia Powell, Kelly Johnson, and Adrian J. Scott. *Image-Based Sexual Abuse: A Study on the Causes and*

Consequences of Non-Consensual Nude Or Sexual Imagery. London: Routledge, 2020.

Henry, Nicola, and Anastasia Powell. "Embodied Harms: Gender, Shame, and Technology-Facilitated Sexual Violence." *Violence against Women* 21, no. 6 (2015): 758–79. https://doi.org/10.1177/1077801215576581.

Henry, Nicola, Anastasia Powell, and Asher Flynn. *Rape Justice: Beyond the Criminal Law*. Hampshire, UK: Springer, 2015.

Henry, Nicola, and Alice Witt. "Governing Image-Based Sexual Abuse: Digital Platform Policies, Tools, and Practices." In *The Emerald International Handbook of Technology-Facilitated Violence and Abuse*, edited by Jane Bailey, Asher Flynn, and Nicola Henry, 749–68. Bingley, UK: Emerald Publishing, 2021.

Herring, Susan C. "The Rhetorical Dynamics of Gender Harassment On-Line." *Information Society* 15, no. 3 (1999): 151–67. https://doi.org/10.1080/019722499128466.

Hess, Kristy, and Lisa Waller. "The Digital Pillory: Media Shaming of 'Ordinary' People for Minor Crimes." *Continuum* 28, no. 1 (2014): 101–11. https://doi.org/10.1080/10304312.2013.854868.

Hessick, Carissa Byrne. "The Limits of Child Pornography." *Indiana Law Journal* 89, no. 4 (2014): Article 4.

Hill, Kashmir. "Imagine Being on Trial: With Exonerating Evidence Trapped on Your Phone." *New York Times*, November 22, 2019. www.nytimes.com/2019/11/22/business/law-enforcement-public-defender-technology-gap.html.

Hinduja, Sameer, and Justin W. Patchin. "Digital Dating Abuse among a National Sample of U.S. Youth." *Journal of Interpersonal Violence* 36, nos. 23–24 (2021): 11088–108. https://doi.org/10.1177/0886260519897344.

Hirsch, Jennifer S., and Shamus Khan. *Sexual Citizens: A Landmark Study of Sex, Power, and Assault on Campus*. New York: W. W. Norton, 2020.

Hirsch, Jennifer S., Shamus R. Khan, Alexander Wamboldt, and Claude A. Mellins. "Social Dimensions of Sexual Consent among Cisgender Heterosexual College Students: Insights from Ethnographic Research." *Journal of Adolescent Health* 64, no. 1 (2019): 26–35. https://doi.org/10.1016/j.jadohealth.2018.06.011.

Hirsh, Jesse, and Kent Glowinski. *Surveillance and Spectacle: Eighty-Four Observations on Citizen Journalism, Social Media, Mobile Devices and Mobs*. Office of the Privacy Commissioner of Canada, November 2011. https://www.priv.gc.ca/en/opc-actions-and-decisions/research/explore-privacy-research/2011/cj_201111/.

Hlavka, Heather R. "Normalizing Sexual Violence: Young Women Account for Harassment and Abuse." *Gender and Society* 28, no. 3 (2014): 337–58.

Hlavka, Heather R., and Sameena Mulla. *Bodies in Evidence: Race, Gender, and Science in Sexual Assault Adjudication*. New York: NYU Press, 2021.

———. "'That's How She Talks': Animated Text Message Evidence in the Sexual Assault Trial." *Law & Society Review* 52, no. 2 (2018): 401–35.

Hobbs, Renee, and Amy Jensen. "The Past, Present, and Future of Media Literacy Education." *Journal of Media Literacy Education* 1, no. 1 (2013). https://digitalcommons.uri.edu/jmle/vol1/iss1/1.

Hockett, Jericho M., Sara J. Smith, Cathleen D. Klausing, and Donald A. Saucier. "Rape Myth Consistency and Gender Differences in Perceiving Rape Victims: A Meta-Analysis." *Violence against Women* 22, no. 2 (2016): 139–67. https://doi.org/10.1177/1077801215607359.

Hogan, Bernie. "The Presentation of Self in the Age of Social Media: Distinguishing Performances and Exhibitions Online." *Bulletin of Science, Technology & Society* 30, no. 6 (2010): 377–86.

Hohl, Katrin, and Elisabeth A. Stanko. "Complaints of Rape and the Criminal Justice System: Fresh Evidence on the Attrition Problem in England and Wales." *European Journal of Criminology* 12, no. 3 (2015): 324–41. https://doi.org/10.1177/1477370815571949.

Holley, Peter. "Chicago Police Have 'No Formal Suspects' in Teen's Alleged Sexual Assault on Facebook Live." *Washington Post*, March 22, 2017. www.washingtonpost.com/news/post-nation/wp/2017/03/21/police-say-dozens-watched-a-teens-sexual-assault-on-facebook-live-and-no-one-reported-it/.

hooks, bell. *Feminist Theory from Margin to Center*. London: South End Press, 1984.

Horeck, Tanya, Kaitlynn Mendes, and Jessica Ringrose. "Digital Defence in the Classroom: Developing Feminist School Guidance on Online Sexual Harassment for Under 18s." In *The Palgrave Handbook of Gendered Violence and Technology*, edited by Anastasia Powell, Asher Flynn, and Lisa Sugiura, 631–49. Cham: Springer International, 2021.

Hoxmeier, Jill C., Julia O'Connor, and Sarah McMahon. "'She Wasn't Resisting': Students' Barriers to Prosocial Intervention as Bystanders to Sexual Assault Risk Situations." *Violence against Women* 25, no. 4 (2019): 485–505. https://doi.org/10.1177/1077801218790697.

Hrick, Pam. "The Potential of Centralized and Statutorily Empowered Bodies to Advance a Survivor-Centered Approach to Technology-Facilitated Violence against Women." In *The Emerald International Handbook of Technology-Facilitated Violence and Abuse*, edited by Jane Bailey, Asher Flynn, and Nicola Henry, 595–615. Bingley, UK: Emerald Publishing, 2021.

Hymes, Robert W., Mary Leinart, Sandra Rowe, and William Rogers. "Acquaintance Rape: The Effect of Race of Defendant and Race of Victim on White Juror Decisions." *Journal of Social Psychology* 133, no. 5 (1993): 627–34. https://doi.org/10.1080/00224545.1993.9713917.

In the Matter of Ma'lik Richmond and Trenton W. Mays. The Court of Common Pleas of Jefferson County, Ohio, Juvenile Division (2012). www.framingpaterno.com/sites/default/files/13.01.08-Transcript_Preliminary_Hearing.pdf.

INCITE! Women of Color Against Violence. *Color of Violence: The INCITE! Anthology*. Durham, NC: Duke University Press, 2016.

Jackson, Stevi, and Sue Scott. "Sexual Antinomies in Late Modernity." *Sexualities* 7, no. 2 (2004): 233–84. https://doi.org/10.1177/1363460704042166.

James, Allison, Chris Jenks, and Alan Prout. *Theorizing Childhood*. Cambridge, UK: Polity, 1998.

James, Carrie. *Disconnected: Youth, New Media, and the Ethics Gap*. The John D. and Catherine T. MacArthur Foundation Series on Digital Media and Learning. Cambridge, MA: The MIT Press, 2014.

Jane, Emma A. "Feminist Flight and Fight Responses to Gendered Cyberhate." In *Gender, Technology and Violence*, edited by Marie Segrave and Laura Vitis, 14–27. London: Routledge, 2017.

Janzen, Sydney. "Amending Rape Shield Laws: Outdated Statutes Fail to Protect Victims on Social Media." *John Marshall Law Review* 48, no. 4 (2015): 1087–1118.

Jemielniak, Dariusz. "Breaking the Glass Ceiling on Wikipedia." *Feminist Review* 113, no. 1 (2016): 103–8. https://doi.org/10.1057/fr.2016.9.

Jewkes, Yvonne. *Media and Crime*. London: Sage, 2015.

Joh, Elizabeth E. "Automated Policing." *Ohio State Journal of Criminal Law* 15 (2018): 559–63.

Jones, Lisa M., and Kimberly J Mitchell. "Defining and Measuring Youth Digital Citizenship." *New Media & Society* 18, no. 9 (2016): 2063–79. https://doi.org/10.1177/1461444815577797.

Jones, Sam. "Protests in Spain as Five Men Cleared of Teenager's Gang Rape." *Guardian*, April 26, 2018. www.theguardian.com/world/2018/apr/26/protests-spain-five-men-cleared-of-teenagers-gang-rape-pamplona.

Jørgensen, Clara Rübner, Annalise Weckesser, Jerome Turner, and Alex Wade. "Young People's Views on Sexting Education and Support Needs: Findings and Recommendations from a UK-Based Study." *Sex Education* 19, no. 1 (2019): 25–40. https://doi.org/10.1080/14681811.2018.1475283.

Jozkowski, Kristen N., Tiffany L. Marcantonio, and Mary E. Hunt. "College Students' Sexual Consent Communication and Perceptions of Sexual Double Standards: A Qualitative Investigation." *Perspectives on Sexual and Reproductive Health* 49, no. 4 (2017): 237–44. https://doi.org/10.1363/psrh.12041.

Judge, Abigail M. "'Sexting' among U.S. Adolescents: Psychological and Legal Perspectives." *Harvard Review of Psychiatry* 20, no. 2 (2012): 86–96.

Katz, James E., and Mark A. Aakhus, eds. *Perpetual Contact: Mobile Communication, Private Talk, Public Performance*. Cambridge: Cambridge University Press, 2002.

Keen, Caroline. "Apathy, Convenience or Irrelevance? Identifying Conceptual Barriers to Safeguarding Children's Data Privacy." *New Media & Society* 24, no. 1 (2022): 50–69. https://doi.org/10.1177/1461444820960068.

Keierleber, Mark. "When Sexual-Violence Victims Attend K–12 Schools." *Atlantic*, August 10, 2017. www.the74million.org/article/forgotten-in-the-devos-debate-over-campus-sex-assaults-the-154-pending-k-12-investigations.

Keller, Jessalynn, Kaitlynn Mendes, and Jessica Ringrose. "Speaking 'Unspeakable Things': Documenting Digital Feminist Responses to Rape Culture." *Journal of Gender Studies* 27, no. 1 (2018): 22–36. https://doi.org/10.1080/09589236.2016.1211511.

Kelly, Liz. "Standing the Test of Time? Reflections on the Concept of the Continuum of Sexual Violence." In *Handbook on Sexual Violence*, edited by Jennifer Brown and Sandra Walklate, xvii–xxv. London: Routledge, 2012.

———. *Surviving Sexual Violence*. Cambridge, UK: Polity, 1988.

Kessler, Gary C. "Judges Awareness, Understanding, and Application of Digital Evidence." *Journal of Digital Forensics, Security & Law* 6, no. 1 (2011): 55–72. https://doi.org/10.15394/jdfsl.2011.1088.

Khan, Isaan. "Rape Victims Face FOUR Year Wait for Justice over Evidence Backlog." *Mail Online*, February 24, 2022. www.dailymail.co.uk/news /article-10545187/Rape-victims-face-FOUR-year-wait-justice-phone-evidence -backlog.html.

Killean, Rachel, Anne-Marie McAlinden, and Eithne Dowds. "Sexual Violence in the Digital Age: Replicating and Augmenting Harm, Victimhood and Blame." *Social & Legal Studies* 31, no. 6 (2022): 871–92. https://doi.org/10 .1177/09646639221086592.

Killias, Martin. "The Emergence of a New Taboo: The Desexualisation of Youth in Western Societies since 1800." *European Journal on Criminal Policy and Research* 8, no. 4 (2000): 459–77. https://doi.org/10.1023/A:1008792013662.

Kim, Mimi E. "The Carceral Creep: Gender-Based Violence, Race, and the Expansion of the Punitive State, 1973–1983." *Social Problems* 67, no. 2 (2020): 251–69. https://doi.org/10.1093/socpro/spz013.

Kimmel, Michael S. *The Gender of Desire: Essays on Male Sexuality.* Albany: SUNY Press, 2005.

Kingkade, Tyler. "Chicago Public Schools Routinely Mishandled Sexual Assault Cases and Violated Title IX: Experts Warn It's No Outlier." *The74million* (blog), September 18, 2019. www.the74million.org/article/chicago-public -schools-routinely-mishandled-sexual-assault-cases-and-violated-title-ix -experts-warn-its-no-outlier/.

———. "High Schools Are Failing Girls Who Report Sexual Assault." *Huff-Post* (blog), March 17, 2016. www.huffpost.com/entry/high-schools-sexual -assault-investigations_n_56e05a06e4b065e2e3d45f6f.

———. "Schools Keep Punishing Girls—Especially Students of Color—Who Report Sexual Assaults, and the Trump Administration's Title IX Reforms Won't Stop It." *The74million* (blog), August 6, 2019. www.the74million .org/article/schools-keep-punishing-girls-especially-students-of-color-who -report-sexual-assaults-and-the-trump-administrations-title-ix-reforms -wont-stop-it/.

Kinlaw, Alisha. "A Snap of Justice: Carving Out a Space for Revenge Porn Victims within the Criminal Justice System." *Temple Law Review*, no. 2 (2019): 407–46.

Klonick, Kate. "The New Governors: The People, Rules, and Processes Governing Online Speech." *Harvard Law Review* 131 (2018): 1598–1670.

Kohm, Steven A. "Naming, Shaming and Criminal Justice: Mass-Mediated Humiliation as Entertainment and Punishment." *Crime, Media, Culture: An International Journal* 5, no. 2 (2009): 188–205. https://doi.org/10.1177 /1741659009335724.

Konradi, Amanda. *Taking the Stand: Rape Survivors and the Prosecution of Rapists.* Westport, CT: Praeger, 2007.

Koss, Mary P. "The RESTORE Program of Restorative Justice for Sex Crimes: Vision, Process, and Outcomes." *Journal of Interpersonal Violence* 29, no. 9 (2014): 1623–60. https://doi.org/10.1177/0886260513511537.

———. "Restoring Rape Survivors: Justice, Advocacy, and a Call to Action." *Annals of the New York Academy of Sciences* 1087 (2006): 206–34. https:// doi.org/10.1196/annals.1385.025.

Krueger, Richard A., and Mary Anne Casey. *Focus Groups: A Practical Guide for Applied Research*. 4th ed. Thousand Oaks, CA: Sage, 2009.

Kushner, Alexandra. "The Need for Sexting Law Reform: Appropriate Punishments for Teenage Behaviors." *University of Pennsylvania Journal of Law and Social Change* 16, no. 3 (2013): 281.

La Ganga, Maria L., and Kate Mather. "More Twists in Audrie Pott Case." *Los Angeles Times*, April 15, 2013. http://articles.latimes.com/2013/apr/15/local/la-me-audrie-pott-20130416.

Lamb, Sharon, Elena V. Kosterina, Tangela Roberts, Madeline Brodt, Meredith Maroney, and Lucas Dangler. "Voices of the Mind: Hegemonic Masculinity and Others in Mind during Young Men's Sexual Encounters." *Men and Masculinities* 21, no. 2 (2017): 254–75. https://doi.org/10.1177/1097184X17695038.

Lane, Jeffrey, Fanny A. Ramirez, and Katy E. Pearce. "Guilty by Visible Association: Socially Mediated Visibility in Gang Prosecutions." *Journal of Computer-Mediated Communication* 23, no. 6 (2018): 354–69. https://doi.org/10.1093/jcmc/zmy019.

Lane, Jeffrey, Fanny Anne Ramirez, and Desmond Upton Patton. "Defending against Social Media: How Public Criminal Defense Helps Us Address Social Media Governance." *AoIR Selected Papers of Internet Research*, October 5, 2020. https://doi.org/10.5210/spir.v2020i0.11256.

Lang, Nico. "We Need to Talk about Steubenville." *Huffington Post* (blog), March 25, 2013. www.huffingtonpost.com/nico-lang/steubenville-rape-culture_b_2944752.html.

Langlois, Ganaele, and Andrea Slane. "Economies of Reputation: The Case of Revenge Porn." *Communication and Critical/Cultural Studies* 14, no. 2 (2017): 120–38. https://doi.org/10.1080/14791420.2016.1273534.

Langston, Jennifer. "How PhotoDNA for Video Is Being Used to Fight Online Child Exploitation." *Microsoft/On the Issues* (blog), September 12, 2018. https://news.microsoft.com/on-the-issues/2018/09/12/how-photodna-for-video-is-being-used-to-fight-online-child-exploitation/.

Larcombe, Wendy. "Falling Rape Conviction Rates: (Some) Feminist Aims and Measures for Rape Law." *Feminist Media Studies* 19 (2011): 27–45. https://doi.org/10.1007/s10691-011-9169-2.

Lawson, Caitlin E. "Platform Vulnerabilities: Harassment and Misogynoir in the Digital Attack on Leslie Jones." *Information, Communication & Society* 21, no. 6 (2018): 818–33. https://doi.org/10.1080/1369118X.2018.1437203.

Leavy, Patricia. "Why Girls and Women Participate in Rape Culture: More Lessons from Steubenville." *Huffington Post* (blog), March 20, 2013. www.huffingtonpost.com/patricia-leavy-phd/why-girls-and-women-parti_b_2909542.html.

Lefkowitz, Bernard. *Our Guys: The Glenn Ridge Rape and the Secret Life of the Perfect Suburb*. Berkeley: University of California Press, 1997.

Legal Services NYC. "NYC Schools Required to Change Sexual Assault Policies, Pay Survivors $700,000, and Provide Additional Educational Supports to Impacted Students in New Settlement." *Legal Services NYC* (blog), August 24, 2021. www.legalservicesnyc.org/news-and-events/press-room

/1701-nyc-schools-required-to-make-changes-to-sexual-assault-policies
-pay-survivors-700000-and-provide-additional-education-supports-in-new
-settlement.

Levy, Ariel. "Trial by Twitter." *New Yorker*, July 29, 2013. www.newyorker.com
/magazine/2013/08/05/trial-by-twitter.

Ley, Tom. "'She Is So Raped Right Now': Partygoer Jokes about the Steubenville
Accuser the Night of the Alleged Rape." *Deadspin* (blog), January 2, 2013.
https://deadspin.com/she-is-so-raped-right-now-partygoer-jokes-about-the
-5972527.

Lezon, Dale. "2 Suspects Arrested in #jadapose Rape Case." *Houston Chronicle*,
December 17, 2014. www.chron.com/houston/article/2-suspects-arrested-in
-jadapose-rape-case-5963112.php.

Lichty, Lauren F., and L. Kris Gowen. "Youth Response to Rape: Rape Myths
and Social Support." *Journal of Interpersonal Violence* 36, nos. 11–12
(2021): 5530–57. https://doi.org/10.1177/0886260518805777.

Lim, Megan S. C., Elise R. Carrotte, and Margaret E. Hellard. "The Impact
of Pornography on Gender-Based Violence, Sexual Health and Well-Being:
What Do We Know?" *Journal of Epidemiology and Community Health* 70,
no. 1 (2016): 3–5. https://doi.org/10.1136/jech-2015-205453.

Lim, Sun Sun, Shobha Vadrevu, Yoke Hian Chan, and Iccha Basnyat. "Facework
on Facebook: The Online Publicness of Juvenile Delinquents and Youths-at-
Risk." *Journal of Broadcasting & Electronic Media* 56, no. 3 (2012): 346–
61. https://doi.org/10.1080/08838151.2012.705198.

Lim, Wei Ying, Chun Ming Tan, Muhamad Nizam, Wencong Zhou, and Swee
Meng Tan. "Toward Digital Citizenship in Primary Schools: Leveraging on
Our Enhanced Cyberwellness Framework." In *Future Learning in Primary
Schools*, edited by Ching Sing Chai, Cher Ping Lim, and Chun Ming Tan,
97–108. Singapore: Springer, 2016.

Lippman, Julia R., and Scott W. Campbell. "Damned If You Do, Damned If You
Don't . . . If You're a Girl: Relational and Normative Contexts of Adolescent
Sexting in the United States." *Journal of Children and Media* 8, no. 4 (2014):
371–86. https://doi.org/10.1080/17482798.2014.923009.

Lisak, David, Lori Gardinier, Sarah C. Nicksa, and Ashley M. Cote. "False Allegations of Sexual Assault: An Analysis of Ten Years of Reported Cases." *Violence against Women* 16, no. 12 (2010): 1318–34. https://doi.org/10.1177
/1077801210387747.

Livingstone, Sonia, and David R. Brake. "On the Rapid Rise of Social Networking Sites: New Findings and Policy Implications." *Children & Society* 24
(2010): 75–83.

Lloyd, Jenny. "Abuse through Sexual Image Sharing in Schools: Response and
Responsibility." *Gender and Education* 32, no. 6 (2020): 784–802. https://
doi.org/10.1080/09540253.2018.1513456.

Loewen, Kim. "Rejecting the Purity Myth: Reforming Rape Shield Laws in the
Age of Social Media." *UCLA Journal of Gender and Law* 22, no. 2 (2015).
https://doi.org/10.5070/L3222028849.

Loney-Howes, Rachel. *Online Anti-Rape Activism: Exploring the Politics of the
Personal in the Age of Digital Media*. Bingley, UK: Emerald Publishing, 2020.

Losavio, Michael, Kathryn C. Seigfried-Spellar, and John J. Sloan. "Why Digital Forensics Is Not a Profession and How It Can Become One." *Criminal Justice Studies* 29, no. 2 (2016): 143–62. https://doi.org/10.1080/1478601X.2016.1170281.

Loughnan, Steve, Nick Haslam, Tess Murnane, Jeroen Vaes, Catherine Reynolds, and Caterina Suitner. "Objectification Leads to Depersonalization: The Denial of Mind and Moral Concern to Objectified Others." *European Journal of Social Psychology* 40, no. 5 (2010): 709–17. https://doi.org/10.1002/ejsp.755.

Lumsden, Karen, and Emily Harmer. *Online Othering: Exploring Digital Violence and Discrimination on the Web.* Cham: Springer International, 2020.

Lynch, Mona. *Hard Bargains: The Coercive Power of Drug Laws in Federal Court.* New York: Russell Sage Foundation, 2016.

Mack, Ashley Noel, and Bryan J. McCann. "Critiquing State and Gendered Violence in the Age of #MeToo." *Quarterly Journal of Speech* 104, no. 3 (2018): 329–44. https://doi.org/10.1080/00335630.2018.1479144.

Macur, Juliet, and Nate Schweber. "Rape Case Unfolds Online and Divides Steubenville." *New York Times*, December 16, 2012. www.nytimes.com/2012/12/17/sports/high-school-football-rape-case-unfolds-online-and-divides-steubenville-ohio.html.

Madigan, Sheri, Anh Ly, Christina L. Rash, Joris Van Ouytsel, and Jeff R. Temple. "Prevalence of Multiple Forms of Sexting Behavior among Youth: A Systematic Review and Meta-Analysis." *JAMA Pediatrics* 172, no. 4 (2018): 327–35. https://doi.org/10.1001/jamapediatrics.2017.5314.

Maier, Shana L. *Rape, Victims, and Investigations: Experiences and Perceptions of Law Enforcement Officers Responding to Reported Rapes.* London: Routledge, 2014.

Manay, Natalia, and Delphine Collin-Vézina. "Recipients of Children's and Adolescents' Disclosures of Childhood Sexual Abuse: A Systematic Review." *Child Abuse & Neglect* 116, no. 1 (2021). https://doi.org/10.1016/j.chiabu.2019.104192.

Mandau, Morten Birk Hansen. "'Directly in Your Face': A Qualitative Study on the Sending and Receiving of Unsolicited 'Dick Pics' among Young Adults." *Sexuality & Culture* 24, no. 1 (2020): 72–93. https://doi.org/10.1007/s12119-019-09626-2.

Marques, Olga. "Intimate Image Dissemination and Consent in a Digital Age: Perspectives from the Front Line." In *The Emerald International Handbook of Technology-Facilitated Violence and Abuse*, edited by Jane Bailey, Asher Flynn, and Nicola Henry, 309–28. Bingley, UK: Emerald Publishing, 2021.

Marshall, P. David. *Celebrity and Power: Fame in Contemporary Culture.* Minneapolis: University of Minnesota Press, 2014.

Martellozzo, Elena, Andrew Monaghan, Julia Davidson, and Joanna Adler. "Researching the Affects That Online Pornography Has on U.K. Adolescents Aged 11 to 16." *Sage Open* 10, no. 1 (2020). https://doi.org/10.1177/2158244019899462.

Martin, Rachel. "Social Media Posts May Complicate Prosecution of Sexual Assault." *NPR*, November 20, 2017. www.npr.org/2017/11/20/565288712/social-media-posts-may-complicate-prosecution-of-sexual-assault.

Marwick, Alice, Claire Fontaine, and danah boyd. "'Nobody Sees It, Nobody Gets Mad': Social Media, Privacy, and Personal Responsibility among Low-SES Youth." *Social Media + Society* 3, no. 2 (2017). https://doi.org/10.1177/2056305117710455.

Massanari, Adrienne. "#Gamergate and The Fappening: How Reddit's Algorithm, Governance, and Culture Support Toxic Technocultures." *New Media & Society* 19, no. 3 (2017): 329–46. https://doi.org/10.1177/1461444815608807.

Matamoros-Fernández, Ariadna. "Platformed Racism: The Mediation and Circulation of an Australian Race-Based Controversy on Twitter, Facebook and YouTube." *Information, Communication & Society* 20, no. 6 (2017): 930–46. https://doi.org/10.1080/1369118X.2017.1293130.

Mateescu, Alexandra, Douglas Brunton, Alex Rosenblat, Desmond Patton, Zachary Gold, and danah boyd. "Social Media Surveillance and Law Enforcement." *Data & Civil Rights*, October 27, 2015. www.datacivilrights.org/2015/.

Mathen, Carissima. "Crowdsourcing Sexual Objectification." *Laws* 3 (2014): 529–52.

McClennen, Joan C., Anne B. Summers, and Charles Vaughan. "Gay Men's Domestic Violence." *Journal of Gay & Lesbian Social Services* 14, no. 1 (2002): 23–49.

McGlynn, Clare, Julia Downes, and Nicole Westmarland. "Seeking Justice for Survivors of Sexual Violence: Recognition, Voice and Consequences." In *Restorative Responses to Sexual Violence: Legal, Social and Therapeutic Dimensions*, edited by Marie Keenan and Estelle Zinsstag, 179–91. London: Routledge, 2017.

McGlynn, Clare, Kelly Johnson, Erika Rackley, Nicola Henry, Nicola Gavey, Asher Flynn, and Anastasia Powell. "'It's Torture for the Soul': The Harms of Image-Based Sexual Abuse." *Social & Legal Studies* 30, no. 4 (2021): 541–62. https://doi.org/10.1177/0964663920947791.

McGlynn, Clare, and Erika Rackley. "Image-Based Sexual Abuse." *Oxford Journal of Legal Studies* 37, no. 3 (2017): 534–61. https://doi.org/10.1093/ojls/gqw033.

McGlynn, Clare, Erika Rackley, and Ruth Houghton. "Beyond 'Revenge Porn': The Continuum of Image-Based Sexual Abuse." *Feminist Legal Studies* 25, no. 1 (2017): 25–46. https://doi.org/10.1007/s10691-017-9343-2.

McGlynn, Clare, and Nicole Westmarland. "Kaleidoscopic Justice: Sexual Violence and Victim-Survivors' Perceptions of Justice." *Social & Legal Studies* 28, no. 2 (2018): 1–23. https://doi.org/10.1177/0964663918761200.

McGovern, Alyce, Thomas Crofts, Murray Lee, and Sanja Milivojevic. "Media, Legal and Young People's Discourses around Sexting." *Global Studies of Childhood* 6, no. 4 (2016): 428–41. https://doi.org/10.1177/2043610616676028.

McMillan, Lesley. "Police Officers' Perceptions of False Allegations of Rape." *Journal of Gender Studies* 27, no. 1 (2018): 9–21.

McNamara, Brittney. "This Is Why You Shouldn't Trash Talk Sexual Assault Survivors." *Teen Vogue*, April 3, 2017. www.teenvogue.com/story/safe-baa-quit-it-sexual-assault-trash-talking-awareness-campaign.

Mead, George Herbert. *Mind, Self, and Society*. Chicago: University of Chicago Press, 1934.

Meehan, Claire. "'It's Like Mental Rape I Guess': Young New Zealanders' Responses to Image-Based Sexual Abuse." In *The Palgrave Handbook of Gendered Violence and Technology*, edited by Anastasia Powell, Asher Flynn, and Lisa Sugiura, 281–95. Cham: Springer International, 2021.

Mendes, Kaitlynn, Jessica Ringrose, and Jessalynn Keller. "#MeToo and the Promise and Pitfalls of Challenging Rape Culture through Digital Feminist Activism." *European Journal of Women's Studies* 25, no. 2 (2018): 236–46. https://doi.org/10.1177/1350506818765318.

Mendoza, Martha. "Lawyer: Assaulted Teen Had Drawings, Name on Body." *Associated Press*, April 15, 2013. www.apnews.com/8e2ddfb8f31446e9a7 b90a99cf4863eb.

Messerschmidt, James W. *Gender, Heterosexuality, and Youth Violence: The Struggle for Recognition*. Lanham, MD: Rowman & Littlefield, 2012.

Messner, Michael A. *Taking the Field: Women, Men, and Sports*. Minneapolis: University of Minnesota Press, 2002.

Meyer, Elizabeth J., and Andrea Somoza-Norton. "Addressing Sex Discrimination with Title IX Coordinators in the #MeToo Era." *Phi Delta Kappan* 100, no. 2 (2018): 8–11. https://doi.org/10.1177/0031721718803562.

Miller, Elizabeth, Kelley A. Jones, Lisa Ripper, Taylor Paglisotti, Paul Mulbah, and Kaleab Z. Abebe. "An Athletic Coach–Delivered Middle School Gender Violence Prevention Program: A Cluster Randomized Clinical Trial." *JAMA Pediatrics* 174, no. 3 (2020): 241–49. https://doi.org/10.1001/jamapediatrics .2019.5217.

Miller, Jody. *Getting Played: African American Girls, Urban Inequality, and Gendered Violence*. New York: NYU Press, 2008.

Mnookin, Jennifer L. "The Image of Truth: Photographic Evidence and the Power of Analogy." *Yale Journal of Law & the Humanities* 10, no. 1 (1998): 1–75.

Moore, Dawn, and Rashmee Singh. "Seeing Crime, Feeling Crime: Visual Evidence, Emotions, and the Prosecution of Domestic Violence." *Theoretical Criminology* 22, no. 1 (2018): 116–32.

Moreno, Megan A., Leslie R. Briner, Amanda Williams, Leslie Walker, and Dimitri A. Christakis. "Real Use or 'Real Cool': Adolescents Speak Out about Displayed Alcohol References on Social Networking Websites." *Journal of Adolescent Health* 45, no. 4 (2009): 420–22. https://doi.org/10.1016 /j.jadohealth.2009.04.015.

Morgan, Rachel E., and Alexandra Thompson. *Criminal Victimization, 2020*. Bureau of Justice Statistics, October 2021. https://bjs.ojp.gov/library/publications /criminal-victimization-2020.

Naezer, Marijke, and Lotte van Oosterhout. "Only Sluts Love Sexting: Youth, Sexual Norms and Non-Consensual Sharing of Digital Sexual Images." *Journal of Gender Studies* 30, no. 1 (2021): 79–90. https://doi.org/10.1080 /09589236.2020.1799767.

Naffine, Ngaire. *Feminism and Criminology*. London: Wiley, 2014.

Nagel, Barbara, Hisako Matsuo, Kevin Mcintyre, and Nancy Morrison. "Attitudes toward Victims of Rape: Effects of Gender, Race, Religion, and Social

Class." *Journal of Interpersonal Violence* 20, no. 6 (2005): 725–37. https://doi.org/10.1177/0886260505276072.

Nagle, Angela. *Kill All Normies: Online Culture Wars from 4Chan and Tumblr to Trump and the Alt-Right.* Winchester, UK: Zero Books, 2017.

Nagy, Peter, and Gina Neff. "Imagined Affordance: Reconstructing a Keyword for Communication Theory." *Social Media + Society* 1, no. 2 (2015): 1–9.

Novak, Martin. "Improving the Collection of Digital Evidence." *National Institute of Justice* (blog), December 16, 2021. https://nij.ojp.gov/topics/articles/improving-collection-digital-evidence.

Noveck, Jocelyn. "Social Media Double-Edged Sword in Steubenville Rape Case." *NBC News*, March 19, 2013. www.nbcnews.com/tech/tech-news/social-media-double-edged-sword-steubenville-rape-case-flna1c8958979.

Oliver, Kelly. "Rape as Spectator Sport and Creepshot Entertainment: Social Media and the Valorization of Lack of Consent." *American Studies Journal*, no. 10 (2015): 1–16.

O'Neill, Tully. "'Today I Speak': Exploring How Victim-Survivors Use Reddit." *International Journal for Crime, Justice and Social Democracy* 7, no. 1 (2018): 44–59. http://dx.doi.org/10.5204/ijcjsd.v7i1.402.

Oppel, Richard A. "Ohio Teenagers Guilty in Rape That Social Media Brought to Light." *New York Times*, March 17, 2013. www.nytimes.com/2013/03/18/us/teenagers-found-guilty-in-rape-in-steubenville-ohio.html.

Pangrazio, Luci, and Neil Selwyn. "'It's Not Like It's Life or Death or Whatever': Young People's Understandings of Social Media Data." *Social Media + Society* 4, no. 3 (2018). https://doi.org/10.1177/2056305118787808.

Park, Chang Sup, and Barbara K. Kaye. "Smartphone and Self-Extension: Functionally, Anthropomorphically, and Ontologically Extending Self via the Smartphone." *Mobile Media & Communication* 7, no. 2 (2019): 215–31. https://doi.org/10.1177/2050157918808327.

Pavan, Elena. "Internet Intermediaries and Online Gender-Based Violence." In *Gender, Technology and Violence*, edited by Marie Segrave and Laura Vitis, 62–78. London: Routledge, 2017.

Pearson, Michael. "Steubenville, Weary of Investigation, Not Done Yet." *CNN*, March 18, 2013. www.cnn.com/2013/03/18/justice/ohio-steubenville-case/index.html.

Pecsenye, Magda. "A Letter to My Sons about Stopping Rape." *Huffington Post* (blog), March 18, 2013. www.huffingtonpost.com/magda-pecsenye/steubenville-rape-mother-letter_b_2902943.html.

Pennington, Rosemary, and Jessica Birthisel. "When New Media Make News: Framing Technology and Sexual Assault in the Steubenville Rape Case." *New Media & Society* 18, no. 11 (2016): 2435–51. https://doi.org/10.1177/1461444815612407.

Penny, Laurie. "This Is Rape Culture's Abu Ghraib Moment." *New Statesman*, March 19, 2013. www.newstatesman.com/laurie-penny/2013/03/steubenville-rape-cultures-abu-ghraib-moment.

Pesta, Abigail. "'Thanks for Ruining My Life.'" *Newsweek*, December 10, 2012. www.newsweek.com/thanks-ruining-my-life-63423.

Peter, Jochen, and Patti M. Valkenburg. "Adolescents and Pornography: A Review of 20 Years of Research." *Journal of Sex Research* 53, nos. 4–5 (2016): 509–31. https://doi.org/10.1080/00224499.2016.1143441.

Pfaff, John. *Locked In: The True Causes of Mass Incarceration—and How to Achieve Real Reform*. New York: Basic Books, 2017.

Phillips, Nickie D. *Beyond Blurred Lines: Rape Culture in Popular Media*. Lanham, MD: Rowman & Littlefield, 2017.

Phillips, Nickie D., and Nicholas Chagnon. "'Six Months Is a Joke': Carceral Feminism and Penal Populism in the Wake of the Stanford Sexual Assault Case." *Feminist Criminology* 15, no. 1 (2020): 47–69. https://doi.org/10.1177/1557085118789782.

Pollack, Wendy. "Student Survivors of Violence Are Saying #MeToo: When Will We Listen?" *Shriver Center on Poverty Law* (blog), January 7, 2019. www.povertylaw.org/article/student-survivors-of-violence-are-saying-metoo-when-will-we-listen/.

Powell, Anastasia. "Seeking Rape Justice: Formal and Informal Responses to Sexual Violence through Technosocial Counter-Publics." *Theoretical Criminology* 19, no. 4 (2015): 571–88. https://doi.org/10.1177/1362480615576271.

Powell, Anastasia, and Nicola Henry. *Sexual Violence in a Digital Age*. London: Palgrave Macmillan, 2017.

Pugliese, Joseph. "Abu Ghraib and Its Shadow Archives." *Law and Literature* 19, no. 2 (2007): 247–76. https://doi.org/10.1525/lal.2007.19.2.247.

Pyrooz, David C., Scott H. Decker, and Richard K. Moule Jr. "Criminal and Routine Activities in Online Settings: Gangs, Offenders, and the Internet." *Justice Quarterly* 32, no. 3 (2015): 471–99.

Rackley, Erika, Clare McGlynn, Kelly Johnson, Nicola Henry, Nicola Gavey, Asher Flynn, and Anastasia Powell. "Seeking Justice and Redress for Victim-Survivors of Image-Based Sexual Abuse." *Feminist Legal Studies* 29, no. 3 (2021): 293–322. https://doi.org/10.1007/s10691-021-09460-8.

RAINN. "Victims of Sexual Violence: Statistics." Accessed May 12, 2022. www.rainn.org/statistics/victims-sexual-violence.

Ramirez, Fanny. "The Digital Divide in the US Criminal Justice System." *New Media & Society* 24, no. 2 (2022): 514–29. https://doi.org/10.1177/14614448211063190.

Ramirez, Fanny, Vincent Denault, Sarah Carpenter, and Jessica Wyers. "'But Her Age Was Not Given on Her Facebook Profile': Minors, Social Media, and Sexual Assault Trials." *Information, Communication & Society* 25, no. 15 (2022): 2282–98. https://doi.org/10.1080/1369118X.2021.1934065.

Randall, Melanie. "Sexual Assault Law, Credibility, and 'Ideal Victims': Consent, Resistance, and Victim Blaming." *Canadian Journal of Women and the Law* 22, no. 2 (2010): 397–433.

Ransom, Jan. "'Nobody Believed Me': How Rape Cases Get Dropped." *New York Times*, July 18, 2021. www.nytimes.com/2021/07/18/nyregion/manhattan-da-rape-cases-dropped.html.

Ravn, Signe, Julia Coffey, and Steven Roberts. "The Currency of Images: Risk, Value and Gendered Power Dynamics in Young Men's Accounts of Sexting."

Feminist Media Studies 21, no. 2 (2021): 315–31. https://doi.org/10.1080 /14680777.2019.1642229.

Reed, Lauren A., Siobhan M. Lawler, Jenny McCullough Cosgrove, Richard M. Tolman, and L. Monique Ward. "'It Was a Joke:' Patterns in Girls' and Boys' Self-Reported Motivations for Digital Dating Abuse Behaviors." *Children and Youth Services Review* 122 (2021): 105883. https://doi.org/10.1016/j .childyouth.2020.105883.

Reed, T. V. *Digitized Lives: Culture, Power and Social Change in the Internet Era*. 2nd ed. New York: Routledge, 2018.

Regehr, Kaitlyn, Arija Birze, and Cheryl Regehr. "Technology Facilitated Re-Victimization: How Video Evidence of Sexual Violence Contributes to Mediated Cycles of Abuse." *Crime, Media, Culture* 18, no. 4 (2021): 597–615. https://doi.org/10.1177/17416590211050333.

Rentschler, Carrie A. "Rape Culture and the Feminist Politics of Social Media." *Girlhood Studies* 7, no. 1 (2014): 65–82. https://doi.org/10.3167/ghs.2014 .070106.

Rich, Adrienne. "Compulsory Heterosexuality and Lesbian Existence." *Signs* 5, no. 4 (1980): 631–60.

Richie, Beth E. *Arrested Justice*. New York: NYU Press, 2012.

Richie, Beth E., Valli Kalei Kanuha, and Kayla Marie Martensen. "Colluding with and Resisting the State: Organizing against Gender Violence in the U.S." *Feminist Criminology* 16, no. 3 (2021): 247–65. https://doi.org/10.1177/155 7085120987607.

Righi, Mary Kirtley, Katherine W. Bogen, Caroline Kuo, and Lindsay M. Orchowski. "A Qualitative Analysis of Beliefs about Sexual Consent among High School Students." *Journal of Interpersonal Violence* 36, nos. 15–16 (2021). https://doi.org/10.1177/0886260519842855.

Ringrose, Jessica, Laura Harvey, Rosalind Gill, and Sonia Livingstone. "Teen Girls, Sexual Double Standards and 'Sexting': Gendered Value in Digital Image Exchange." *Feminist Theory* 14, no. 3 (2013): 305–23. https://doi.org /10.1177/1464700113499853.

Ringrose, Jessica, Katilyn Regehr, and Sophie Whitehead. "'Wanna Trade?': Cis-heteronormative Homosocial Masculinity and the Normalization of Abuse in Youth Digital Sexual Image Exchange." *Journal of Gender Studies* 31, no. 2 (2021): 243–61. https://doi.org/10.1080/09589236.2021.1947206.

Roberts, Sarah T. *Behind the Screen*. New Haven, CT: Yale University Press, 2019.

Robinson, Kerry. "Reinforcing Hegemonic Masculinities through Sexual Harassment: Issues of Identity, Power and Popularity in Secondary Schools." *Gender & Education* 17, no. 1 (2005): 19–37. https://doi.org/10.1080/0954 02504200301285.

Robinson, Laura. "The Cyberself: The Self-Ing Project Goes Online: Symbolic Interaction in the Digital Age." *New Media & Society* 9, no. 1 (2007): 93–110.

Rodríguez-Castro, Yolanda, Rosana Martínez-Román, Patricia Alonso-Ruido, Alba Adá-Lameiras, and María Victoria Carrera-Fernández. "Intimate Partner Cyberstalking, Sexism, Pornography, and Sexting in Adolescents: New

Challenges for Sex Education." *International Journal of Environmental Research and Public Health* 18, no. 4 (2021): 2181. https://doi.org/10.3390 /ijerph18042181.

Roeder, Tara. "'You Have to Confess': Rape and the Politics of Storytelling." *Journal of Feminist Scholarship* 9, no. Fall (2015): 18–29.

Rogers, Leoandra Onnie, Marc A. Scott, and Niobe Way. "Racial and Gender Identity among Black Adolescent Males: An Intersectionality Perspective." *Child Development* 86, no. 2 (2015): 407–24. https://doi.org/10.1111/cdev .12303.

Rostad, Whitney L., Daniel Gittins-Stone, Charlie Huntington, Christie J. Rizzo, Deborah Pearlman, and Lindsay Orchowski. "The Association between Exposure to Violent Pornography and Teen Dating Violence in Grade 10 High School Students." *Archives of Sexual Behavior* 48, no. 7 (2019): 2137–47. https://doi.org/10.1007/s10508-019-1435-4.

Rumney, Philip, and Duncan McPhee. "The Evidential Value of Electronic Communications Data in Rape and Sexual Offences Cases." *Criminal Law Review*, no. 1 (2021): 20–33. https://doi.org/10.3316/agispt.20210401044144.

Russell, Scott, and Diane Crocker. "The Institutionalisation of Restorative Justice in Schools: A Critical Sensemaking Account:" *Restorative Justice* 4 (2016): 195–213. https://doi.org/10.1080/20504721.2016.1197524.

Safronova, Valeriya, and Rebecca Halleck. "These Rape Victims Had to Sue to Get the Police to Investigate." *New York Times*, May 23, 2019. www.nytimes .com/2019/05/23/us/rape-victims-kits-police-departments.html.

Salinas, Sara. "Facebook Says It Made an A.I. Tool That Can Detect Revenge Porn before It's Reported." *CNBC* (blog), March 15, 2019. www.cnbc.com /2019/03/15/facebook-ai-tool-detects-revenge-porn-before-its-reported .html.

Salter, Michael. *Crime, Justice and Social Media*. London: Routledge, 2017.

———. "Justice and Revenge in Online Counter-Publics: Emerging Responses to Sexual Violence in the Age of Social Media." *Crime, Media, Culture* 9, no. 3 (2013): 225–42. https://doi.org/10.1177/1741659013493918.

———. "Privates in the Online Public: Sex(Ting) and Reputation on Social Media." *New Media & Society* 18, no. 11 (2016): 2723–39.

———. "Publicising Privacy, Weaponising Publicity: The Dialectic of Online Abuse on Social Media." In *Digital Intimate Publics and Social Media*, edited by Amy Shields Dobson, Brady Robards, and Nicholas Carah, 29–43. Cham: Springer International, 2018.

Salter, Michael, Thomas Crofts, and Murray Lee. "Beyond Criminalisation and Responsibilisation: Sexting, Gender and Young People." *Current Issues in Criminal Justice* 24, no. 3 (2013): 301–16. https://doi.org/10.1080/10345329 .2013.12035963.

Sambor, Alyssa Lauren. "Sexual Assault as Spectacle: Understanding Steubenville's Role in the Production of Rape Culture." Thesis, Texas Tech University, 2015. https://ttu-ir.tdl.org/handle/2346/62379.

Samuel, Sigal. "It's Hard to Be a Moral Person: Technology Is Making It Harder." *Vox*, July 27, 2021. www.vox.com/the-highlight/22585287/technology-smart phones-gmail-attention-morality.

Sanday, Peggy R. *Fraternity Gang Rape: Sex, Brotherhood, and Privilege on Campus*. 2nd ed. New York: NYU Press, 2007.

Sandberg, Sveinung, and Thomas Ugelvik. "Why Do Offenders Tape Their Crimes? Crime and Punishment in the Age of the Selfie." *British Journal of Criminology* 57, no. 5 (2016): 1023–40. https://doi.org/10.1093/bjc/azw056.

Sassen, Saskia. "Towards a Sociology of Information Technology." *Current Sociology* 50, no. 3 (2002): 365–88.

Savage, Jon. *Teenage: The Creation of Youth Culture*. New York: Viking, 2007.

Schambelan, Elizabeth. "Everybody Knows." *N+1*, December 10, 2018. https://nplusonemag.com/issue-33/essays/everybody-knows/.

Schilt, Kristen, and Laurel Westbrook. "Doing Gender, Doing Heteronormativity: 'Gender Normals,' Transgender People, and the Social Maintenance of Heterosexuality." *Gender & Society* 23, no. 4 (2009): 440–64. https://doi.org/10.1177/0891243209340034.

Schippers, Mimi. "Recovering the Feminine Other: Masculinity, Femininity, and Gender Hegemony." *Theoretical Sociology* 36 (2007): 85–102.

Schrock, Andrew. "Communicative Affordances of Mobile Media: Portability, Availability, Locatability, and Multimediality." *International Journal of Communication* 9 (2015): 1229–46.

Schrock, Douglas, and Michael Schwalbe. "Men, Masculinity, and Manhood Acts." *Annual Review of Sociology* 35, no. 1 (2009): 277–95. https://doi.org/10.1146/annurev-soc-070308-115933.

Segal, Murray D. *Independent Review of Rehtaeh Parson's Case*. 2015. https://novascotia.ca/segalreport/Parsons-Independent-Review.pdf.

Segrave, Marie, and Laura Vitis, eds. *Gender, Technology and Violence*. London: Routledge, 2017.

Serazio, Michael. "Shooting for Fame: Spectacular Youth, Web 2.0 Dystopia, and the Celebrity Anarchy of Generation Mash-Up." *Communication, Culture and Critique* 3 (2010): 416–34.

Serisier, Tanya. *Speaking Out: Feminism, Rape and Narrative Politics*. Cham: Springer International, 2018.

Setty, Emily. *Risk and Harm in Youth Sexting: Young People's Perspectives*. London: Routledge, 2020.

Shaikh, Rafia. "Violence against Women Online: What Next Steps Intermediaries Should Take." *GenderIT.Org* (blog), January 8, 2015. www.genderit.org/articles/violence-against-women-online-what-next-steps-intermediaries-should-take.

Shariff, Shaheen, and Ashley DeMartini. "Defining the Legal Lines: EGirls and Intimate Images." In *EGirls, ECitizens*, edited by Jane Bailey and Valerie Steeves, 282–307. Ottawa: University of Ottawa Press, 2017.

Shepherd, Tamara, Alison Harvey, Tim Jordan, Sam Srauy, and Kate Miltner. "Histories of Hating." *Social Media + Society* 1, no. 2 (2015). https://doi.org/10.1177/2056305115603997.

Sills, Sophie, Chelsea Pickens, Karishma Beach, Lloyd Jones, Octavia Calder-Dawe, Paulette Benton-Greig, and Nicola Gavey. "Rape Culture and Social Media: Young Critics and a Feminist Counterpublic." *Feminist Media Studies* 16, no. 6 (2016): 935–51. https://doi.org/10.1080/14680777.2015.1137962.

Simon, Kim. "Prevent Another Steubenville: What All Mothers Must Do for Their Sons." *Huffington Post* (blog), March 18, 2013. www.huffingtonpost .com/kim-simon/prevent-another-steubenville-moms-of-sons_b_2896131 .html.

Skinner, Olivenne D., Beth Kurtz-Costes, Dana Wood, and Stephanie J. Rowley. "Gender Typicality, Felt Pressure for Gender Conformity, Racial Centrality, and Self-Esteem in African American Adolescents." *Journal of Black Psychology* 44, no. 3 (2018): 195–218. https://doi.org/10.1177/0095798418764244.

Sleath, Emma, and Ray Bull. "Police Perceptions of Rape Victims and the Impact on Case Decision Making: A Systematic Review." *Aggression and Violent Behavior* 34 (2017): 102–12. https://doi.org/10.1016/j.avb.2017.02.003.

Sloan, Luke, and Anabel Quan-Haase. *The SAGE Handbook of Social Media Research Methods*. London: Sage, 2017.

Smart, Carol. *Feminism and the Power of Law*. London: Routledge, 1989.

Smith, Earl, and Angela J. Hattery. "Race, Wrongful Conviction & Exoneration." *Journal of African American Studies* 15, no. 1 (2011): 74–94. https:// doi.org/10.1007/s12111-010-9130-5.

Smith, Olivia, and Tina Skinner. "How Rape Myths Are Used and Challenged in Rape and Sexual Assault Trials." *Social & Legal Studies* 26, no. 4 (2017): 441–66. https://doi.org/10.1177/0964663916680130.

Sokoloff, Natalie J., and Ida Dupont. "Domestic Violence at the Intersections of Race, Class, and Gender: Challenges and Contributions to Understanding Violence against Marginalized Women in Diverse Communities." *Violence against Women* 11, no. 1 (2005): 38–64. https://doi.org/10.1177 /1077801204271476.

Sommers, Samuel R. "Race and the Decision Making of Juries." *Legal and Criminological Psychology* 12, no. 2 (2007): 171–87. https://doi.org/10 .1348/135532507X189687.

Spencer, Dale, Alexa Dodge, Rose Ricciardelli, and Dale Ballucci. "'I Think It's Re-Victimizing Victims Almost Every Time': Police Perceptions of Criminal Justice Responses to Sexual Violence." *Critical Criminology* 26, no. 2 (2018): 189–209. https://doi.org/10.1007/s10612-018-9390-2.

Spohn, Cassia, and Katharine Tellis. "The Criminal Justice System's Response to Sexual Violence." *Violence against Women* 18, no. 2 (2012): 169–92.

———. "Justice Denied? The Exceptional Clearance of Rape Cases in Los Angeles." *Albany Law Review* 74 (2011): 1379.

Stanko, Elizabeth. *Intimate Intrusions: Women's Experience of Male Violence*. London: Routledge, 1985.

Stanton, Andrew. "Sexual Assault Victims Say NYPD Fails to Handle Cases, 'I Identified My Own Rapist.'" *Newsweek*, October 19, 2021. www.newsweek .com/sexual-assault-victims-say-nypd-fails-handle-cases-i-identified-my-own -rapist-1640451.

Stewart, Alicia W. "#IamJada: When Violence Becomes a Teen Meme." *CNN* (blog), July 17, 2014. www.cnn.com/2014/07/18/living/jada-iamjada-teen -social-media/index.html.

Stonard, Karlie E. "'Technology Was Designed for This': Adolescents' Perceptions of the Role and Impact of the Use of Technology in Cyber Dating

Violence." *Computers in Human Behavior* 105 (2020): 106211. https://doi .org/10.1016/j.chb.2019.106211.

Strauss, Anselm, and Juliet Corbin. *Basics of Qualitative Research*. Newbury Park, CA: Sage, 1990.

Stuart, Hunter. "Anonymous Focuses on Maryville Sexual Assault Case." *HuffPost* (blog), October 15, 2013. www.huffpost.com/entry/anonymous -maryville-missouri-sexual-assault_n_4098773.

Sturken, Marita, and Douglas Thomas. "Introduction: Technological Visions and the Rhetoric of the New." In *Technological Visions: The Hopes and Fears That Shape New Technologies*, edited by Marita Sturken, Douglas Thomas, and Sandra Ball-Rokeach, 1–18. Philadelphia, PA: Temple University Press, 2004.

Sulek, Julia Prodis. "San Jose: Boys Apologize in Wrongful Death Lawsuit Settlement over Girl's Suicide." *Mercury News*, April 3, 2015.

Susman, Tina. "Ohio Teens Guilty of Rape, but Town's Ordeal Isn't Over." *Los Angeles Times*, March 17, 2013. http://articles.latimes.com/2013/mar/17 /nation/la-na-steubenville-rape-verdict-20130318.

Sutton, James E. "Athlete Multiple Perpetrator Rape (MPR) as Interactional and Organizational Deviance: Heuristic Insights from a Multilevel Framework." *Violence against Women* 28, no. 14 (2022): 3608–30. https://doi.org /10.1177/10778012211070312.

Suzor, Nicolas, Molly Dragiewicz, Bridget Harris, Rosalie Gillett, Jean Burgess, and Tess Van Geelen. "Human Rights by Design: The Responsibilities of Social Media Platforms to Address Gender-Based Violence Online." *Policy & Internet* 11, no. 1 (2019): 84–103. https://doi.org/10.1002/poi3.185.

Suzor, Nicolas P. *Lawless: The Secret Rules That Govern Our Digital Lives*. Cambridge: Cambridge University Press, 2019.

Taddicken, Monika, and Cornelia Jers. "The Uses of Privacy Online: Trading a Loss of Privacy for Social Web Gratifications?" In *Privacy Online: Perspectives on Privacy and Self-Disclosure in the Social Web*, edited by Sabine Trepte and Leonard Reinecke, 143–56. Heidelberg: Springer, 2011.

Tambe, Ashwini. "Reckoning with the Silences of #MeToo." *Feminist Studies* 44, no. 1 (2018): 197–203. https://doi.org/10.15767/feministstudies.44.1 .0197.

Taslitz, Andrew. *Rape and the Culture of the Courtroom*. New York: NYU Press, 1999.

Thacker, Lily. "Rape Culture, Victim Blaming, and the Role of Media in the Criminal Justice System." *Kentucky Journal of Undergraduate Scholarship (KJUS)* 1, no. 1 (May 15, 2017). https://encompass.eku.edu/kjus/vol1/iss1/8.

Thiel-Stern, Shayla. *From the Dance Hall to Facebook: Teen Girls, Mass Media, and Moral Panic in the United States, 1905–2010*. Amherst: University of Massachusetts Press, 2014.

Thompson, John B. "The New Visibility." *Theory, Culture & Society* 22, no. 6 (2005): 31–51.

Thorkelson, Erika. "How Camera Phones Stunt Bravery and Short-Circuit Human Decency." *Hazlitt* (blog), March 18, 2014. https://hazlitt.net/blog/how -camera-phones-stunt-bravery-and-short-circuit-human-decency.

Thorne, Barrie. *Gender Play: Girls and Boys in School*. Buckingham, UK: Open University Press, 1993.

Thuma, Emily L. "Lessons in Self-Defense: Gender Violence, Racial Criminalization, and Anticarceral Feminism." *WSQ: Women's Studies Quarterly* 43, no. 3 (2015): 52–71. https://doi.org/10.1353/wsq.2015.0065.

Tillman, Shaquita, Thema Bryant-Davis, Kimberly Smith, and Alison Marks. "Shattering Silence: Exploring Barriers to Disclosure for African American Sexual Assault Survivors." *Trauma, Violence, & Abuse* 11, no. 2 (2010): 59–70.

Tilly, Charles. *Credit and Blame*. Princeton, NJ: Princeton University Press, 2014.

Tolman, Deborah L., Brian R. Davis, and Christin P. Bowman. "'That's Just How It Is': A Gendered Analysis of Masculinity and Femininity Ideologies in Adolescent Girls' and Boys' Heterosexual Relationships." *Journal of Adolescent Research* 31, no. 1 (2015): 3–31. https://doi.org/10.1177/0743558415587325.

Tolman, Deborah L., Renée Spencer, Myra Rosen-Reynoso, and Michelle V. Porche. "Sowing the Seeds of Violence in Heterosexual Relationships: Early Adolescents Narrate Compulsory Heterosexuality." *Journal of Social Issues* 59, no. 1 (2003): 159–78.

Trottier, Daniel. "Policing Social Media." *Canadian Review of Sociology* 49, no. 4 (2012): 411–25. https://doi.org/10.1111/j.1755-618X.2012.01302.x.

Tuchman, Gaye. *Making News: A Study in the Construction of Reality*. New York: Free Press, 1978.

Turner, Graeme. "The Mass Production of Celebrity: 'Celetoids', Reality TV and the 'Demotic Turn.'" *International Journal of Cultural Studies* 9, no. 2 (2006): 153–65.

Tyner, Kathleen. *Literacy in a Digital World: Teaching and Learning in the Age of Information*. London: Routledge, 2014.

Ullman, Sarah E. "Comparing Gang and Individual Rapes in a Community Sample of Urban Women." *Violence and Victims* 22, no. 1 (2007): 43–51. https://doi.org/10.1891/vv-v22i1a003.

Ullman, Sarah E., and Liana Peter-Hagene. "Social Reactions to Sexual Assault Disclosure, Coping, Perceived Control and PTSD Symptoms in Sexual Assault Victims." *Journal of Community Psychology* 42, no. 4 (2014): 495–508. https://doi.org/10.1002/jcop.21624.

Uncel, Megan. "Facebook Is Now Friends with the Court: Current Federal Rules and Social Media Evidence." *Jurimetrics* 52, no. 1 (2011): 43–69.

Urbina, Ian. "Social Media, a Trove of Clues and Confessions." *New York Times*, February 16, 2014.

Valentine, Gill. *Public Space and the Culture of Childhood*. Hants, UK: Ashgate, 2004.

van Dijck, Jose. *The Culture of Connectivity: A Critical History of Social Media*. Oxford: Oxford University Press, 2013.

Van Doorn, Niels. "The Ties That Bind: The Networked Performance of Gender, Sexuality and Friendship on MySpace." *New Media & Society* 12, no. 4 (2010): 583–602.

Varandani, Suman. "13-Year-Old South Carolina Girl's Sexual Assault Lives-treamed on Facebook, Suspects Arrested." *International Business Times*, May 5, 2020. www.ibtimes.com/13-year-old-south-carolina-girls-sexual-assault-livestreamed-facebook-suspects-2970660.

Vincze, Eva A. "Challenges in Digital Forensics." *Police Practice and Research* 17, no. 2 (2016): 183–94. https://doi.org/10.1080/15614263.2015.1128163.

Vingiano, Ali. "Daisy Coleman Publishes a Personal Essay about Her Sexual Assault." *BuzzFeed News* (blog), October 18, 2013. https://www.buzzfeed news.com/article/alisonvingiano/daisy-coleman-publishes-a-personal-essay -about-her-sexual-as.

Vitis, Laura, and Laura Naegler. "Public Responses to Online Resistance: Bringing Power into Confrontation." In *The Palgrave Handbook of Gendered Violence and Technology*, edited by Anastasia Powell, Asher Flynn, and Lisa Sugiura, 693–709. Cham: Springer International, 2021.

Vogels, Emily A., Risa Gelles-Watnick, and Navid Massarat. *Teens, Social Media and Technology 2022*. Pew Research Center, August 10, 2022. https://www .pewresearch.org/internet/2022/08/10/teens-social-media-and-technology -2022/.

Wade, Lisa. "Responses to the Steubenville Verdict Reveal Rape Culture." *Sociological Images* (blog), March 19, 2013. https://thesocietypages.org /socimages/2013/03/19/this-is-rape-culture-responses-to-the-steubenville -verdict/.

Wajcman, Judy. "Feminist Theories of Technology." *Cambridge Journal of Economics* 34, no. 1 (2010): 143–52.

———. *TechnoFeminism*. Cambridge, UK: Polity, 2004.

Walker, Kate, and Emma Sleath. "A Systematic Review of the Current Knowledge Regarding Revenge Pornography and Non-Consensual Sharing of Sexually Explicit Media." *Aggression and Violent Behavior* 36 (2017): 9–24. https://doi.org/10.1016/j.avb.2017.06.010.

Wallis, Jim. "Men and Boys Behaving Badly: Where Are Their Fathers?" *Huffington Post* (blog), March 26, 2013. www.huffingtonpost.com/jim-wallis /men-and-boys-behaving-bad_b_2957865.html.

Wang, Esther. "Why the NYPD's Horrific Mishandling of Rape Investigations Won't Go Away." *New Republic*, October 28, 2021. https://newrepublic.com /article/164186/nypd-svd-rape-investigations.

Wang, Vivian, and Cheryl P. Weinstock. "Yale Student Found Not Guilty in Rape Trial." *New York Times*, March 7, 2018. www.nytimes.com/2018/03 /07/nyregion/yale-student-not-guilty-saifullah-khan.html#story-continues-1.

Watson, Colin, and Laura Huey. "Technology as a Source of Complexity and Challenge for Special Victims Unit (SVU) Investigators." *International Journal of Police Science & Management* 22, no. 4 (2020): 419–27. https://doi .org/10.1177/1461355720962525.

Weinstein, Emily, and Carrie James. *Behind Their Screens: What Teens Are Facing (and Adults Are Missing)*. Cambridge, MA: MIT Press, 2022.

Wetzel, Dan. "Steubenville High School Football Players Found Guilty of Raping 16-Year-Old Girl." *Yahoo*, March 17, 2013. https://sports.yahoo.com

/news/highschool--steubenville-high-school-football-players-found-guilty-of
-raping-16-year-old-girl-164129528.html.

Whittier, Nancy. "Carceral and Intersectional Feminism in Congress: The Violence against Women Act, Discourse, and Policy." *Gender & Society* 30, no. 5 (2016): 791–818. https://doi.org/10.1177/0891243216653381.

Widman, Laura, Sophia Choukas-Bradley, Sarah W. Helms, and Mitchell J. Prinstein. "Adolescent Susceptibility to Peer Influence in Sexual Situations." *Journal of Adolescent Health* 58, no. 3 (2016): 323–29. https://doi.org/10.1016/j.jadohealth.2015.10.253.

Williams, Raymond. *Television: Technology and Cultural Form*. Glasgow: Fontana, 1974.

Willis, Malachi, Sasha N. Canan, Kristen N. Jozkowski, and Ana J. Bridges. "Sexual Consent Communication in Best-Selling Pornography Films: A Content Analysis." *Journal of Sex Research* 57, no. 1 (2020): 52–63. https://doi.org/10.1080/00224499.2019.1655522.

Willis, Malachi, Kristen N. Jozkowski, and Julia Read. "Sexual Consent in K–12 Sex Education: An Analysis of Current Health Education Standards in the United States." *Sex Education* 19, no. 2 (2019): 226–36. https://doi.org/10.1080/14681811.2018.1510769.

Wolak, Janis, David Finkelhor, Wendy Walsh, and Leah Treitman. "Sextortion of Minors: Characteristics and Dynamics." *Journal of Adolescent Health: Official Publication of the Society for Adolescent Medicine* 62, no. 1 (2018): 72–79. https://doi.org/10.1016/j.jadohealth.2017.08.014.

Wood, Mark, Evelyn Rose, and Chrissy Thompson. "Viral Justice? Online Justice-Seeking, Intimate Partner Violence and Affective Contagion." *Theoretical Criminology* 23, no. 3 (2018): 375–93. https://doi.org/10.1177/1362480617750507.

Yar, Majid. "Crime, Media and the Will-to-Representation: Reconsidering Relationships in the New Media Age." *Crime, Media, Culture* 8, no. 3 (2012): 245–60.

Yar, Majid, and Jacqueline Drew. "Image-Based Abuse, Non-Consensual Pornography, Revenge Porn: A Study of Criminalization and Crime Prevention in Australia and England & Wales." *Zenodo*, March 13, 2020. https://doi.org/10.5281/zenodo.3709306.

Ybarra, Michele L., and Kimberly J. Mitchell. "Prevalence Rates of Male and Female Sexual Violence Perpetrators in a National Sample of Adolescents." *JAMA Pediatrics* 167, no. 12 (2013): 1125–34. https://doi.org/10.1001/jamapediatrics.2013.2629.

Yin, Robert K., ed. *Case Study Research: Design and Methods*. 5th ed. Thousand Oaks, CA: Sage, 2014.

Young, Alison. "From Object to Encounter: Aesthetic Politics and Visual Criminology." *Theoretical Criminology* 18, no. 2 (2014): 159–75. https://doi.org/10.1177/1362480613518228.

Young, Amy, Melissa Grey, Antonia Abbey, Carol J. Boyd, and Sean Esteban McCabe. "Alcohol-Related Sexual Assault Victimization among Adolescents: Prevalence, Characteristics, and Correlates." *Journal of Studies on*

Alcohol and Drugs 69, no. 1 (2008): 39–48. https://doi.org/10.15288/jsad.2008.69.39.

Youth Risk Behavior Survey Data Summary & Trends Report: 2011–2021. Centers for Disease Control & Prevention, 2023. www.cdc.gov/healthyyouth/data/yrbs/pdf/YRBS_Data-Summary-Trends_Report2023_508.pdf.

Zanobini, Annie. "Protecting Victims: Limiting Discovery of Child Pornography in California." *Georgetown Journal of Legal Ethics* 29, no. 4 (2016): 1461–81.

Index

Founded in 1893,
UNIVERSITY OF CALIFORNIA PRESS
publishes bold, progressive books and journals
on topics in the arts, humanities, social sciences,
and natural sciences—with a focus on social
justice issues—that inspire thought and action
among readers worldwide.

The UC PRESS FOUNDATION
raises funds to uphold the press's vital role
as an independent, nonprofit publisher, and
receives philanthropic support from a wide
range of individuals and institutions—and from
committed readers like you. To learn more, visit
ucpress.edu/supportus.

www.ingramcontent.com/pod-product-compliance
Lightning Source LLC
Chambersburg PA
CBHW030830270326
41928CB00007B/973